Volume One

OHIO Furniture Makers

1790 to 1845

Jane Sikes Hageman

Dedicated...

to my husband Edward M. Hageman
and to my family who were my staff

Acknowledgements

It is with greatest humility and gratitude that I extend my appreciation to those kind people who have given so much of their knowledge and time to this research project which could not have been completed without them.

To the Ohio Historical Society staff member, Douglas White, and Library staff members, Conrad F. Weitzel, Arlene Peterson, Gary Arnold and Carol Bell.

To my research assistants Carolyn B. Lewis, Suzanne Elder Rogan, Wendy Shepherd, Barbara Macke Sikes and Dawn Vanderzee.

To those kind people who encouraged me along the way - Robert Andrews, Gary Arnold, Carol Bell, Mrs. Margaret Bennett, Mrs. Mary Biggs, Jean Bolger, Ann Braxton, Mary Brown, Mr. Marshall Burt, Mrs. David Case, Mrs. James Connell, Mrs. Edward Cook, Mrs. Donald Cowden, Mike Clum, Lee Daniels, Mrs. Ray David, Mr. Jerry Devol, Carol Dewey, Mr. and Mrs. John Diehl, Mrs. Charles Drinkle, Mr. Bruce Evans, Mrs. Falter, Patrick Foltz, Ted Foster, William Gilmore, Mrs. Allen Gough, John Grabb, Mrs. Herbert Hadley, Mrs. Charles Hall, Mr. and Mrs. George Harold, Ione Hiestand, Mr. and Mrs. Robert Jones, Theda Keever, Mrs. Cary Kinder, Mrs. Carolyn Lewis, Mrs. James Lowder, David Mairs, Mrs. Pearl Markley, Mrs. A. Fullerton Miller, Mrs. Mary M. Miller, Mrs. Polly Miller, Mr. and Mrs. James Mitchell, Charles Muller, Mrs. Westley Newkirk, Arlene Peterson, Mrs. Catherine Remley, Thomas Rentschler, William Reynolds, Mrs. Jack Reynolds, Sarah E. Rusk, Mrs. John Ruthven, Mr. and Mrs. Ted Schmidt, Norris Schneider, David Sheely, Mrs. Charles Stahl, Mrs. Donald Stuck, Mrs. James Sutherland, Mrs. George Utley, Mrs. Susan Vaaler, Mrs. Helen Van Meter, Victoria VanHarlingen, Eileen Whitt, Elmer Webster, Conrad F. Weitzel, Judith Wehn, Douglas White, Larry Wilson, Mrs. Jean Williamson.

Special gratitude and acknowledgement is given to John Grabb, of the Ross County Historical Society who had researched Ross County cabinetmakers for 10 years when he most graciously shared all of his extensive research with me. Also Norris Schneider, Bill Reynolds and Ruth Drinkle who did the same in their areas.

The book could not have been produced without the patient, skillful editing of Barbara Macke Sikes, the meticulous detail work, humor and graphic design of Edward M. Hageman, the typography of Pagemakers and the photography of Frank Lukas, who drove many thousands of miles to get that last photograph, aided by Joseph Worley, Todd Weier, Edward Betz, Alan Haines, Nancy Farrar, Judy Morehead, Edward M. Hageman, Jeffrey Schenck and Judy Wehn. With greatest appreciation to The Merten Company, especially Skip Merten, for their excellent work always accomplished within an impossible time frame. To them all, I extend special and heartfelt thanks.

Western migration, oil on canvas, artist unknown, privately owned.

Transportation by flatboat.

Introduction

In *Ohio Furniture Makers: Volume I,* Jane Sikes Hageman has made a significant contribution to the history of the material culture of the region during the first half of the nineteenth century. Her fascinating chronicle of the lives of the men who pushed westward across the Alleghenies will serve historians and antiquarians as a unique source for in-depth studies of these entrepreneurs.

In her first book, *The Furniture Makers of Cincinnati, 1790 to 1849,* Mrs. Hageman focused on the craftsmen of her home city. The research for that book forced a realization of the need for the same sort of work to be done on a statewide basis. Thus she has continued her study, and in this first volume broadens her territory to the Ohio counties south of Route 40, the National Road that was the main artery bringing settlers into the state. Traveling thousands of miles, she has visited libraries, court houses, historical societies, and private homes, ever searching for another piece of the puzzle. Her work has indeed been a labor of love, both of the state and of its people with whom she has met and shared information.

In *Ohio Furniture Makers: Volume I,* life is depicted in the region before 1840 as interpreted through its furniture. Using diaries, letters, business ledgers, and advertisements, she documents not only the furniture makers but reveals fascinating facts about the economy of the state as well as about the tastes of her people. Interviews with descendants and examination and photographs of the actual pieces of furniture further enhance this documentary of the furniture making business in the newly-settled state.

The findings reveal a sophisticated business community of experienced tradesmen following the settlers to fill their bare cabins and houses with furnishings built from Ohio's hardwood forests. The research reinforces once again the age-old formula of supply and demand: new homes with empty rooms and an endless supple of maple, cherry and walnut woods beckoned to ambitious young craftsmen from the East who were able to fashion the needed cupboards, bedsteads, and tables.

Jane Sikes Hageman's search has resulted in the documentation of many of these small businessmen. They were the backbone that held the frontier together and, as a result of their labor, Ohio was, by 1820, one of the most industrial states in the nation. Her fascinating chronicle of their lives and how they were affected by their environment will interest all who seek to understand the past by what remains of it today.

Ann K. Lowder, *Editor*
Ohio Antique Review

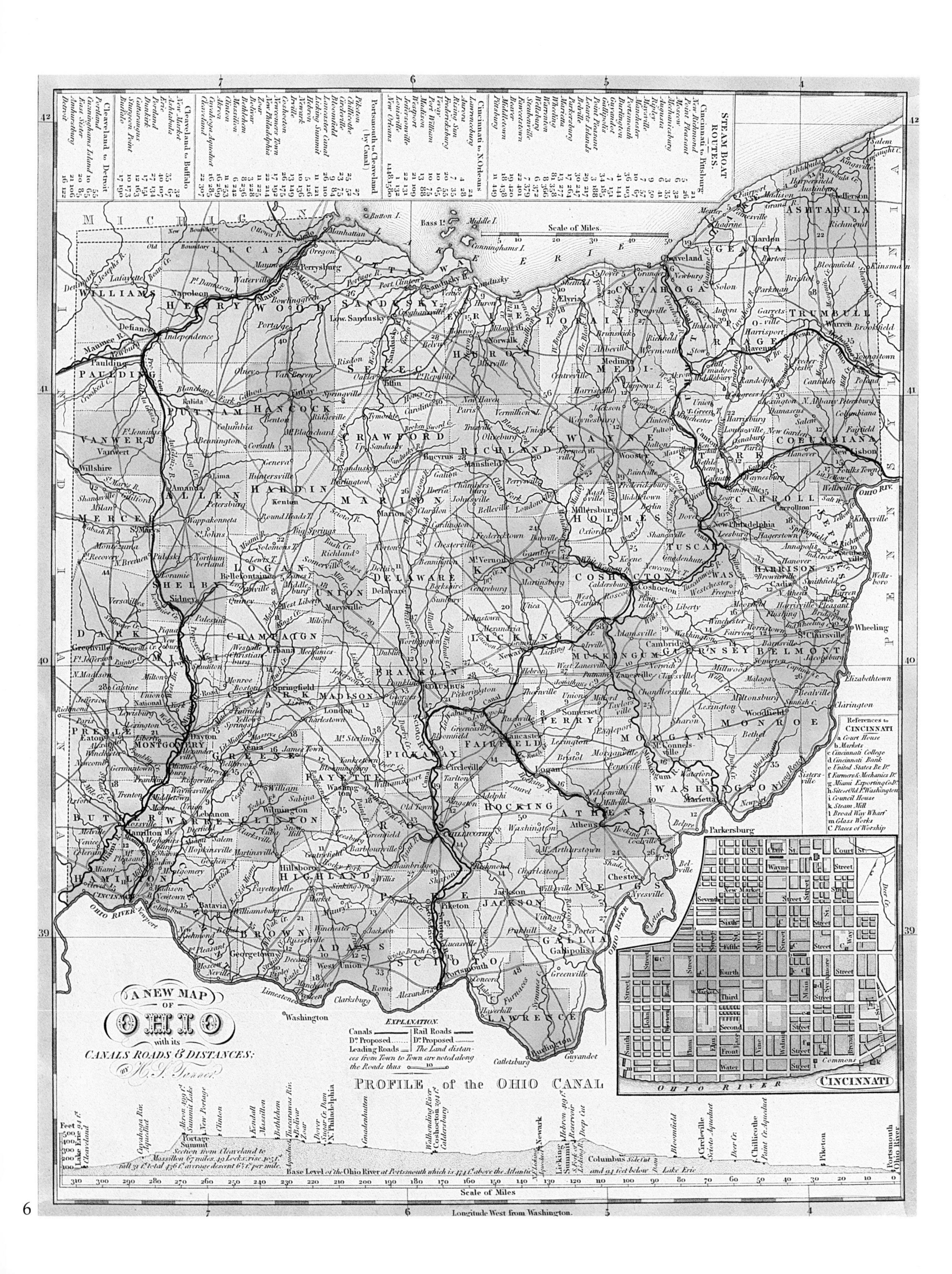
A NEW MAP OF OHIO with its CANALS ROADS & DISTANCES; BY H. S. Tanner.
STEAM BOAT ROUTES.
EXPLANATION.
Canals
Dº Proposed
Leading Roads
Rail Roads
Dº Proposed
The Land distances from Town to Town are noted along the Roads thus
Scale of Miles.
References to CINCINNATI
a Court House
b Markets
c Cincinnati College
d Cincinnati Bank
e United States Br. Dº
f Farmers & Mechanics Dº
g Miami Exporting Co. Dº
h Site of Old Fᵗ Washington
i Council House
k Steam Mill
l Bread Way Wharf
m Glass Works
C Places of Worship
CINCINNATI
OHIO RIVER
PROFILE of the OHIO CANAL
Section from Cleaveland to Massillon 67 miles. 49 Locks: rise 103 ft. fall 31 ft. total 436 ft. average descent 6½ ft. per mile.
Base Level of the Ohio River at Portsmouth which is 474 ft. above the Atlantic and 94 feet below Lake Erie
Scale of Miles
Longitude West from Washington.

Westward Migration

In the early 1800s Ohio was the gateway to the Northwest Territory. Geographically, the western migration of this era funneled into Ohio from all states in the Union.

Those who moved west did so by choice to find larger property holdings, more fertile fields and an opportunity to build a society in a more moderate climate. They came from a variety of backgrounds and their diversified origins made for a complicated cultural pattern. Some were men of wealth and learning. Many were educated craftsmen who possessed the skills needed to shape a thriving community from a rough wilderness: surveyors, housewrights, cabinetmakers, joiners, potters and silversmiths, to name but a few.

The boundless forests of the Northwest Territory presented a new opportunity to those who found farming unproductive in areas of New England or Pennsylvania, land too expensive in the middle coastal states, or religious intolerance repressive in other areas. Thus, with the defeat of the Indians by General Anthony Wayne in 1795, Ohio lands opened for settlement. "Old America was breaking up and moving Westward."[1]

Travel was difficult; diaries such as that of Paul Furson, who came in May, 1815 from New Hampshire, describe conditions on the road. "We came by wagon, the roads were monstrously rough mountain roads which led to the United States turnpike. 'It equals in beauty and smoothness any of the best turnpikes in New England,' it will be completed in five years," and "I must confess the Ohio River thus far does not equal my expectations in its magnitude and appearance." He found that the river increased greatly in magnitude - "In twenty-four hours we have run a hundred miles...The richest verdure covers the whole earth."[2]

Some families had easy and rather uneventful trips west. Melinda Hyde in September 1818 wrote home to Connecticut to say, "Just two months after we left Griswold, we arrived at our new home. I hardly know what to say about it but I think I like (it) as well as expected."[3] And yet there were grievous situations which occurred along the way, such as that described by this notice in the American Friend (Marietta) of May 14,1814:

Information Wanted

My husband Thaddeus Andrew Middleton parted with me at a place about three miles below Pittsburgh to meet in Springfield, Muskingum County, Ohio. He was to go by land with two horses (one of these had a woman's saddle) while I was to go by water with our baggage and two small children. After a passage of two weeks, I came to Springfield on the 17th instant and although it is upward to four weeks since we parted, he has not reached this place, neither have I heard a syllable from him. Any person who may be acquainted with his situation will confer on a poor distressed woman by giving me information.

Rachel Middleton

Springfield, 26 April 1814

continued on next page

This notice appeared in the Dayton Watchman on 6 November 1821:

Information Wanted
About 20 years ago, a certain William Eaton who was married to Rebecca McCann, my parents, moved to the Blue Ridge Mountains in Virginia...and to the Westward and are no doubt in Kentucky, Ohio or Indiana. At the time that they left Virginia, they left three children, myself and two younger brothers. I was bound to a certain James Rose with whom I remained until I was of age. I have never heard of them since they left me. Any information sent to me at Dayton, Ohio by letter or otherwise will be most gratuitously received.
Joseph Eaton

In the earliest years of wagon and flatboat travel, the migrants could bring very little with them. William Shepherd of Miamisburg walked out with his wooden Revolutionary War canteen and a cane.[4] Some of the pioneers who came in 1790 "brought with them a few light articles of household furniture, but many were mostly destitute."[5] "The road conditions were such to forbid the emigrants taking any articles but those of indispensable necessity for a six-horse wagon at a slow gait could not carry more and the boats carried cows, horses and sheep as to have little room for anything else but a few articles of family housekeeping of the first necessity."[6] Along the great river floated flatboats, piroques and arks, all of which were excellent conveyances of family goods. "Came to Pittsburgh...procured things for keeping our crockery, glass and ironware we purchased there and have been fortunate to get it here. We broke nothing worth mentioning that we broat(sic) from Connecticut."[7] Still, the emigrants did not mention bringing furniture or buying it along the way. By 1819, there were seventy steamboats plying the waters between Pittsburgh and New Orleans, and this form of transportation was the most common means of travel during its general usage (1819-1850).

Finally, the canals were cut through Ohio, giving much greater accessibility to the interior. Crops grown in the central towns could be exported to New Orleans and goods could be brought in. The canal was used by families who came west to Ohio, however, it was expensive. Benjamin Conrad who moved to Highland County in 1850 stated:

But first let me say to all who move out here after let them come in their own conveyance, as we did, and not by canal, as Joseph did. His expenses were $88.00 and $10.00 to get his carriage out, and then he had no wagon or horses to go to work with. I would also advise any two persons coming out to see the country to come in a buggy, then they can see it right and get more useful information than they can get by traveling in a public conveyance and if time is not precious they can travel cheaper.[8]

Although steam boats and canal boats were extremely important to shipping produce east and west, many of the settlers who came to Ohio continued to come by wagon via the National Road and into the interior via flatboats. By the 1830s Ohio was flourishing.

Land Office, Marietta, 1800.

The Economic Climate

The economic ties between the eastern states and Ohio were very frail. The merchant returned to restock his store with goods from Philadelphia and New York. Ocean-going ships were built in Marietta from 1801 until 1808. These ships sailed from that town down the Mississippi to New Orleans, to the West Indies, to England and back to Philadelphia. Of course, the ship could not return to Marietta; however, the captain and his goods returned in wagons traveling overland. Herds of cattle were driven from Ohio to Baltimore to market. Goods were imported from the eastern markets; produce grown and items manufactured in the Ohio Territory had to be sent to New Orleans for sale. This created an imbalance of trade, which, by 1819 became disastrous.

The merchants who sold their Ohio produce in New Orleans had to buy in Philadelphia, New York and Baltimore. The credits in New Orleans had to offset debts owed in the east. This created an "adverse balance between imports and exports and there was no way of liquidating debts owed by Ohioans to the U.S. Government and to eastern creditors."[9] Until 1818 banks offered unlimited paper money and easy credit which created out of hand inflation; however, in July of that year the United States Bank reversed its policy of easy loans and they suspended all credit. Wholesale bankruptcy ensued.

During this time merchants in Zanesville, Hamilton and Cincinnati were desperately working to restore economic strength at home by encouraging home manufacture. One newspaper article after another extolls

BENJAMIN ADAMSON,
CABINET-MAKER,
SYCAMORE STREET,
Has on hand a variety of articles, particularly—
MAHOGANY SIDEBOARDS,
SECRETARIES, BUREAUS, &c. &c.
Which he will dispose of at very reasonable prices for cash.
He will exchange, or make to order, any kind of furniture, for a pair of OXEN, which are immediately wanted—and twenty MILCH COWS, to be delivered in the month of March next.
Cincinnat, Dec 29, 1812. 25tf

the merit of buying in one's own town in order to keep those dollars which were formerly spent over the mountains at home in Ohio. Such an active policy helped the young furniture and chair manufactories a great deal.

On the whole, the settlers had to depend on themselves for survival. This independent situation created a lack of capital on the frontier during the early 1800s. Barter was always the method of payment for cabinet and chair goods. John Lyons of Mt. Healthy stated in his advertisement of 1800 that wheat could be delivered at Goudy's Mills in exchange for his cabinetware.[10] In 1822, William M. Wiles of Lebanon accepted linsey, sugar, pork, wood, chickens, turkies(sic), geese, eggs, and any other article from the Western Market.[11] Even as late as 1840 David West of Springfield said, "Sometimes we would hardly ever see a dollar for maybe weeks and weeks. The greater part of our business was done by trading."[12] If someone paid by cash, he was given a great advantage. Often it took a year or more to pay off a debt in cash.

There was always a scarcity of labor. Craftsmen advertised continuously for apprentices and journeymen and it is not known whether they filled those positions or not. In most census records and business schedules indications are that cabinet and chair makers had one or two men working for them at the time. These small businesses were called factories. It was a rare factory indeed which had as many as five to eight men working for it in 1820. Therefore, "it is a matter of wonder that in 1820 Ohio was one of the leading industrial states in the Union."[13] The manufacturing concerns were very small but very numerous.

By 1829 the economy was on a sound footing again. Affluency was returning; the steamboats and canals were bringing more wealth to the interior of Ohio and furnituremakers could sell their goods again. In 1831 there was a devastating flood and a cholera epidemic which affected the rivertowns especially, and in 1837 there was another depression, but somehow the

Joel Williams.

WANTED by the Subscribers, a Journeyman or two, who understand Cabinet Making, to whom good wages will be given by

Campbell and Williams.

Cincinnari, *Sept.* 11, 1795.

Flatboats on the Ohio River.

furniture and chair makers continued to produce and sell nevertheless. The demand for furniture goods was always greater than the supply, and although a great deal of money did not change hands the industry continued to prosper. By 1840 many small factories were established and Cincinnati was well on its way to being the leading furniture manufacturer in the West and eventually in the entire country.

A few words must be said about Cincinnati since it was the great manufacturing center in Ohio. "For modern Americans it is impossible to appreciate fully the surpassing importance of Cincinnati among the cities of the State (Ohio) before 1850. In population it was totally without rival in Ohio - situated at the mouth of the Miami Canal opposite the mouth of the Licking its location on the Ohio and the early enterprise of business leaders made it an important canal and river port. But manufacturing was the chief support of the city."[14]

This aptly describes Cincinnati, the Queen City of the West during the early 1800s. Her manufacturing interest in furniture was one of her mighty industries. Daniel Drake in his *Picture of Cincinnati 1815* says "the principle manufacture in wood are sideboards, secretaries, bureaus and other cabinetware, all of which may be had of a superior quality made of our beautiful cherry and walnut and of mahogany freighted up the Mississippi." Charles Cist relates in *Cincinnati in 1841 its Early Annals* that Cincinnati was producing 538,000 dollars worth of cabinetware in 48 shops and 131,000 dollars worth of chairs in 11 shops employing 128 hands. When these statistics are combined with those from allied fields, such as bedstead makers, upholsterers and clockmakers, the total production of these combined manufacturers was over a million dollars annually in 1840. It is small wonder that Cincinnati was the largest furniture manufacturing center in the entire country by the mid century.

NewCabinet Wareroom.

CHARLES LEHMAN,

CABINET AND CHAIR MAKER,

From Philadelphia,

TENDERS his services to the public in the line of his profession, and will execute all orders, upon the most reasonable terms, with punctuality and despatch, in a style of workmanship equal to any west of the mountains. For satisfactory proof of his abilities he invites Ladies and Gentlemen to his Ware room on

SEVENTH STREET,

Between Main and Sycamore-sts.

Next door but one east of Watson's Clock Manufactory, where orders will be thankfully received.

Being well acquainted with the newest and most fashionable patterns of Cabinet work executed in Philadelphia, he feels the most perfect confidence in inviting public patronage.

Cincinnati, Dec. 11, 1819. 88 3t&m1y.

FANCY CHAIR STORE.

THE Subscribers most respectfully inform their friends and the public, that they have, in addition to their large establishment on Sycamore, opened a factory and ware room on Main, a few doors above Sixth street, where they intend to keep a general assortment of *Chairs, Settees*, &c. of the latest and most approved patterns. Their friends and customers in the upper part of the city, wishing to purchase, will please to favor them with a call.

Their former experience in the Chair making business, together with the very liberal patronage that has been given them, assures them in warranting their work to be equal to any manufactured West or East of the mountains, and they will sell on the most *liberal terms*.

They intend to manufacture and keep on hand an assortment of Curled Maple Chairs and Settees of the newest patterns.

They continue to keep a large assortment at their old stand on Sycamore street near the river.

Steam Boats and Hotels furnished with Chairs and Settees at the shortest notice and on the most reasonable terms.

P. & C. C. SKINNER.

Feb. 25, 1830 2-tf

FOR NEW ORLEANS.

THE new and splendid steamer LOUISIANA, N. Beckwith master, will leave this place for the above port on Saturday next. For freight or passage, (having spacious and elegant accommodations,) apply to Capt. Beckwith, or to

OWEN & HAYDEN

Black walnut cupboard built in Marietta by Jonathan Sprague before 1800. Ohio Historical Society - Campus Martius.

First Furniture - A Matter of Necessity

The thousands of settlers who came to Ohio made their first homes in simple cabins. In almost every community, the interior furnishings of these cabins were described as handmade by the owner: a table, a chair, tree stumps for seats and a bed attached to the wall.

"Tables were made of planks laid on trestles, trunks and blocks served as chairs, wooden bowls and trenchers for dishes, gourds for drinking vessels. Bedsteads were made of poles held by two outer posts and the other sticking into holes in the wall. Skins were laid across to serve as a mattress and also for bed coverings; children slept in the loft."[15]

"The furniture of the first rude dwellings was made of puncheons. Cupboards, seats and tables were thus made by the settler himself. Flintlock, powder horn and bullet pouch were hung over the door. Almost every family had its own spinning wheel for flax and its big wheel for wool."[16]

Stretcher table of hewn planks made by Truman Guthrie for his own use in Belpre, before 1800. Ohio Historical Society - Campus Martius.

Some cabins were more elegantly furnished, such as that of Susan Howell Connor, who later married Nicholas Longworth I. "The furniture of the cabin was superior to the house itself. Excellent tables, cupboards, benches were made of beech and poplar," reminisced Mrs. Longworth.

Ohio Log home, North Bend, Ohio.

Candlestand and ratchet belonging to James Kemper, ca. 1800.

Log house in Oregonia, "Rhonda's Old Home." Oil on canvas by Marcus Mote, Quaker artist.

The James Kemper family built their log house in 1804 on Walnut Hill in Cincinnati and lived in it for their lifetime. Mrs. Kemper mentions in her will quilts, split bottomed chairs, an old desk, a carpet, a dining table, a candlestand, much silver and a sideboard.

One of the more elegant log houses belonged to the Thomas Worthingtons of Chillicothe. In 1802 their daughter, Sarah, described the house as a double pen log house; the space between the two sections was the drawing room, adorned by pier glass and the old mahogany and cherry tables from Virginia, brass andirons, carpets and net curtains.[17]

The Rufus Putnam House still standing in Marietta is visual proof that a frontier home can be reasonably comfortable, spacious and well-furnished. Other cabins such as the Newcom Cabin, Dayton, and the Overfield home in Troy, Ohio, remain to give testimony to the furniture used in such homes.

Cherry salt box, Montgomery County, Ohio.

Ladderback chair, Ohio.

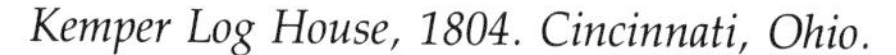

Kemper Log House, 1804. Cincinnati, Ohio.

Early farm house in Preble County.

Very early receipts are extant to prove that many people did indeed make furniture for themselves. Michael Brokaw of Cincinnati, "bought of Smith and Findlay 1780-1800:

1 pr. of chest hinges
1 1/2 doz. screws
4-4 keyd locks
8 desk handles
8 brass knobbs (sic)
2 doz. screws[18]

William Mason bought of Mr. Woodbridge on the 9th of September, 1793:

16 knobs
1 brass desk lock
2 pair of brass hinges
2 cupbord (sic) locks
2 1/2 doz. screws[19]

Woodbridge also sold hardware in 1793-1794 to Stephen Guthrie, Samuel Mitchell and Thomas Hutchinson. He sold kitchen cupboard locks and hinges, brass hinges, locks, etc.; however, these hardware items were sold in such small quantity and at such irregular intervals that they would be only for the personal use of the customer, and do not indicate that he had a shop.

It did not take long for Ohioans to begin to build frame, brick and stone houses. Some were town houses and many were farm dwellings. The ones that remain today seem most fine.

By 1820 and 1830, living conditions were generally much more comfortable and in many cases luxurious. There was a great desire to achieve the ease of living which the families had known before and left behind. The merchant could supply many things such as dishes, dyes, hardware, glass, tea, fabrics for clothing, and trinkets for the ladies, but it was the rare merchant who sold furniture or pottery.

In a few cases merchants were the agents between the client and the local cabinetmaker. In Cincinnati, John H. Piatt & Company, merchant and banker, bought furniture from Benjamin A. Porter. An extant 1817 receipt from Porter indicates for whom the furniture is being made:

Benjamin A. Porter - for John H. Piatt & Co.
17 Feb.,1817 (Piatt acted as agent for Porter)

one table (for) store	*$ 4.50*
1 portable desk	*10.00*
1 bedstead	*3.50*
Repair bedstead for T. Sloo	*1.00*
1 Table - Armstrong	*8.00*
1 Counting Room Desk for store	*10.00*
1 Pembroke table - Reeded legs	*10.00*
1 Common table with drawers	*4.00*
1 Common Bedstead - P. Grandin	*3.25*
1 Sofa - P. Grandin	*80.00*
1 Field Bedstead	*14.00*
1 Fancy Bedstead	*7.00*
1 pr. small end tables	*15.00*
2 common bedstead @ $3.00	*6.00*
1 small dining room table	*10.00*
1 walnut table	*3.00*
1 portable desk	*6.00*
	$ 215.25
Countra	
14 Oct. by cash pd	
George Porter	*25.00*
Received above	*$ 190.00*
In full [20]	

It is worth noting that it took 8 months to pay this bill.

In Leesburg, Ohio several local cabinetmakers were indicated as making furniture for the merchant John Henley in 1823 and 1824.[21] It is also known that Dudley Woodbridge of Marietta was engaging the services

Stone house built by Christian Waldschmidt in 1804, Camp Dennison, Ohio.

Brick house with portico, Chillicothe, Ross County, Ohio.

of a cabinetmaker by the name of John Richardson to make furniture for the Blennerhassett Mansion House in 1806. However, these examples are unusual ones; generally, cabinetmakers advertised independently and worked as separate entities from the merchants.

While merchants and peddlers sold many things, they seldom sold furniture. Therefore, since people brought little with them and merchants rarely dealt in desks, chairs and bureaus, except as agents, it must be assumed that the local cabinetmaker and chairmaker supplied all the needs of the burgeoning community. Judge Johnson of Licking County said, "There were a few quaint specimens of cabinetwork dragged into the Wilderness, but they were sporadic and not common."[22] Further, the Citizens Book states, "It was found cheaper to import local craftsmen to make furniture than to import marketable goods."[23]

We know that small shops existed in Cincinnati as early as 1795, selling cabinetware and chairs.[24] In 1806 Margaret Blennerhassetts wrote to Dudley Woodbridge, "Tell Mr.Richardson I wish him down with the chairbacks, as soon as he can come, I shall buy them and engage him to furnish us with a bedstead and two small chest of drawers."[25] Thomas Worthington brought George McCormick to Chillicothe to help build his home Adena and an extant receipt remains concerning furniture made on the place by McCormick in 1809.[26] In 1809 William Lytle of Cincinnati built a home often referred to as a Mansion House and it too was furnished locally by Benjamin Porter in 1815.[27]

In 1820 the Federal Manufacturer's Census described a shop managed by "George Egnon, Owner, Piketon, Pike County, Ohio, who made chairs and wheels, used wood, paints, oils - $200; employed 2 men operating a turning lathe, wages $130 annually; extra expenses $100; market sold fifty wheels and 200 chairs, bringing $600 per year." The same census lists a cabinetmaker named William M.

Brick house with portico and carved cornice molding, Lancaster, Ohio, 1834.

Wiles from Lebanon, Warren County, Ohio, who "made sideboards, secretaries, desks, bookcases, Madison tables, ladies cabinets, wardrobes, Grecian card tables, washstands with bucket, bedsteads of various qualities, bureaus, portable desks, dining and breakfast room tables; used cherry, walnut, mahogany, poplar boards and scantling. Glue, nails, beeswax and varnish."

By 1830, local cabinetmakers were using newspaper advertisements to eloquently describe their wares to the people of the town. In Springfield, the Farmers Chronicle and Clark County Advertiser, 10 January 1833 stated:

> *Cabinet and Warerooms - Spencer and Smith*
>
> *Wish to announce that they have taken a large commodious room one door west of Greens Hotel, South Street, Springfield.*
>
> *Cabinet Furniture: Chairs, Secretaries, Sofas, Sideboards, Bureaus, Tables, Stands, field and common Bedsteads, cane seat, fancy and plain chairs and settees.*

Federal house built by Daniel Sifford for John Grubb, Lancaster, Ohio 1834.

In the Hamilton Intelligencer of February 1, 1831 there appeared the following:

> *Monsier P. Frederick Nardin, informs the citizens of Butler County and the public generally that he has recently commenced business in Hamilton on Basin Street a few doors east of the Intelligencer Office and South of the Court House.*
>
> *Monsier Nardin having learned his trade with the best workmen in France, from which he has recently removed, feels no hesitancy in saying that his work will be found equal to any heretofor offered to the public in the Western Country. He warrants his work to bear a polish that will stand washing equal to glassware. He feels a delicacy in speaking of his own manufacture well knowing that the work itself will pay a greater compliment to him as a mechanic than any eulogies he can publish.*
>
> *He therefore invites judges of good work and all who wish to furnish themselves with cabinetware to call and examine for themselves.*

It was during the 1830s that the local cabinet and chair makers truly came into their own. The homes were larger, times were good, populations were doubling and tripling, and the canals meant that central Ohio could market its produce and products. Homes remain today with furniture which almost always dates to the 1830 period.

Brick house, Virginia influence, built for Allen Trimble, Hillsboro, Ohio, 1804.

Wilksville November 30th 1834.

Dear Grandmother,

I now take this opportunity (for the first time as I have never wrote since we left there). for the ~~first~~ purpose of letting you know that we are all well and I hope these lines will find you the same and all the rest of my Dear relations. I am to work in the shop with my father at my trade Cabinet making. I have been to work in the shop two years next January father is now making a cupboard for uncle Ziba. uncle Ziba is in very good health and aunt Becca also Lewis and Elzada are the same Elzada and Lawson and Charles comes running in saying send my love to Grandmam send my love to Grandmam and they bother me so I cant write as well as I would like to. likewise aunt Pettiplace is in good health and Ruth also

The Life of the Average Cabinetmaker

The cabinetmaker's life was a mobile one. He often made his first move at the age of 14; he would leave his boyhood home and move to another town to become an apprentice to a working cabinetmaker. He then would strike out on his own to work as a journeyman in a place where work could be found - usually moving west. If all went well, he would continue in his own shop for a lifetime; if not, he moved on. There are numerous examples of this search for prosperity. In the case of Alexander Pinkerton, he trained in Pittsburgh; moved to Beaver County, Pennsylvania; lost title to his land and everything he owned; moved to New Castle, Pennsylvania until 1819, when the Depression helped him decide to move to Ohio. He was heading for Zanesville when he happened to stop in McConnelsville where he stayed for good.

Hector Sanford was orphaned at an early age in Fairfax County, Virginia and overseers of the poor apprenticed him to Ephraim Evans, a chairmaker. It is believed that he came to Ohio in 1797 in a canoe and went to Chillicothe. However, he was back in Georgetown, Virginia by 1802 where he advertised that he would paint, gild and japan anew tea-urns, waiters, etc. in his Windsor chair manufactory on Bridge Street. By 1805, he was advertising in Chillicothe where he made chairs for Thomas Worthington, the governor of Ohio. He remained in Chillicothe through 1813 and perhaps longer, but the last known of him was as a circuit-riding preacher in Brown County, Ohio in 1837. He died in May of that year.

William T.S. Manly, another cabinetmaker, was born near Poolesville, Maryland, moved to Virginia and then to Springfield, Ohio, on to Richmond and Indianapolis, Indiana, finally settling in Logansport, Cass County,Indiana.[28]

As one learns about these men, it is difficult not to become sympathetic toward them, considering the hard times which caused them to search for security and prosperity. How often a mechanic seemed blessed with land, home, a small shop--then, for one reason or another he was suddenly left with absolutely nothing. With his wife and children packed in a wagon, he moved onward to greener pastures and possible success.

When he finally found the town where he felt he could be established for good, he had a small shop, usually as a part of his home or a shop in the town--its location well described in his opening advertisement in the local papers as being across from the Court House, three doors west of Mr. Gregg's store on Main Street. Before long, he was advertising for an apprentice or journeyman. For example, Dan Thompson was a Wilkesville cabinetmaker who lived and worked in his home which stood on sixty acres adjoining the public green in 1831. He made furniture for members of his family and the community and also built an organ. His young son William was his apprentice.[29] Perhaps the chair and furniture maker would have from two to five apprentices working for and boarding with him. James Caldwell, a cabinetmaker from Zanesville, had nineteen people listed as living in his home in 1820. Since he was only twenty-eight years old, he could not have had so many children, so some of these would have been apprentices. He had a large furniture manufactory for the times.

John L. Tabb,
Cabinet Maker,

MOST refpectfully informs his friends and the public in general, that he has commenced bufinefs in the town of Chillicothe, in Water-ftreet, oppofite Mr. John Mantle's tan-yard, where he will, by fhort notice, accommodate all gentlemen and ladies with quick difpatch and on very reafonable terms, for cafh or country produce;— he will execute his work in the neweft fafhion and moft durable manner. He will alfo exchange furniture for good feafon'd inch and half inch cherry and walnut plank.

Dec 12, 1805.

When the cabinetmaker finally achieved success, he would have a wareroom where he could display his cabinetwares, usually in a different location from his shop. At this time in his career the furnituremaker was handling business matters while his journeymen were producing the furniture. The Read brothers, who worked north of Xenia, were described by their neighbor, Elizah T. Fisher, in 1817:

The way the Reads get hold of so much money, they have 8 hands working at cabinetwork, which is a cash article and they carry on the manufacturing of clocks. They carry that business so large that it keeps one business (man) in collections, one in peddling clocks, and one in selling cabinetwork and settling for timber.[30]

As this letter indicates, Abner and Amassa Read were now handling the accounts, ordering the timber and generally overseeing the business while their journeymen did the manufacturing.

A young lad began his apprenticeship in the cabinet business at the age of fourteen and continued until he was twenty-one. He received his room and board, and was taught a trade in return for his labor; no money changed hands. In many cases, this was an agreeable arrangement for both the master and his apprentice. However, occasionally it was not. The newspaper at times carried advertisements about the young apprentice running away, sometimes wearing his master's clothing. In the Columbus Gazette, July 1, 1819 appeared the following:

RUN AWAY FROM THE SUBSCRIBER ...living in Charlestown, an apprentice to the cabinetmaking business, John Craig; he had on a blue coat, brown cashmere pantaloons, yellow vest, etc. Find him and receive $1.00 reward.
A. Woods - cabinetmaker - Charlestown

In the same paper, John Craig, the apprentice and absconder, was also advertising:

To the inhabitants of the county of Franklin that he commences the cabinetmaking business at the corner of Water and Main streets - Furniture of the finest quality and newest fashions from Baltimore - John Craig.

After this confrontation in print, nothing more was heard from either one of the above gentlemen. It was an intriguing situation and one wonders how it was resolved.

Much is unknown about the many men who worked in this field. Often they advertised once and then never again -- Did they stay or leave town? If they left, where did they go? Perhaps they worked for a while and then changed professions. There seems to be a high correlation between furniture making and tavern keeping -- Alexander Mitchell, William M. Wiles and James Reeves all did both. Some became grocers; others became involved in politics.

A great number of the men who stayed in the furniture business also made significant contributions to their city and county. Ephraim Carmack became Justice of the Peace in Shandon; Alexander Mitchell of Eaton became County Treasurer; William Keyes of Hillsboro was Auditor of Highland County in 1804 and had his cabinetmaking shop in his magistrate's office. It is noted that many others contributed to the spiritual welfare of their community. Hector Sanford was a traveling minister; Robert Merrie was an overseer of the poor; Matthew Patton was an elder in the Presbyterian church. Examples such as these are endless.

JOHN JEFFORDS

CABINET MAKER,

High Street, Columbus Ohio,

RESPECTFULLY informs the citizens of Columbus and its vicinity, and the public in general, that has now on hand a handsome and elegant assortment of Cabinet Furniture, consisting of
SIDE BOARDS,
SECRETARYS with book cases,
PLANE, SWELLED, and
ELIPTIC BURE US
BREAKFAST, DINING, and
TEA TABLES.
CANDLE and WASH STANDS.
FRENCH, HIGH POST and
common BEDSTEADS
With every other article in his line of business. All of which he offers cheap for cash, approved notes or country produce. He returns his sincere thanks to the public for their liberal patronage, and hopes to merit a continuance of their favors, by having his work well done.
Wanted as an apprentice to the above business, a boy from fourteen to sixteen years of age, who can be well recommended.
Columbus, April 8, 1819.

On the other hand, not all early cabinetmakers were reputable individuals, as seen in this newspaper notice in the American Friend, 11 July 1817:

$50 REWARD - STOP THE SWINDLER

Made his escape from the constable of Hocking Tsp., Fairfield County, a presence by the name of Andrew Cavett or A.M. Cavett having been taken on capias for debt. He is a tall man, sandy complexion, red hair, heavy eyebrows, occupation cabinetmaker, though he generally follows gambling and defrauding for a livelihood. He is an arch villain and well calculated for taking the unwary and unsuspecting. He is a noted liar which is easily detected by his shortness of memory. The above reward will be given to any person to secure the said Cavett in any jail in this state.

John E. Baker

Columbus, 26 June 1817

There is a certain pathos to be found in notices such as this one which appeared in the Marietta newspaper of December 1815:

Help the Poor...

The subscriber is anxious to settle his business in the close of the year and requests that those indebted to him make payments---Windsor chairs of the newest fashion and most substantial manner for sale at his shop.

Nathaniel Smith

continued on next page

On Friday, 25 April 1817, the American Friend carried this notice:

> *Died in this town; Sunday evening last of a long illness which he bore with patience and resignation, Captain Nathaniel Smith, age 25. On Tuesday morning, an infant son of Captain Smith, both interred in one grave.*

During the working years of the mechanic, he bought his tools from the local merchant, or second-hand at household sales or he made them himself. He bought hardware from the local merchant - glass knobs, locks, keyhole escutcheons, etc..He acquired his veneer and inlay from a large town merchant who sold it. To date, Andrew McAlpin of Cincinnati and John Mansfield of Chillicothe were two of the many men known to have sold inlay and veneers in Ohio during the period under review.

We can get a good idea of the contents of the average chairmaker's shop from the shop inventory of Robert K. Foresman of Circleville, who first advertised in 1822. He died in 1823 and his shop tools were sold. The inventory includes one glue pot, one hammer, one hand ax, one small chair, one window sash, one set paint brushes, one drawing knife, one grindstone and frame, one shaving horse, one whetstone, one file, one vise, one file, one chissel (sic), one gauge, and five paint pots, one quart measure, one square, one saddle bag, two pocket books, one trunk, one foot adz, one lot paint crocks, one holdfast, one brace and bits, one taper auger and one pan shovel and tongs.[31]

As well as can be discerned the men who made chairs and furniture were a diversified group. Some worked for a year and some for a lifetime. They were careful, prudent and very hardworking. They kept long hours and worked under difficult and often inferior conditions. Their pay was very frugal by todays standards and they began a lifetime of toil at the age of 14. Many times they worked with brothers or fathers in family units. Success came slowly but the final advancements and good fortune must have tasted very sweet after so many years of struggle.

PUBLIC SALE.

THERE will be exposed to public sale, on Saturday the 15th inst. at the house of Sally Jeffords, in Columbus, all the remaining personal property of John Jeffords, deceased, consisting of all kinds of cabinet makers' tools, 10,000 feet of seasoned lumber, (of different descriptions,) a variety of cabinet furniture, viz. sideboards, secretaries, bureaus, desks, tables, &c. &c. together with considerable other property too tedious to mention. Sale to commence at 11 o'clock, A. M. Three months' credit will be given for all sums over five dollars, by giving notes with approved security.

SALLY JEFFORDS,
Adm'x of the estate of John Jeffords.

Fancy and Windsor
CHAIR MAKING.

The subscriber respectfully informs his friends and the public, that he has removed his shop next door West of the Printing Office, where he intends carrying on the above business in all its various branches; he also makes high and low post Bedsteads of a superior quality—all of which he will sell as reasonable as any work in his line can be had in the state. His work is all warranted, and in case of any failure in the first twelve months, it is made good free of charge

Approved country produce will be taken in payment for Chairs Bedsteads &c.

Walter M'Donald.

Lancaster, April 9, 1818.

Mr Thomas Worthington Dr 1593

to George McCarmick

to 4 Dressing tables	$14.50
to 1 Clockcase	30..00
to 1 Sideboard	40..00
to 2 highposts Bedsteds	18..00
to 2 Cardtables	30..00
to a Set of Northumberlin tables	30..00
to Making a Cellar Door	5..00
	167..50
	5:00
	162:50

1806 Thomas Watherington 1593

to George McCarmick Dr

February 19	to laying a Square of floor	$ 5..00
19	to Making Steps for Springhouse	2..50
	to hanging Door and locking	..50
27	to Making a bedsted	2..50
	to Making a Safe	4..00
	to Mending table and making a Case	2..00
	to Making a bookcase	6..00
	to 152 lights of Bel Sash at /53 per l	80..56
	to 152 lights of Ovelo Sash at /40 per l	60..80
November 8	to a Calf	2..00
	to boarding john Scot 12 weeks	18..00
1806 june 17	to boarding 70 weeks at 1.50	105..00
		$208..86

Brookcase of tiger maple made by William Hawkins, 1829-1839. Cincinnati Art Museum.

Furniture Style

From 1780 until 1840, the cabinetmaking trade remained much the way it had been for one hundred years - "a craft based on skills learned through apprenticeship and dependent on the artistry and ability of the cabinetmaker."[32]

Ohio furniture styles were influenced by the maker and his memory. He built furniture the way that he had been taught; therefore, his style was similar to the region from which he came.

Thomas Renshaw, who worked with Henry May in Chillicothe, had recently come from Baltimore. Their advertisement in 1816 states, "they flatter themselves that they can finish work in a stile (sic) equal to any imported; they have on hand an extensive variety of Bent-backs, Broadtops with landscapes, gilt and plain chairs. N.B. Orders from a distance will be promptly attended to and chairs put up so as to receive no injury from carriage."[33] Broadtop with landscapes is a well known Baltimore chair characteristic.

In Zanesville, the Muskingum Messenger of 18 August 1819 carried this ad:

> CABINETMAKING...
>
> *The subscriber...carries on in all of its various branches for he has long been acquainted with above business and working in the principal shops in the eastward -*
>
> *John Sheward*
>
> *A quantity of curled maple wanted*

Numerous examples remain of work which has Maryland or Pennsylvania influence such as that of Christopher Shively, or German influence such as that of Jacob Bopes.

Cupboard by Christian Shively, Jr. Wolf Creek settlement, Montgomery County, Ohio, 1810-1820.

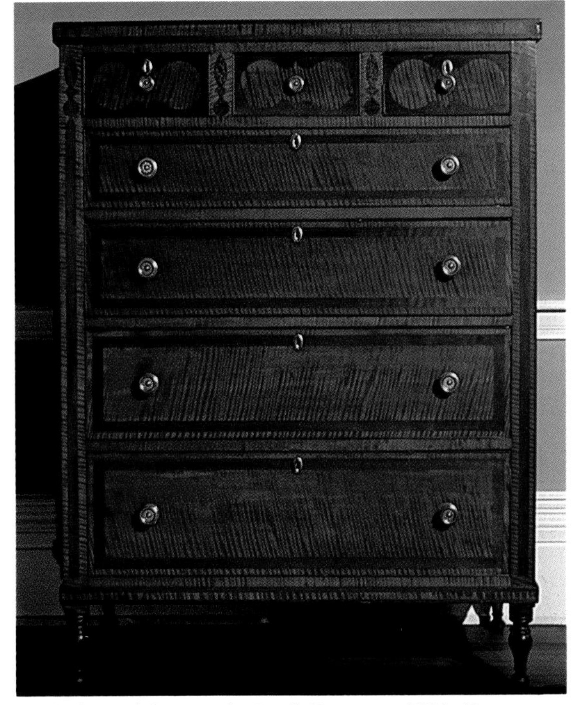

High chest of drawers by Jacob Bope, ca. 1830. Bopes Corner, Fairfield County, Ohio.

Sideboard by George McCormick. Ohio Historical Society, Adena.

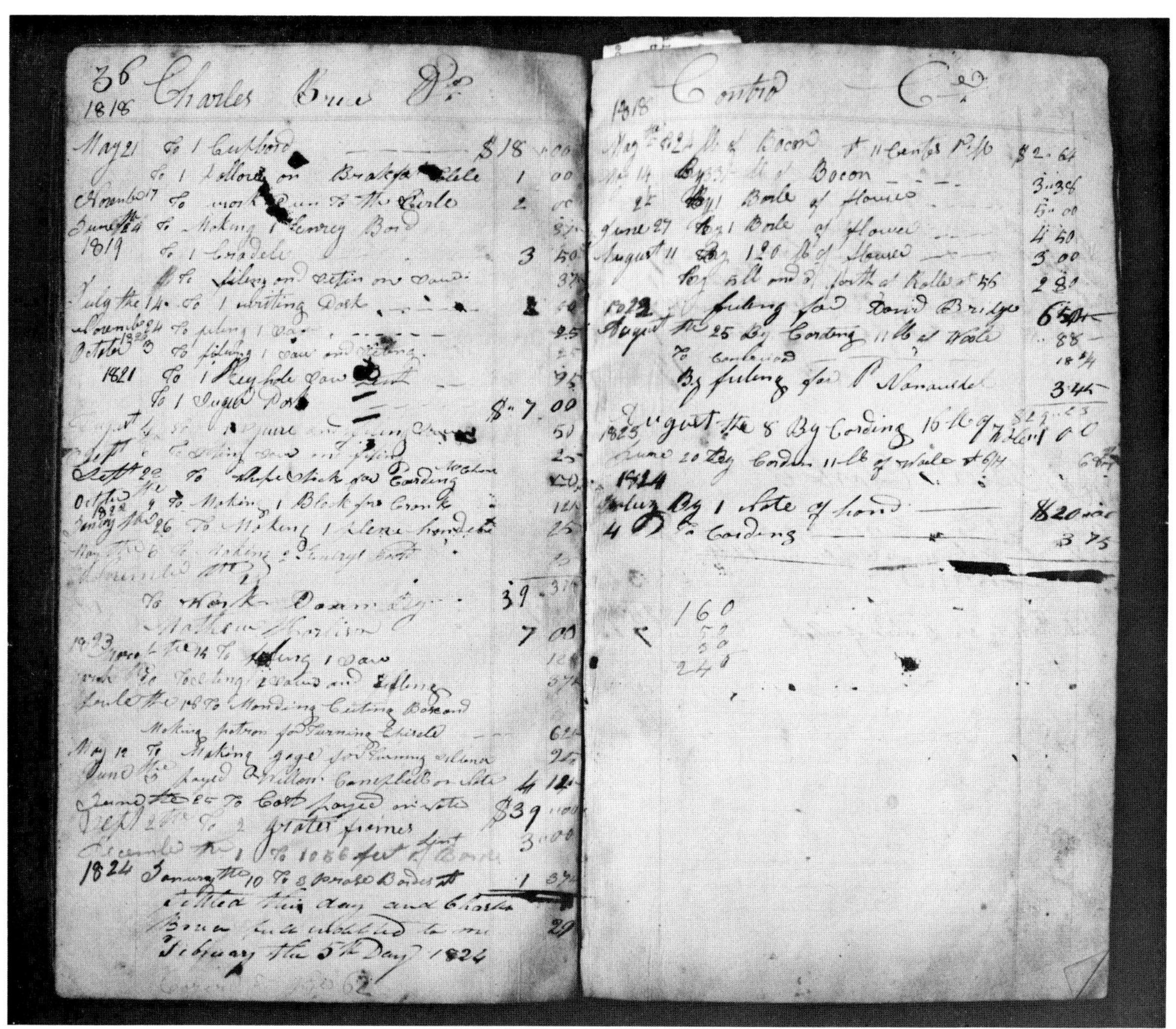

Thomas Morgan Account Book, Preble County, Ohio.

Older patterns lingered from thirty to fifty years after they were seen in the English pattern books, or were made in shops in the east. "On studying old furniture it is of prime importance to remember that basic forms continued to be made for long periods."[34] This is especially true in Ohio.

Styles were not inspired particularly by printed sources. There were no American or Midwestern pattern books concerning furniture or chairmaking until 1840.[35] In 1840 John Hall published the Cabinet Makers Assistant - Design, Drawn and Published by John Hall, Architect, Baltimore.[36] There were price books which stipulated how much a manufacturer could charge for his wares by the piece. Cincinnati has two of these, one published in 1831 and the other published in 1836 (see illustration).[37] The influence of these books may have been of importance in Cincinnati only. They are illustrated and give a great deal of description about every form of furniture and chairs. It is generally believed that the only manuscript books which we can rely on for assistance in style outside of urban centers are the hard-to-find ledger books of which to date we have only three: that of Alexander and Robert Pinkerton of McConnelsville; Leonard Perry Bailey of Zanesville; and Thomas Morgan of Eaton.

Household inventories render some insight into the kinds of woods used and number of chairs owned and so forth. Newspaper advertisements describe very clearly the type of furniture that was made;

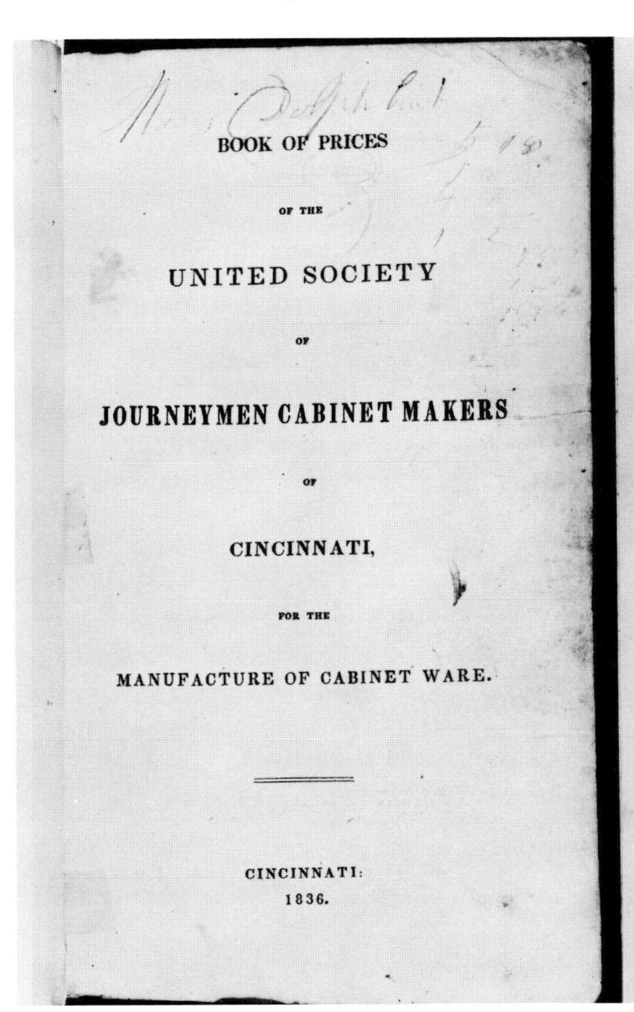
BOOK OF PRICES

OF THE

UNITED SOCIETY

OF

JOURNEYMEN CABINET MAKERS

OF

CINCINNATI,

FOR THE

MANUFACTURE OF CABINET WARE.

CINCINNATI:

1836.

42 A CHERRY BREAKFAST TABLE.

For drawers—*See Table of ditto.*

If ditto are made to draw out either way, to be double.

Each extra leg	25
If guides are framed between ditto, each	12
If stretchers at bottom, each	25
If bottom or shelf start size, one inch thick or under	62
If notched to fit the legs, each corner	5
Each inch longer than two feet six inches, or wider than eighteen inches	2
If top is hinged at front edge, and a horse to support ditto	50
Each extra horse, when hinged	25
When over three to five feet long	75
A bottom in frame as start	25
Ditto from three to five feet long	37
If top, or bottom shelf, is made of pine, deduct per foot, superfice	2

A CHERRY BREAKFAST TABLE.

Three feet long, three feet six inches wide when open, one swivel on each side of top, to support the leaves, framing four inches deep, four plain turned legs, the edge of top square	$2 00
Each inch less in length or width	4
Each inch more in width	4
Each inch more in length	6
Each inch more in depth of framing	8
Rounding or canting corners of leaves, each corner	3
Shaping ditto elliptic, each	5
Ditto double elliptic	10
Treble elliptic	13
Shaping whole top elliptic	40
If drawer in end of frame	50
Veneering the head of legs, and end rail, each end	15
If the head of legs is veneered under the leaf, each	3
If ends are veneered, when with drawer	20
When drawer is made to draw out either way	1 00
Making drawer front to lap over edge of rail, each rail	6
Making sham drawer fronts when veneered, each	12
If astragal, bead, or band, on lower edge of frame	8
If ditto extends across the leg, each leg	4
If joint rails with single fly, each	45
Each extra fly	20
If rule joints extra from square, each joint	10
Scalloping the fly rail ogee, each fly	10
If leaves are hung with square joint, deduct, per foot run	6
If legs of table are mahogany, each leg extra	2
If top is made of mahogany, per foot superfice, extra	3
If table is made of pine, deduct per cent	25
If tops are stained and polished	20
If under side of leaves are polished, each leaf	4

Courtesy of Henry Francis DuPont, Winterthur Museum.

also household receipts or bills are helpful in understanding amounts paid for various furniture items. There are several shop inventories which still exist, inventories of cabinet and chairmakers who died while they were in the prime of life and still working actively at their businesses. The tools they used are, of course, very interesting, as are such notations as "case for bureau - small," "unfinished bedsteads and bedposts," or "6 Winser chears (sic)." Census reports also help to give an accurate picture of the average cabinet and chairmakers shop. The *1820 Federal Manufacturers Census* describes the amount and type of wood used, the number of people employed and the type of equipment used, such as turning lathes and the number and types of tools used. It mentions the amount of wages paid to the employees, the capital invested in the shop and the amount of sales for the year 1819-1820. The *1850 Industry Schedule* of 436 cabinetmakers listed the power used:

Type of Power	*Total Number*	*Percentage*
Hand	*325*	*75%*
Horse	*47*	*11%*
Steam	*25*	*6%*
Hand & Horse	*22*	*5%*
Water	*12*	*3%*
Dog	*1 less than*	*1%*[38]

With such resources we are able to identify the style and type of furniture used in Ohio homes from 1790 until 1845. Thus, combined with the furniture itself, Ohioans of the present day can establish proof of style.

Furniture of the plain sort was made in shops in Cincinnati as early as 1795. Newspaper ads for John Humes, a chairmaker, and Campbell and Williams, cabinetmakers, still remain[39] and very shortly after 1800 there were men working

The Subscriber

Begs leave to inform the public, that he has commenced a

CHAIR MANUFACTORY,

AT the upper end of Water street, nearly opposite the governor's, at the sign of the WINDSOR CHAIR, where he intends to carry on the business in all its branches. He makes gilt ornamented chairs of various patterns, Windsor chairs, with round and square backs, settees, rocking chairs and children's chairs of various kinds and colours. He will also mend, paint, and varnish old chairs; draw, paint and letter signs of every description, in the neatest manner, on the shortest notice, and on terms that cannot fail to please all those who may favor him with their custom.

HECTOR SANFORD.

Chillicothe, December 11, 1805.

AARON S. RICHARDSON,

CHAIRMAKER,

VERY respectfully informs the citizens of Dayton and its vicinity that he has commenced the Chairmaking Business in Market-street, directly opposite Mr. Matthew Patterson's Cabinetmakers' shop, where he is prepared to make

CHAIRS of every description,

in the neatest manner, and hopes to merit and receive a part of the public patronage.

N. B. Orders from a distance will be thankfully received and punctually attended to.

Dayton, June 11. 26,3t

in Chillicothe, Zanesville, Dayton and Hamilton, to name only a few. During this period, furniture was made by hand, and was seldom signed by the maker.

This furniture was sturdy, functional and easily assembled with the minimum of hardware. Case pieces could be assembled with wooden pins. Chairs such as Windsors and fancies were assembled ingeniously with certain woods adhering the spindles tightly to crest rails and seats. Wooden knobs were used for pulls; morticed and dovetailed joints were used. However, hardware such as chestlocks, hinges and escutcheons was available for sale as early as 1793 in Marietta and Cincinnati.[40] Advertisements and household inventories prove that cherry, walnut and maple were used as primary woods, with butternut and sycamore used occasionally. Mahogany was imported as early as 1811 and used throughout the entire time under review. Poplar was used almost exclusively as a secondary wood. Pine did not grow locally except in Fairfield County, but it was imported from the Alleghenies via the Ohio River and used occasionally by cabinetmakers who worked in river towns.[42] Furniture in the majority of shops was finished with varnish. Jesse Woltz of Lancaster mentions in his advertisement, "Varnished off in style."[43] Chairmakers used paint, of course, and some country furniture was painted. Sayre and Donohoe who were working in Eaton in 1839 advertised their chair business in the Eaton Register and stated that they could make imitations of the "following woods and marbles---oak, mahogany, sattan (sic), rosewood, curl and Birdseye maple, Egyptian, Italian, Irish and American marble."[44]

The styles which were in vogue were influenced by the Hepplewhite and Sheraton, generally grouped as the Federal Style in America. In the earlier years, there is often a feeling of delicacy, with straight lines and incomplete curves. By the 1840s, bedsteads and case furniture became heavier.

Fancy chairs by Ross and Geyer, Cincinnati, 1832-1839.

Corner cupboard, Gano family, Cincinnati, ca. 1810-1820.

There are many examples of the tapered leg and scalloped aprons with gently arched cyma curve. Often furniture of the plain sort was enhanced by the magnificent glowing curly and striped cherry woods used throughout a chest - plain, crotched walnut many times used as a veneer, sometimes throughout a cupboard or chest.

One of the most common types of foot used between 1800 and 1830 is the graceful, attenuated, outswept foot. It can be seen in Hepplewhite and Directoire furniture and is generally referred to as a "French foot." This foot is used on plain and elegant pieces.

Ohio furniture abounds with the turned Sheraton foot on chests, clocks, sideboards, and other pieces. Plain case pieces had any number of varieties of turned foot, such as ring, vase and ball shapes. Half turned columns often decorate Ohio chests, hanging corner cupboards, regular cupboards, etc. These turnings are executed in every variety imaginable. Beds have intricately turned posts in many varieties. Ohio furniture was frequently decorated and trimmed with turnings.

The candlestands which were advertised had square, oval, or round tops with a latch for turning the top down; they stood on a well turned center post which ends in a concave or convex tripod foot.

Cherry chest, french feet, scalloped base.

Tea table, hepplewhite legs, scalloped apron.

Walnut hanging corner cupboard, half turned columns, scalloped skirt.

Maple bed with distinctive turned finials, Clark County, Ohio.

Bed deeply carved finials, Gratis, Ohio.

Cherry bed, hand carved ball finial, ca. 1845.

Candlestand, bird cage, tilt top construction, turned pedestal, Belmont County, Ohio.

Because turning was such an essential part of the cabinetry of the 1800-1840s, it is important to describe how it was done. The first turning that was known to have been done was on a floating mill devised by Jonathan Deval which floated on the Muskingum river. This 40 foot diameter undershot wheel did rough sawing and turning for furniture in 1800. A great deal of turning was done by foot power by the master, or by the apprentice working in country shops. According to Robert Pinkerton's account book, he made his own furniture and did the turning for it also:

Making tab(tablet) bureau	*6.50*
Turning columns for Do(ditto)	*.12½*
Making drop bureau, 5 drawers	*5.50*
Turning for Do	*.18¾*[45]

In Cincinnati, Josiah Haines advertised proudly that he was turning with horse power in 1817. Sayre and Donohoe were also using horse power as late as 1839 in Eaton. There are many examples in the years in between. In one case, dog power was mentioned and it is very probable that water power was used occasionally for turning, although it was mentioned only once in advertisements or accounts.

Sometimes carving was done to enhance a piece. In the case of the Watson clock, the carving had definite eastern influence as seen in the Adamesque medallion and the pineapple carving, but the feathers were most likely a figment of the imagination of the carver. Carving was frequently done on table legs as twisted reeding and as reeding and fluting on bedposts (Gilmore tables, Clum tables).

Simple inlay was used as early as 1800 in Ohio - applewood, walnut, holly, maple and satin woods were inlaid. Stringing was often used in decorating. These inlays and stringing may have been ordered from New York or Philadelphia. Andrew McAlpin and nine other concerns of Cincinnati and J. Mansfield of Chillicothe advertised inlay and veneering materials and sold them to those in the area.

Luman Watson clock case with elaborately carved door.

Leaf and vine inlay on John Magee desk, also banded inlay.

There are a few types of furniture which have not been attributed to Ohio in the past but inventories, receipts and account books prove that such pieces of furniture as sugar chests were made locally. In his ledger book, Thomas Morgan of Eaton bills a client for one and Eleanor Worthington mentions a sugar chest in her will. In another instance, card tables remain in Adena and there is a bill from George McCormick with them for a pair of card tables as well as for other items such as sideboards, etc.

A Madison table is often mentioned in ads and inventories; although it is not known at present exactly what type of table this is, it could perhaps be a 2 part dining table. Another term used by George McCormick in his bill to Thomas Worthington was a Northumberland table - but the characteristics of this particular type of table remain a mystery. Double dining tables and swelled and elliptic bureaus were also mentioned.

After a long search for furniture made in Ohio it is generally believed that local furnituremakers could produce almost every style of furniture that would be found at that time in the eastern states.

From 1815 to 1840 the time was at hand for elegance and eclat. Great homes were being built by the wealthy; the Greek Revival and Federal homes were going up in high style. Examples of these are the Martin Baum House, 1819; The Worthington home called Adena in Chillicothe; the Georgian and the Stansberry home, Lancaster; Glendower in Lebanon and the Matthews home in Zanesville.

In order to supply such a demand, the furniture shops were producing the high style furniture. Their ads proclaimed it;

Hand carved spiral fluting.

Elaborately carved sideboard by Jacob Ware, Ross County, Ohio.

Samuel Herr of Lancaster was making furniture in the most approved styles; Samuel Neigh (Nye) in 1830 made first-rate mahogany sideboards, two mahogany secretaries, 12 cherry bureaus, full and half column; William M. Wiles of Lebanon sold at vendue an elegant sideboard, an elegant secretary and bookcase, an elegant circular bureau and others; John Anthony of Zanesville sold furniture in the most fashionable manner - Grecian sofas and chairs "according to the latest fashion;" William Crumpton of West Union stated that "having employed experienced workmen, he warrants his work to be equal to any in the country."

John D.Conwell had the latest luxury items of the New York trade - pier tables and sideboards. In Chillicothe, another center of distinction, worked Thomas Renshaw of Baltimore fame and John Peebles, who expounded, "Having wrought in the best shops in Philadelphia and from his long experience in business, he hopes to give satisfaction to those who may please to favor him with their custom." William Robinson intended to make furniture of the "best quality and newest fashion (1815)."

These are just a few examples of high styled Ohio furniture. There is a secretary in Marietta with french feet, inlaid vines along the corner post, inlaid paterae on the corner block and inlaid escutcheons (see illustration). A fine Hepplewhite sideboard made in Zanesville of cherry has oval medallions, round brass pulls, mahogany veneer - there is also a sideboard and a pair of card tables of solid mahogany at Adena.

The high style furniture was advertised and undoubtedly made in large quantities in Cincinnati. Several examples remain - The William Hawkins secretary, a maple high post bed and the Samuel Best clock - to name only a few.

There were other centers where the finest furniture was produced. In Chillicothe, Ohio's first capital, George McCormick made card tables, sideboards and clock cases for Thomas Worthington. Other fine examples come from such commercial centers as Zanesville and Lancaster, and from the Montgomery County area.

Secretary with inlaid paterae, french feet.

There is a Perry County cupboard made of cherry wood, veneered with burled maple and mahogany; it has elaborate half turnings, pineapple decoration, twisted reeding and hairy paw feet.

These are examples of high styled furniture made in Ohio before 1840.

Advertisements as late as 1839 noted dressing tables, french bedsteads, ladies washstands and a painted washstand.

Further evidence that furniture for the grand homes was made locally are manuscript receipts that exist, such as the following:

John Ward Mason - Cincinnati May 1822

To: General William Lytle (one of Cincinnati's leading and most affluent citizens.)

1 large bookcase	*$ 30.00*
1 reeded bedstead large size	*30.00*
Repairing stand/new lock	*1.00*
Clockcase all mahogany	*45.00*
Coffin raised lid - cherry	*20.00*
Moulding	*5.00*
Fancy bedstead	*8.50*
	$ 139.50
Contra	*68.72*
	70.78

Inasmuch as an average bedstead sold for $3.50, we can safely assume that a bed for $30 was elegant; and a mahogany clockcase for $45 would have been very high style.

Barton White - To Messrs Wayne & Co. - (1838)

1 Secretary and Bookcase	*$ 108.00*
The frame for one bedstead	*1.00*
	$ 109.00
Credit for crib	*7.00*
	$ 102.00
Rec'd payment by load of wood	*3.00*
Cincinnati 1 Jan.1839	*$ 99.60*

A secretary bookcase for $108.00 would have been of the highest style and latest fashion since the average bookcase would have cost $30.00 at the most.

Household inventories such as that of Romeo Lewis, Oxford, who owned a barouch (a four-wheeled carriage with a drivers seat and a folding top), 18 dining room chairs, a french closet worth $42.00 and a dressing bureau worth $30.00, indicate that he was considered a wealthy man.

Following the trial of Aaron Burr and Harman Blennerhassett, the Blennerhassett Mansion across from Belpre on the Ohio River was appraised in 1807. Amongst the household goods were 2 sofas, one candlestand and seven white flowered chairs - the Blennerhassetts had household goods on a grand scale.

Thus we have much proof that high styled furniture was made and used in Ohio from 1800 until 1845. Because there were so many men working in Ohio a checklist has been assembled and appears in the section following the photographs.

Bed with carved post, acanthus leaf and pineapple carving.

Adams County

Ladderback chair, brown paint, unusual finials and unusual back treatment, mixed woods, Gilmore Collection.

Cherry stand, one drawer, Hepplewhite legs and interesting scalloping on skirt. Gilmore Collection.

Cherry two drawer stand with crisp turnings and reeded decoration, Harsha Township.

Five drawer chest of curly cherry has quarter turnings which are carved in a spiral design. An unknown cabinet maker made this as a wedding present for a Harsha Township bride. The chest has remained in the family for whom it was made. Gilmore Collection.

Cherry dining table, flame cherry apron with maple inlay - one end of a two part table. Descended in family. Privately owned - Hageman photograph.

Cherry tilt top, bird cage candle stand. Center post with vase turning, feet of a Queen Anne style. Privately owned - Hageman photograph.

Cherry one drawer stand, top has cut out corners, wooden drawer pull, interesting turnings on legs, original finish. Descended in family. Privately owned.

Cherry dressing table, one drawer, Hepplewhite legs, original brass pulls, original finish. Privately owned - Hageman photograph.

Brown County

Ladderback rocking chair, belonged to Jesse Grant, father of Ulysses Simpson Grant. Grant Homestead, Georgetown, Ohio. Hageman photograph.

Butler County

Cherry five drawer chest with large bonnet drawers with slight hang over graduated drawers accentuated vase turnings and double casters. Millville area. Privately owned.

Child's cherry four drawer chest. Exact replica of large, full sized chest. First drawer is large and has overhang, with three graduated drawers below. Hand carved half columns with spiral and vase turning. Drawers have locking mechanism. Interesting heart inlay . From the Millville area. Privately owned.

Miniature or child's chest of cherry wood. Half turnings, vase and ring turning with ball feet. Jones Collection - Sikes photograph.

Grecian fancy chair, green paint decorated with gilt stenciled design, mixed woods, signed - W. Coles - chairmaker, Springfield area. Collection of the Miami Purchase Association.

Stenciled signature of William Coles - chairmaker - Springfield, Ohio. Courtesy of Miami Purchase Association.

Solid birdseye maple trinket box with poplar bottom, dovetailed ends. Attributed to the Springfield area. Privately owned.

Clark County

Clock case made for Melwyn Baker, Clark County, by Ezra Read. Clark County History dates this case 1809. Works and face are replaced. Privately owned - Sikes photograph.

Cherry pie safe, two small drawers, six original tin panels with pinwheel decoration. Unusual cherry gallery around the top. South Charleston area. Privately owned.

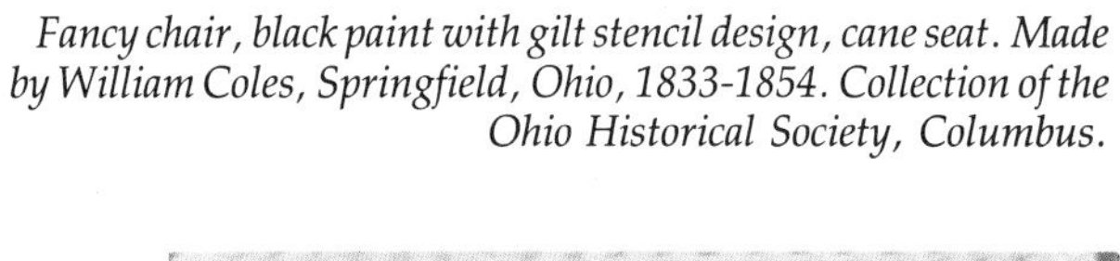

Fancy chair, black paint with gilt stencil design, cane seat. Made by William Coles, Springfield, Ohio, 1833-1854. Collection of the Ohio Historical Society, Columbus.

Close-up of stenciled signature of W. Coles

Blanket chest, poplar wood with red paint, bulbous feet. Clermont County. Privately owned.

Cherry pie safe, six tins with rare design in punched tins of church with steeple and arrow on top of steeple, trees and diamond decoration.

Poplar food safe, six tin panels with eagle decoration. Attributed to Clermont County. Privately owned.

Chair with vase splat and very simple style, original red paint, signed "made by Philip Drum - Ohio - 1847 - for Samuel Simpson." Samuel Simpson was the uncle of Ulysses Simpson Grant.

Clinton County

Cherry six drawer chest with tiger maple full turned columns. Poplar secondary wood. Wilmington. Privately owned - Alan Haines photograph.

Cherry corner cupboard, single door, 12 glass panes, two blind doors at bottom, plain bracket feet. Wilmington. Privately owned - Alan Haines photograph.

Seven drawer high chest of drawers, tiger maple and walnut with decorative inlays. Secondary wood poplar. Made by Jacob Bope Co. Bopes Corner.
Courtesy Fairfield Heritage Foundation.

Detail of unique form of inlay.

Detail of drawer construction.

Small sideboard of cherry with crotched cherry veneer. Courtesy Fairfield Heritage Foundation.

Striped maple one drawer stand. Inlay of curly walnut. Mike Clum Collection.

Sideboard with appleroot veneer, the fully turned and carved columns are walnut, carved hairy paw feet of walnut. Made by George Hamilton STrode, 1799-1876. Lancaster, Ohio. Courtesy Fairfield Heritage Foundation.

Cherry cupboard with french feet and 16 panes of glass in the doors. Below are 2 blind doors. Lancaster, Ohio. Courtesy Fairfield Heritage Foundation.

Walnut dry sink, traces of black paint. Splash back decorated with carved sunburst. Attributed to Jacob Bope. Bopes Corner. Mike Clum Collection.

Two part dining table with cherry crotched veneer and spiral turnings on legs. Applied carved medallion on posts of the legs. Attributed to George Hamilton Strode, 1799-1876. Lancaster, Ohio. Courtesy Fairfield Heritage Foundation.

Large white walnut corner cupboard. Architectural cornice with delicate half turned columns. Columns applied to cupboard. Sixteen glass panes with three drawers across. Made at Bopes Corner. Privately owned - Farrar photograph.

Cherry tall clock case with brass works. Lancaster, Ohio. Courtesy Fairfield Heritage Foundation.

Cherry drop leaf table, signed on bottom, J. Woltz, Lancaster, Ohio, 1824. Morehead and Farrar photograph.

Cherry candle stand by Issiah Vorhis, interestingly scrolled legs with ball foot. Privately owned.

Corner cupboard of cherry wood. Nine pane single door above, two blind doors below, half turned columns with sunburst at center. Made at Bopes Corner. Privately owned - Morehead and Farrar photograph.

Stoutsville cherry chest with paneled ends, herringbone trim on top front and base with graceful fluted and trimmed half turnings. Signed on back by Joseph Stepilton, Stoutsville, Fairfield County, Ohio. Privately owned - Morehead and Farrar photograph.

Franklin County

Bought by an early collector in Franklin County, curly cherry four drawer tall desk, stringing and diagonal decorative veneer. The Cook Collection.

Fancy arrowback Windsor, correctly repainted, Adin G. Hibbs, 1833-1837, name impressed under seat. Columbus, Ohio. The Hunt Collection.

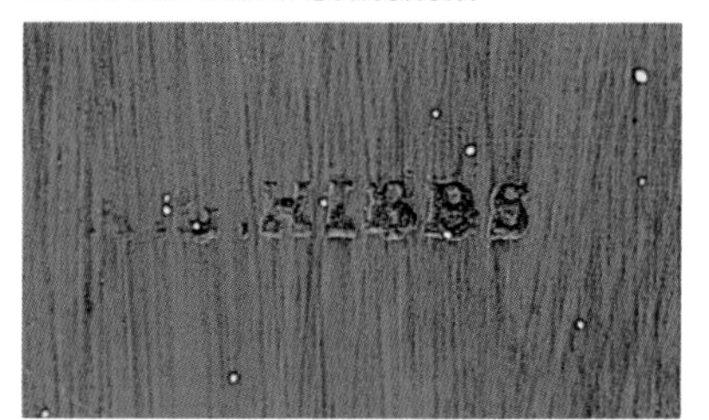

High eight drawer chest, curly cherry with diamond veneer, french feet, Sheraton pulls. Elmer Webster Collection.

Chest of drawers, cherry wood, five drawers. From the Jacob Darst residence, Beaver Creek Township. Interesting geometrical inlay on the underside of the bottom drawer. "This bureau was made and finished the 8th day of March 1809 Abraham L..netz in Greene County Ohio." Owned by the Montgomery County Historical Society. Todd Weier photograph - courtesy of the Columbus Museum of Art, Ohio.

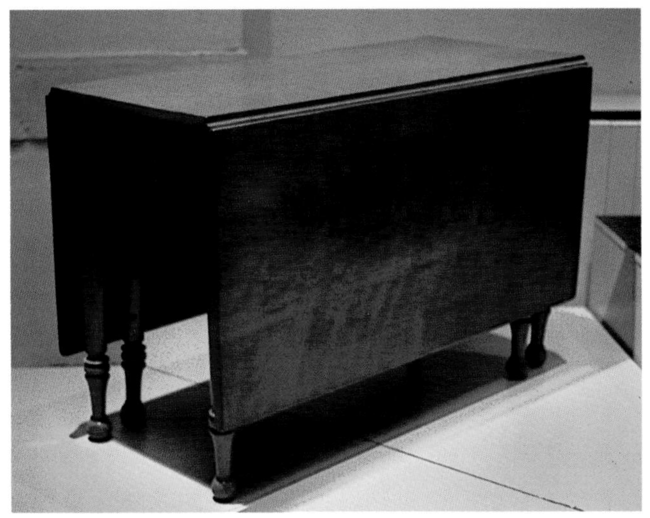

Cherry drop leaf table, circa 1810. In collection of Montgomery County Historical Society. Wehn photograph.

Loop back Windsor chairs made for the James Kemper family. Remain in the family - nine spindles. Betz photograph.

Green painted cupboard, poplar wood, 12 glass panes. Privately owned.

Tall post bed of tiger maple with reeded posts. Part of the original furnishings of Taft Museum, Cincinnati. Elmer Webster Collection.

Luman Watson tall case clock of cherry with unique carving, wooden works, 1820-1830, Cincinnati.

Tall case clock by Samuel Best, cherry wood with flame cherry veneer, french feet, geometrical inlay, 1811. Privately owned.

Cherry chest with full turned pillars, made by Israel Brown - signed. Cincinnati. Privately owned - Betz photograph.

Signature of Israel Brown. Betz photograph.

Fancy Windsor bench painted black with grained and gilt decoration on crest rail. Courtesy Miami Purchase Association, Sharon Woods.

Highland County

Oil painting on canvas of the Barrett home at Barretts Mills, Highland County. Privately owned.

Hocking County

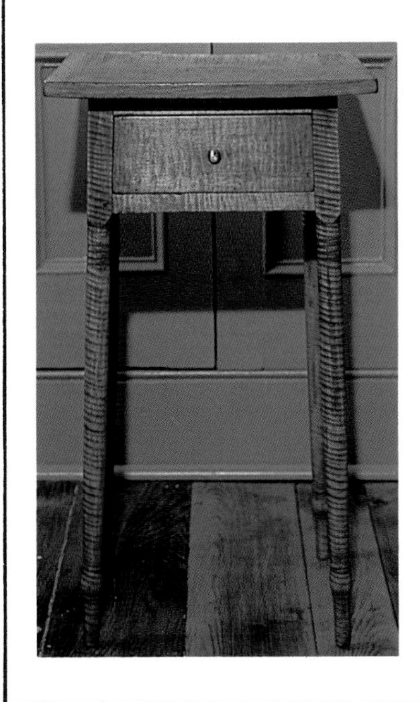

Tiger maple stand with single drawer. The Clum Collection.

Arrowback writing arm Windsor chair from the Allen Trimble estate. Painted black with gilt striping, mixed woods. Privately owned.

Cherry chest with bonnet drawers, interesting carved gallery motif, circa 1842. Privately owned.

Jackson County

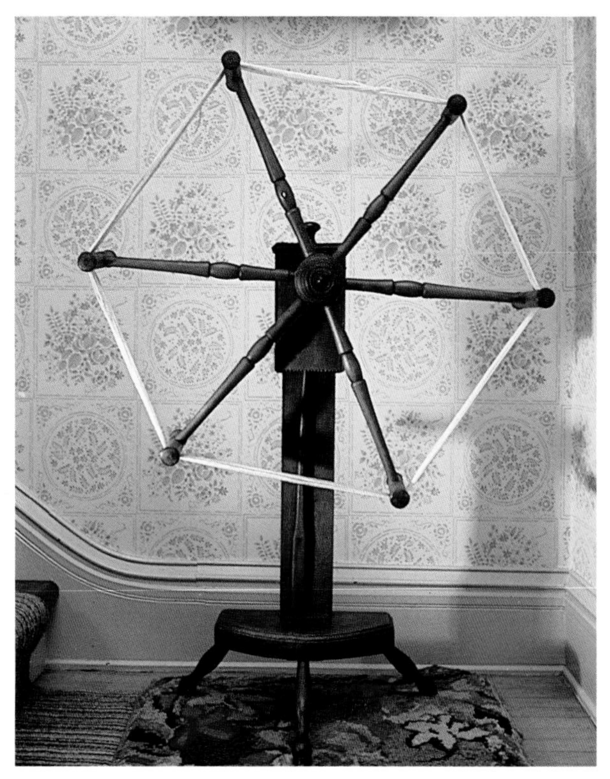

Wool yarn winder of walnut wood, circa 1820-1830. Signed Jesse Stebleton. Privately owned.

Lawrence County

High post bed. Interesting turnings on post, end rail and headboard. Privately owned - Sikes photograph.

Lawrence County

One drawer stand, interesting turnings on the legs, chamfering on the drawer front in the original red paint. Privately owned - Sikes photograph.

Arrowback Windsor chair, original white paint with stenciled design. Privately owned - Sikes photograph.

Maple ladder back chair, hand carved ball finials, replaced seat. Privately owned - Sikes photograph.

Montgomery County

Cupboard of cherry, walnut and maple, New Lebanon - Johnsville area. Made by Christian Shively Jr. The Elmer Webster Collection.

Cradle with turned spindles, cherry wood, original rockers, circa 1830. Courtesy Dayton Art Institute.

Marsh, Williams and Company mantle clock, stenciled decoration and half turned columns, original reverse painting on glass. Dayton, Ohio. Privately owned.

Walnut cupboard, 12 paneled doors, scalloping on cornice, reeded center and corner posts, turned foot. The Elmer Webster Collection.

Tiger maple bookcase, french feet which have been shortened. Attributed to the Dayton area. The Elmer Webster Collection.

Painted box, Germantown, Ohio. Family history attributes this box as having been painted by a 16 year old boy. Montgomery County Historical Society.

Montgomery County

Five drawer chest, french feet, herringbone-chevron inlay, curly cherry. The Elmer Webster Collection.

Eight drawer tall chest of cherry, half turned drops, double paneling on end, turned feet. The Elmer Webster Collection.

Cherry bonnet chest, turned feet, wooden pulls. Attributed to Matthew Patton Shop. Privately owned.

Miniature cherry wood bonnet chest, solid flame cherry drawers front and paneled ends. Attributed to the shop of Matthew Patton, 25" by 25". Privately owned.

Cherry bonnet chest, turned feet with interestingly turned wooden knobs, brass keyhole escutcheons, attributed to the shop of Matthew Patton. Courtesy The Gilmore Collection.

Cherry and tiger maple chest, full turned post with diagonal fluting, bulbous turned feet, solid maple drawer fronts and top. Attributed to the Matthew Patton Shop. Courtesy Dayton Art Institute.

Montgomery County

Cherry chest with flame cherry veneer, paneled ends, turned legs. Made in Matthew Patton Shop, January 7, 1829. The Evans Collection.

One drawer tiger maple table made in Germantown, Ohio. Privately owned.

Detail view of carved leg.

Self portrait of Nathaniel Sprague, chairmaker, who worked in Zanesville, McConnelsville and Malta. Rusk Collection - Family photograph.

Painted fancy chair from Bellbrook, Ohio. Original red paint. Privately owned.

Arrowback Windsor chair by Nathaniel Sprague. Original paint removed. Made in McConnelsville or Malta. Remains in the family. Rusk Collection - Family photograph.

One half of cherry dining table made by Leonard Perry Bailey for his family. The table remains in the family today. The center pediment is carved with rope turnings and four legs are decorated with acanthus leaf carving and brass paw feet, circa 1845. Linn Collection.

Clock case of mahogany veneer, poplar and broken arch pediment, with unengaged columns on either side of the face, full columns decorate the case and face turnings for feet. Made by Leonard Perry Bailey for a member of his family, it has remained in that family, circa 1835-1840.

Walnut secretary bookcase by Leonard Perry Bailey, Zanesville. The desk opens out, the proportions are unusual in that the largest area is for books with several cupboards below. Linn Collection.

Painted and stenciled Grecian settee. It is painted black with flamboyant stenciled flowers and other decoration, rolled over arms. Attributed to Zanesville. Miami Purchase Association, Sharon Woods.

Arrowback Windsor chair, attributed to Muskingum County. Courtesy Miami Purchase Association, Sharon Woods.

Sideboard of crotched walnut veneer, maple and cherry, bulbous feet and turnings. Made by Leonard Perry Bailey and mentioned in his account book. Privately owned.

Fancy half arrowback arm chair, gilt striping and stenciling. Attributed to James Huey. The Clum Collection.

Close-up of crest rail.

Close-up of foot rail.

Painted and decorated settee, half arrowback, painted black with cornucopias, fruit, leaf motifs, original finish. Privately owned.

Stenciled on the bottom of the seat "J. Huey Zanesville."

Perry County

Corner cupboard with interesting and elaborate turnings on sides and top, circa 1840. Made by Hetzer. Remains in the family for whom it was made. The Clum Collection.

Corner cupboard of walnut with interesting half turnings on sides and top. Sixteen glass panes, single drawer and two blind doors below. Mr. and Mrs. Donald Stuck Collection.

Card table, cherry wood, Hepplewhite legs, cherry veneer. Mr. and Mrs. Donald Stuck Collection.

Impressed signature - J. Wilson.

Corner cupboard of elaborate style, veneered with birdseye maple and crotched walnut, hairy paw feet. Half turned columns carved with pineapple motif and spiral turnings. Mr. and Mrs. Donald Stuck Collection - Todd Weier photograph, courtesy of the Columbus Museum of Art, Ohio.

One drawer stand of cherry wood. Maple veneer on drawer, heavy turnings on legs. Mr. and Mrs. Donald Stuck Collection.

Butternut corner cupboard, bracket feet and carved apron, 16 glass panes. Made by Thomas Morgan, Eaton, Ohio. Privately owned.

Cherry secretary with 12 glass panes, glass original, half turning on side of stile and biscuit turned feet with casters. Made in Eaton. Privately owned.

Walnut cupboard, six glass pane upper doors with double paneled doors below. Reeded trim and scalloped cornice. The Elmer Webster collection.

Cherry stand, one drawer with beading and brass knob. Made in Eaton. Privately owned.

Secretary desk of cherry wood, full turned columns with spiral carving, ball feet and gallery, inlaid with maple and curly cherry. Made by Thomas Morgan and descended in family. Privately owned.

Ross County

Courtesy of the Ross County Historical Society.

Oval table built by William Guthrie in 1802 for the Court House, Chillicothe. Black walnut, Hepplewhite legs, 27-3/4" in height. Members of the Constitutional Convention framed the Ohio Constitution on the table in 1802.

Three drawer stand with legs carved with acanthus leaf and pineapple decoration, cherry wood. Gilmore Collection.

Cherry drop leaf table, spiral turnings and spiraling on knob of drawer. Kingston, Ross County. Gilmore Collection.

Part of a cherry banquet table, satinwood veneer crotched walnut center decoration on serpentine front turned foot. Made by George McCormick for Adena, 1806-1809. Ohio Historical Society, Adena, Chillicothe.

Sideboard by Jacob Ware of Frankfort (near Chillicothe), cherry, mahogany and butternut woods. Used in the home of Duncan McArthur, Bainbridge, Ross County, Ohio. Courtesy of the Ross County Historical Society.

Mahogany card table of circular shape. One of a pair. Hepplewhite legs. Made by George mcCormick for Thomas Worthington's home, Adena, 1806-1809.

Painted child's crib made by George McCormick for Thomas Worthington, 1806-1809, Chillicothe. Courtesy Ohio Historical Society - Adena.

Mahogany sideboard with serpentine front, mahogany veneer with beading of a lighter wood. Hepplewhite legs. Made by George McCormick for Thomas Worthington, 1806-1809. Chillicothe. Courtesy Ohio Historical Society - Adena.

Walnut table with scrolled skirt, Hepplewhite legs, Chillicothe. Privately owned.

Fancy chair, original yellow paint and stenciling diamond decoration on chair rail. Courtesy Ohio Historical Society - Adena.

Fancy settee, white paint with blue stencil and leaf decoration, turned foot. Used in the home of Dr. Edward Tiffin, the first governor of Ohio. This bench and a matching chair still in the home of a descendent. Privately owned - Sikes photograph.

Warren County

Cherry chest with half drop decoration, turned feet, two small drawers at top, with large drawer, three graduated drawers below, an interesting arrangement. Made by Paul Lewis. Courtesy of the Glendower State Museum - Worley photograph.

Cherry drop leaf table, turned and reeded legs with casters. Made by Paul Lewis. Gift of Perle Riley. Glendower State Museum - Worley photograph.

Cherry secretary desk, veneered with flame cherry turned feet. Made by Paul Lewis. Gift of Perle Riley. Glendower State Museum - Worley photograph.

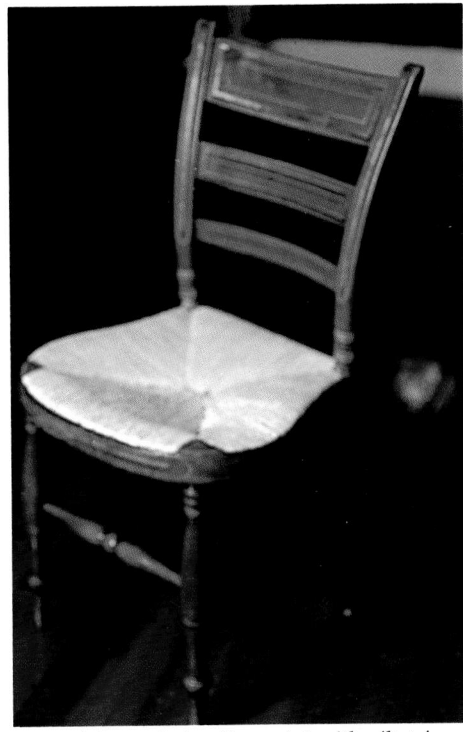

Painted fancy chair, olive paint with gilt trim, one of a set of six. Glendower State Memorial - Worley photograph.

Domed top miniature box with drawer in cherry. Presented to Susanna Steddom in 1838, M. Mote marked on hinge. Lebanon. Privately owned

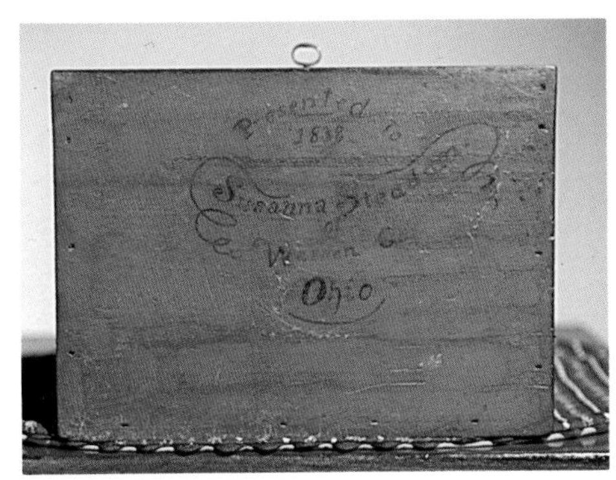

Close-up of inscription.

Washington County

Secretary desk, cherry and walnut, vine and leaf inlay, paterae on doors and stiles, broken arch pedestal with swag detail, French feet. Courtesy Ohio Historical Society - Campus Martius.

Walnut desk from Marietta, signed by John Magee in 1819 on the apron of the desk. Interesting vine and leaf inlay on door and drawers. Geometrical inlay on base and on chamfering cut out ends. Courtesy of the Dayton Collection - Todd Weier photograph, courtesy of the Columbus Museum of Art.

Fall front desk with plain ends and cut out feet. Glass knob probably replaced. Four graduated drawers, secondary wood poplar. Made by William Mason of Marietta in 1793. Courtesy Ohio Historical Society - Campus Martius.

Miniature chest of walnut, "J.M." on skirt, bonnet drawer in center, vine and leaf inlay and geometrical inlay decoration. Strong similarity to John Magee desk. Privately owned - Hageman photograph.

Loop back Windsor chair attributed to Joseph Barker, seven spindles. Courtesy Ohio Historical Society, Campus Martius.

Cherry candle stand, tripod feet. Courtesy Ohio Historical Society - Campus Martius.

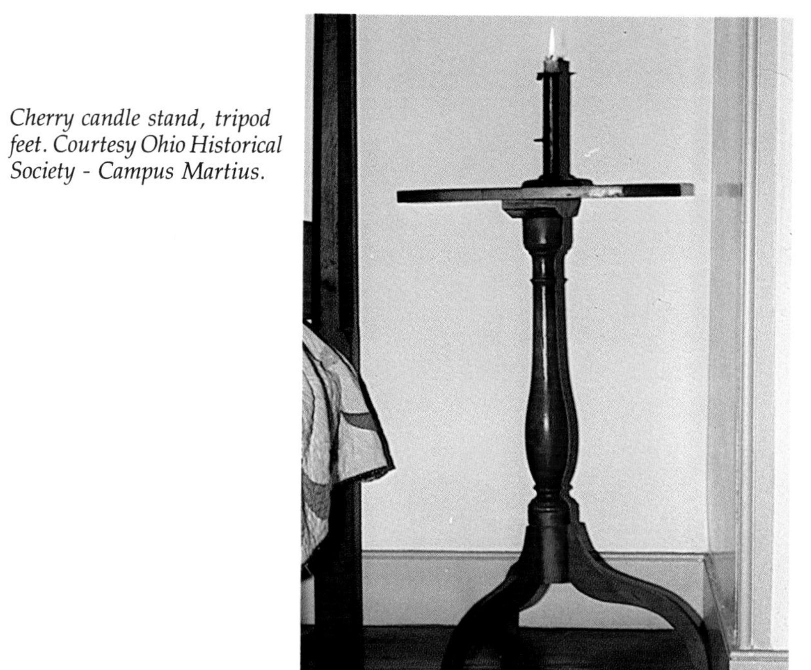

Comb Back Windsor chair, mixed woods, bamboo turning and seven spindles. Courtesy Ohio Historical Society - Campus Martius - Sikes photograph.

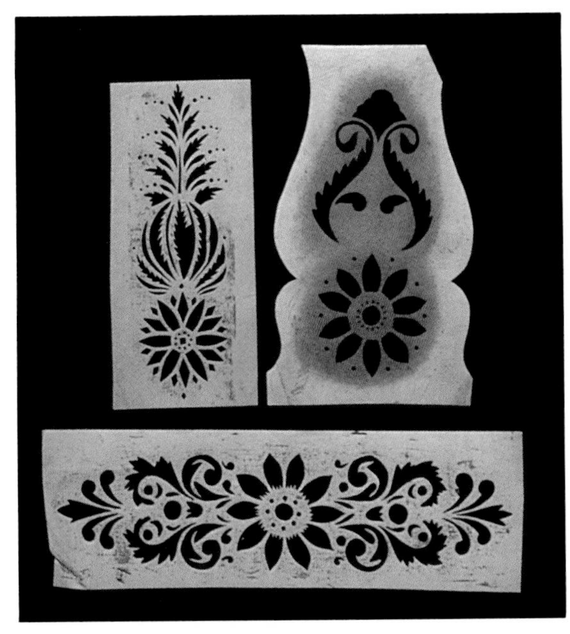

A sampling of stencil and pounce designs used by John Alter for the decoration of his chairs, 1806-1850 Zanesville, Muskingum County, Ohio.

from the collection of John Alter descendants.

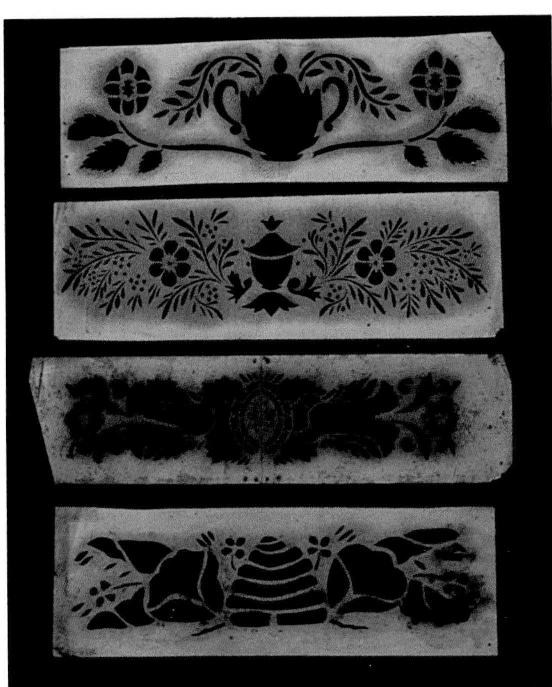

Ohio Furniture Makers listed by county.

ADAMS COUNTY
James Bereman
Thomas Bereman
- Clark
William Crumpton
John Page Hood
Absalom Lafferty
Joseph Page
Robert Warwick Ramsay
Thomas Ramsay
John Waite
David A. Watters
John Wood
Robert H. Wood
Alexander Woodrow

ATHENS COUNTY
William D. Bartlett
William A. Braddock
J. Cook
Patrick W. Develings
Isaac N. Norton

BELMONT COUNTY
Milton Gray
William Noble
William Perrine and Co.
William B. Reynolds
Amos Wilson

BROWN COUNTY
J.M. Blair
Dennis Cassat
Edward Cassat
Issachar Davis
Jacob Fowler
Ebenezer C. Hatch
P.M. Kay
John Maddux
A. Towner

BUTLER COUNTY
Abram Boyd
- Boyer
Joseph Budd
Ephraim Carmack
Joshua Deleplane
David L. Duffield
Robert E. Duffield
Thomas Enyeart
Isaac Falconer
Sebastian Fromm
Adam Gilliland
Samuel Gregg
- Halderman
Stephen Hayden
Reuben Hills
Thomas P. Jester
Francis Kelshymer
Isaac McClelland
P. Frederick Nardin
Hiram Osborn
Aaron Osgood
Isaac Osgood
Andrew Oyler
Samuel Schafer
- Scott
Harrison Watson
George White
- Wilson

CLARK COUNTY
John L. Berry
William Coles Sr.
Benjamin Coles
James Elam
G.B. Fields
William T.S. Manly
Thomas Montjoy
James Smith
J. Francis Spencer
John G. Wood
Robert Wood
A. Woods

CLERMONT COUNTY
W.H. Beall
Brice R. Blair
Andrew Boulware
Jacob Boulware
Jeremiah Cleveland
Nathaniel Conrey
Turpin Daughters
John Dennison
Ezekiel Dimmits
Amos Downey
Phillip Drum
Otis Dudley (and Son)
John Earhart
Robert Earhart
E.A. Hines
William Hooker
Isaac Huling
Totten Jackson
John C. Jefferies
Lemuel John
Joshua P. Jordon
William Lytle
Samuel McAdams
Christopher McNeill
James McNeill
John McNeill
John Meyers
S.D. Mount
Puzzle and White
John Reakirt
David Richey
Andrew Smith
Jeremiah Smith
Vincent Stevens
Doughty Stockton
Job Stockton
Volney Stockton
James Tomkins

CLINTON COUNTY
- Jones
Daniel Marble
David Marble
Eli McGregor
George B. Moore
Haines Moore
John Haines Moore
Joshua Moore
Burgoyne Purcell
Daniel Radcliffe
John Rogers

FAIRFIELD COUNTY
Lumen Baker
Philip Baker
Bennina Black
William Black
- Booth
Jacob Bope
Andrew Cavett
W.S. Clark
William Duffield
Joseph Grubb
S.K. Hazel
Samuel Herr
Jacob Kirtz
John Leist
Walter McDonald
Peter McKee
George K. Miers
Henry Miller
Christian Musser
Samuel Nye (Neigh)
- Pembroke
John B. Reed
John D. Schlich (Schleigh)
S.Z. Selzer
Daniel Sifford
W. Stiler
George Hamilton Strode
Isaiah Voris
James A. Weakly
Samuel Wilhelm
John Wills
Jesse Woltz

FAYETTE COUNTY
John H. Barker
Hamilton Bryant
Jesse Bryant
Clark Gordon

FRANKLIN COUNTY
James Aston
Andrew Backus
Lumen Baker
David Brooks
John Craig
Joseph Dopp
Isoban G. Dryer
Jacob Elmer
T. Garner
S. Fertig
S.K. Hazel
Adin G. Hibbs
John Jeffords
Jacob Reynolds
John Smith
S.Z. Selzer

GALLIA COUNTY
James Gatewood
Peter Noel
John B. Shephard
Daniel Thompson
William Thompson

GREENE COUNTY
Samuel Binckley
David Bratton
James Bratton
James Bunton
George Charters
John Charters
John D. Conwell
Daniel Day
James Edwards
Mills Edwards
Samuel (Samson) Ferguson
William Gordon
Christian Hosteller
James Jeffries
Uriah Jeffries
Daniel Medsker
David Medsker
John Minton (Mitten)
David Monroe
George Monroe
James Monroe
Daniel Murphy
Abner Read
Amassa Read
John Shearer
Samuel Smeigh
Lyman Taft

GUERNSEY COUNTY
William Cosgrove
Samuel Drummond
Joseph Gregg
Joseph C. Hunter
Samuel Lindsey
James Nelson
Peter Sarchet
Samuel Wilson

HAMILTON COUNTY
(excluding Cincinnati)*
Richard Conklin
Thomas McCammon
Samuel Reed

HIGHLAND COUNTY
Edward Bruce
Newton Doggett
Joseph Hampshir
Uriah Horsmann
William Keyes
James A. Peale
Samuel Peale
James Wadman
Soloman Walton

JACKSON COUNTY
Jesse Stebleton

MEIGS COUNTY
John McMaster
William Parker Sr.
William Prall
John Probst

MONTGOMERY COUNTY
John Childs
Henry Diehl
James Elliott
Elizah Githans
Moses Hatfield
James Henderson
Louis P. Hildreth
James Irwin
Daniel Keifer
Matthew Patton
Aaron S. Richardson
Christian Shiveley
Ebenezer Stibbens

MORGAN COUNTY
James Cornelius
William S. Johnson
Alexander Pinkerton
Henry Pinkerton
Solomon Robinson
Nathaniel W. Sprague

MUSKINGUM COUNTY
Barnhart Allwine
Lawrence Allwine
Westle Allwine
John Alter
John Anthony
Leonard Perry Bailey
Thomas Brown
James Caldwell
Jacob Graves and Company
James Guthrie
James Huey
E.A. Miller
James Reeves
John Sheward
Benjamin Sloan
Daniel Stickney
Joseph Taylor

PERRY COUNTY
J. George Daniel

PICKAWAY COUNTY
John Carolus
William Y. Emmett
Robert K. Foresman
John Hedges
Solomon Hedges
William Jacobs
Basil Justice
Michael May
James McCrum
Washington McLain
Jonathon Moore
G.W. Myers
F. Myers
George R. Piper
Michael Pontius
George Wildbahn

PIKE COUNTY
George Egan

PREBLE COUNTY
Joseph Donohoe
Alexander Mitchell
Thomas Morgan
Joseph Peggens
\- Sayres
William Steele
\- Van Trump
William B. Wilson
George F. Zeitzer

**For information on Cincinnati furniture see* "Furniture Makers of Cincinnati" *by Jane E. Sikes, 1976.*

ROSS COUNTY
Benjamin Adamson
Charles A. Baker
t.H. Bringhurst
William W. Caldwell
Harman DeHaven
Nathan Durfee
William Y. Emmett
James Engle
- Gerens
Willis Graham
William Guthrie
- Hillhouse
Joseph Hopkins
James Howard
George Huffman (Hoffman)
David Long
Henry May
George McCormick
John E. Mills
William Mills
Joseph Thoits Moore
Charles F. Parker
John Peebles
James Phillips
Thomas Renshaw
James Robinson
Robert Robinson
William Robinson
Hector Sanford
Joshua Seney
Jonas Shell
Henry Shepherd
Joseph Shepherd Sr.
William Shepherd
George Stine
John L. Tabb
Jocab Ware
Thomas Allen Ware
J.D. Wiley
Graham Willis
Johnson Woolcot
- Young
John Zimmerman

SCIOTO COUNTY
Steven Cameron
Daniel Edwards
Andrew Jackson Erislow
David Glearkey
James W. Huston
James Isenlord
Samuel G. Jones
James Linn
H.H. McCloud
Levi McDougal
Thomas Morgan
John Peebles
Samuel Rauson

WARREN COUNTY
James R. Abbott
William M. Barton
Allen Clutch
James H. Colbert
John W. Colbert
- Cretors
Edmund Geoghagen
William Gordon
William Halsey
John W. Keyes
John King
Alexander Lewis
John Lewis
Peter S. Lewis
John Lloyd
James Longshore
John Lucas
Andrew McBurney
George Miller
Henry B. Miller
John Mitchell
William Moore
William B. Moore
Jacob C. Roll
C.E. Rosenfield
George Sherman
John Smith
Edwin A. Wiles
William Moon Wiles
Robert Wilson
Samuel F. Yeoman

WASHINGTON COUNTY
Joseph Barker
- Beebee
W.S. Clark
Abner Corwin
William Glessner
Stephen Guthrie
J. Hannan
Alexander Hill
Hugh Hill
Henry Huvey
John Huvey
Robert Logue
Seth Lothrup
John Magee
William Mason
- Powers
T. Ramsay
Nathaniel Smith
Jonathan Sprague
Joshua Sprague
Robert Wells, Jr.

Lawrence Allwine Windsor Bench attributed to Zanesville.

He used his Philadelphia stamp.

Ohio Trinket Box – Courtesy Mike Clum.

Windsor Cradle.

Interior construction of an Ohio upholstered settee.

Some examples of Ohio chairs.

Ohio Furniture Makers listed in alphabetical order.

ABBOTT, JAMES R......1819
Lebanon, Warren County

James Abbott advertised in the Western Star of December 21, 1819:

NOTICE: Sold at Public Sale at Jared Scofield, Deerfield Township, Warren Cty, Ohio: 1 set of bench plane tools, carpenters tools, one lot of turning tools: some household furniture and lot.

JAMES R. ABBOTT CYNTHIA ABBOTT

ADAMSON, BENJAMIN.....1811-1812-1815-1819
Chillicothe, Ross County

Benjamin Adamson came from Alexandria, Virginia and he was working in Cincinnati in December, 1811 on Sycamore Street. He was living in the house of Mr. Whetstone and was carrying on the cabinetmaking business in all of its branches.

He was still in Cincinnati in 1812 but was planning to farm for his advertisement of December 29 states that he has on hand a variety of articles particularly, mahogany sideboards, secretaries and bureaus which he will dispose of at reasonable prices for cash. He also stated that he will exchange them for a pair of oxen which he needs immediately and twenty milk cows to be delivered in March.

By October 1815 he was in Chillicothe working and advertising in the Scioto Supporter of October 3, 1815, on page 3, column 3:

CABINETMAKING–BENJAMIN ADAMSON
Respectfully informs that he has commenced the cabinetmaking business in the house formerly occupied as the Indian Tavern on Paint Street. Quantity of mahogany furniture of superior quality. Two journeymen, three apprentices.

October 3, 1815.

However, by 1819 Adamson was back in Cincinnati working at 11 New Market Street. He must have changed locations again for he was not listed as working in Cincinnati in the 1825 directory.

ALLWINE FAMILY
Zanesville, Muskingum County

Lawrence Allwine came from Philadelphia; he had been a chairmaker there. His son, Westle, was a chair painter and also sold chairs. He was married to Mary Bowers on October 7, 1809 in Zanesville. He had two sons, Charles and Harrison.

The August 29, 1816 will of John Allwine, recorded at Muskingum Court House Will Book B, page 123, case no. 206 states "exonerate my father Lawrence Allwine from Philadelphia from all debts, book accounts etc." He also mentions his younger brother Barney (Barnhart), his sister Eliza and his brother Westle's children, Charles and Harrison.

In March 1842, in Will Book C of the town of Zanesville, page 376, Westle Allwine requests of his wife Polly (Mary) Allwine that "a plain durable stone be erected at my grave. Keep the minor children together, educate generally and religiously." Westle died in 1842.

ALLWINE, LAWRENCE......1786-1811-1815-1827
ALLWINE, BARNHART
Zanesville, Muskingum County

In the *Cabinetmakers of America* by Bjerkoe published in 1953, Lawrence Allwine is mentioned as working in Philadelphia in 1786 as a Windsor chairmaker. He made chairs for John Penn. His name is stamped on the bottom of a fan backed Windsor. He claimed to have made "the best Windsor chairs, gilt, plain and variously ornamented, being painted with his own patent colors,,," for which he secured a United States Patent. (Horner)

In the Muskingum Messenger of November 13, 1811,there appeared the following ad:

Take Notice
Removed from his old stand six miles on the New Lancaster Road to the town of Zanesville on Main St.

House of Entertainment

At the sign of the Fountain Pump

where the traveler and customers of every description will be accomodated and he assures them that nothing shall be wanting on his part to give general satisfaction to those who may please to favor him with their commands.
Lawrance(sic) Allwine

Nov. 1, 1811

The diary of Paul Furson mentions stopping at Allwine's mentions stopping at Allwine's tavern seven miles east of Zanesville in 1815.

In March, 1827 Lawrence and his son Barnhart sold whole stocks of Windsor chairs at auction. Since there is no will for either of them perhaps they moved to another location. Barnhart and other Allwine relatives were listed as living in Perry County in 1850.

PUBLIC VENDUE.

THE SUBSCRIBERS, living in Zanesville, at the Stand of the Steam boat tavern, intend selling off by auction on Friday and Saturday, the 16th and 17th of March, all their whole Stock of well made

WINDSOR CHAIRS

&

SETTEES,

of various Colours, and Paterns; also a quantity of well made 12 light, 8 by 10 window Sash, a new ten plate Stove and 2 Coat Stoves with pipe, also several Coal Grates; Glass, Stone, and Earthen ware; some good Rifles and Shot guns; a few good Watches, an excellent wooden Clock, some well made Spinning Wheels and Reels. Cast-Steel chopping Axes, trace-Chains, Castings, and a quantity of well seasoned 2 inch Poplar-plank, and some 1 inch poplar and other Boards; Saddlery, house hold and kitchen furniture, a parcel of hogs and young pigs, and many other articles too tedious to enumerate. Sale to commence on each day at 9 o'clock A. M. Conditions of Sale made known, and attendance given accordingly by

LAWRANCE ALWINE,
BARNHART ALWINE.

Zanesville, Feb. 22, 1827.—ts16.

ALLWINE, WESTLE....1814-1819-1834-1842
Zanesville, Muskingum County

Westle Allwine advertised in the Zanesville Express Republican Standard on Wednesday, May 11, 1814:

Sign Painting and Etc.

Westle Allwine removed from Springfield to Zanesville next to Dr. Evans drug store. He intends to carry on his business of painting in its extensive variety. He paints and letters signs, boards of every description and house paints.

The Springfield mentioned here later became Putnam and is now part of Zanesville. Another advertisement appeared in the Zanesville Express of February 16, 1820:

Fancy chair shop

Grateful for the acknowledgement of his customers, fancy and Grecian chair business of various fashions. He has employed the best workmen from the city and the best materials, chairs made and repaired. He has for sale glass, putty, paints, country produce taken in part for the above articles.

Westle Allwine

Westle Allwine was still in Zanesville in 1834. He died there in 1842, leaving his wife Polly (Mary) and his many children.

Fancy Chair Shop.

THE subscriber returns his grateful acknowledgments to his customers for favors shown him in his line of business, and begs leave to inform them and the public generally, that he has commenced the

Fancy & Grecian Chair Business

OF VARIOUS FASHIONS.

He has employed the best of workmen from the citys, and the best materials to make good substantial work. All orders from a distance will be attended to with dispatch. CHAIRS made & repaired at the shortest notice, and warranted.

House and Sign Painting

EXECUTED IN THE NEATEST MANNER.

N. B. He has for sale Paints, Oil, Glass and Putty. Country Produce taken in part payment for the above articles and for work

Westle Allwine.

Zanesville, Aug. 30, 1819. 37

ALTER, JOHN......L. 1779-1850
Zanesville, Muskingum County

John Alter was born in Reading, Somerset County, Pennsylvania in 1779. He married Elizabeth Miller, the daughter of Josiah Miller of Somerset County in 1802.

John Alter went to Lancaster, Ohio but did not find enough business there and decided to return to Pennsylvania. On his way he stopped in Zanesville in 1806.

Norris Schneider states in the Zanesville Times Recorder, November 13, 1966 - "John Alter was driving his covered wagon back home to Pennsylvania in 1806. Sickness and lack of work had discouraged him at Lancaster, Ohio.

He had only $.25 in his pocket when he stopped at Harvey's tavern at Third and Main."

Hearing that John Alter was a chairmaker and wheelwright, Harvey called Daniel Convers and John McIntire. They offered him a free house, provisions and fire wood if he would stay in Zanesville. He accepted.

People rode for 25 miles to buy spinning wheels from Alter. He often worked half the night to supply the demand. As local residents became more prosperous, Alter made better furniture. In 1841 he advertised that he made "common and fancy chairs, settees and sociables etc. embracing Grecian, French and common chairs, Boston and cane Rocking chairs." Alter wanted it known that he used bronze only for low priced work, for better chairs he applied gold leaf. He also made bureaus, tables and bedsteads.

One authentic piece of Alter cabinetwork is a three piece banquet table Alter made for the Lutheran delegation convention.

John Alter died in Zanesville in 1850.

ANTHONY, JOHN......1823
Zanesville, Muskingum County

John Anthony advertised in the Zanesville, Ohio Republican on Saturday, March 8, 1823:

WANTED - One or two boys, 15 to 16 years of age, as apprentice to cabinetmaking business. Boys from the country preferred.

March 3, 1823 JOHN ANTHONY

N.B. Cabinetware kept constantly on hand at his stand at Main and Third streets.

In the Zanesville, Ohio Republican of July 26, 1823, there appeared the ad:

JOHN ANTHONY, at the upper end of Main and Third streets informs the public that he keeps on hand furniture made in the latest style - Grecian sofas and chairs in the neatest manner, and according to the latest fashion.

And again in the Zanesville, Ohio Republican of December 27, 1823:

JOHN ANTHONY, at the corner of Main and Third street, informs his friends and the public that he keeps on hand furniture of every description made in the most favorable manner, which he will sell very low for cash and country produce. Grecian sofas and chairs.

John Anthony ceased making furniture for in 1850 he was listed as 55 years of age with the profession of water works agent.

ASTON, JOHN......1835
Columbus, Franklin County

The following advertisement appeared in the Western Hemisphere, July 29, 1835:

Upholstery and Cabinetmaking. The subscriber would respectfully inform the citizens of Columbus and the public in general, that he has opened a shop on State Street opposite the public buildings where he will manufacture to order any article in either of the above lines. He hopes his experience in New York City, unremitting attention and an anxious desire to please, will secure to him a share of that patronage, which it shall be his constant study to merit.

James Aston

BACKUS(BACHUS),ANDREW......B.1790..1815-1879
Columbus, Franklin County

From the *History of Franklin and Pickaway Counties, Ohio:*

ANDREW BACKUS, living, son of Simon Backus, was born in Middleborough, Plymouth county, Massachusets, October 3, 1790, in the old homestead that formerly belonged to his grandfather, Rev. Isaac Backus, the Baptist minister and historian. He was a descendant of Stephen Backus, who came from Norwich,

England, about 1635, and lived in Saybrook. Afterwards, in 1660, he moved to Norwich, Connecticut, with his three sons. They were among the first settlers of the place, and he was the first white man that died in Norwich. Hannah Alden, the mother of Andrew Backus, was fifth in lineal descent from John Alden, one of the Mayflower pilgrims that landed at Plymouth, December 1620. Mr. Backus lived with his father, working on the farm and attending school, until he went to Taunton to learn the cabinet trade with William and Henry Washburn. At the age of twenty-one, having finished his trade, he remained some time with them as a journeyman. While living in Raynham, Massachusetts, he was enrolled as a soldier in the War of 1812, under Captain Chase. This company was stationed at Fairhaven. When discharged, he went to Middleborough to live, and was drafted and enrolled as a corporal under Captain Greenleaf Pratt, who joined the remainder of the command at Plymouth beach, September 21, 1814. Mr. Backus received an honorable discharge, also a deed from the government of one hundred and sixty acres of land in Plymouth county, Iowa; further recognition of his services was given him in the form of a pension, by act of congress. He is the oldest living (continuously) citizen of Columbus, and voted at the October election of 1879, in his ninetieth year. He has aided some in building up the city, having built several business and dwelling houses. He came from a long-lived stock, had a strong constitution, and these, together with regular and temperate habits, have given him almost perfect health and freedom from sickness. He rarely knew, by experience, what sickness was, until late years. His brother, Joseph A. Backus, in his eighty-first year, lives in Middleborough, Massachusets, on the old homestead of his father and grandfather.

May 25, 1815, he decided to go to Columbus, Ohio, then a great undertaking, and a long, tedious journey, full of hardship and exposure, taking several weeks to make the trip. At Chenango Point he remained several months. At Franklin, Pennsylvania, he saw the Indians spreading blankets on the river, gathering floating oil, which they sold as a cure for rheumatism. At Pittsburg he took passage on a flat-boat down the Ohio river, to the mouth of the Muskingum, there took passage on a boat to Zanesville, and thence by wagon to Columbus, through forests and over almost impassable mud and corduroy roads, arriving in Columbus the twenty-fifth of October. He immediately made arrangements for the manufacture of furniture, being the first to begin the cabinet trade in Columbus. His shop was on High, north of Mound street. He built, opposite this, a double frame dwelling, with John W. Smith, now the third house north of Mound, on the west side of High street.

May 10, 1817 Mr. Backus started, on horseback, for Middleborough, Massachusetts. He rode as far as Catskill, and then sold his horse and took the boat to Providence. The trip, which took him fifty-four days to complete, was for the purpose of marrying Miss Bathsheba King, daughter of John King, of Raynham, Massachusetts. The happy couple were united, August 24, 1817, and remained at Raynham and Middleborough, visiting with their friends, until 14th, when they bade good-bye to kindred, and set out to try their fortunes on the frontier. They traveled with their own team, in a covered wagon well filled with necessary articles for housekeeping, and were sixty-two days, journeying towards the setting sun, before arriving in Columbus, Ohio. ..They arrived November 16, 1817, with thankful hearts, rejoicing to be at rest in their new home.

The following extract is from the Ohio State Journal, 1866:

The manufacture of furniture and cabinet ware is one of our best developed branches of trade. This is now represented by three powerful firms, whose sales aggregate in amount nearly, or quite, three hundred thousand dollars per annum. It is curious, in this connection, to trace the rise and progress of this business, now so much a specialty, and a retrospective glance will be interesting, as well as instructive. Mr. Andrew Backus, the pioneer in the manufacture of furniture in Columbus, Ohio, moved to this city in 1816, and soon after established himself in this business on High, near Mound streets....Mr. Backus, with his employes, worked in the old shop some seven years, when he moved into more commodious buildings, erected by him in the rear of where the Backus buildings now are, on the east side of High, near Town street. In 1838 he built the brick store-room adjoining, on the north of his dwelling, and occupied by his sons, Orrin and Lafayette Backus, as a family grocery store, and, in 1848, built the three story brick business block adjoining his residence on the south. Mr. Backus carried on the business for some forty years, and retired, leaving an extensive trade to his successors.

---

continued on next page

In the Franklin County Federal Manufacturer's Census of 1820 (as reprinted in the Tri-State Trader) appears the entry:

Andrew Bachus, Owner, made cabinetware using cherry and walnut, costing $100. One man employed. Capital $75.00. Articles sold in the neighborhood.

Andrew Backus advertised in the Daily Ohio State Journal of Thursday, July 20, 1837:

Andrew Backus- cabinetware shop, wareroom and shop on East High Street, south of the city(of Columbus).

BAILEY, LEONARD PERRY......L. 1789-1887
Zanesville, Muskingum County

Leonard Perry Bailey was born in Budd's Ferry, Pennsylvania in 1789; he moved to Pittsburgh for his apprenticeship to an organ and piano maker which he finished in 1814. He came to Zanesville in 1823, and established his shop on Main Street at Court Alley. He married Abigail Matthews, the daughter of Increase Matthews. His shop was on the north side of Main Street at Court Alley. Later he moved to Main Street and Second.

He never advertised in the newspaper but he made a great deal of furniture for the Zanesville people and a great deal remains in the family today.

His account books remain today. The earliest one is dated 1823-1824 and is preserved in Pioneer Society. The candle stand he made for Levi Whipple cost $7.00. He charged $2.00 for a bed, a bureau was $14.00. A High Post bed was $13.00. The most expensive item was a sideboard for $130.00.

There are several photographs of Mr. Bailey's furniture and ledger book. The account book from 1824-1829 which is owned by the Pioneer Society states that Leonard Bailey made : a cradle for $2.00, a trundle bed for $2.50, a cord bed for $2.00, bureau - $14.00, high post bed - $13.00, a sofa - $35.00, night tables - $2.00, breakfast tables for $5.00, and ladies work tables for $50.00. His fancy furniture cost more: pair of harp end tables - $50.00, pair of claw dining tables - $80.00, sideboard - $88.00. A later ledger book was dated 1841. He was making pianos, mahogany chairs, card tables, corner stands, sofa tables and sofas. He was using rosewood, mahogany, birdseye maple and holly veneers.

Mr. Bailey died in 1876 at the age of 87.

BAKER, CHARLES A......1842
Chillicothe, Ross County

APPRENTICE WANTED;

The subscriber pursuing the chair and cabinetmaking business wishes to take a boy as an apprentice to his trade...one from the country from 14 to 16 years old would be preferred.

July 28, 1842 *CHARLES A. BAKER,*
Chillicothe

BAKER, LUMEN......1830
Lancaster, Fairfield County

This ad appeared in the Lancaster Ohio Eagle of November 27, 1830:

LUMEN BAKER has removed from his former shop to the house recently occupied by James H. Smith, deceased, one door west of Mr. Townsend's silver shop and directly opposite the nail factory, where he intends to manufacture and keep for sale plain and fashionable cabinetware: and with promptness and dispatch to make to order every article in his line of business, having spared neither pains nor expense in procuring materials.

BAKER, PHILLIP......1818
Lancaster, Fairfield County

This notice appeared in the Lancaster Ohio Eagle of April 16, 1818:

Tools will be sold on Friday, the last day of May, next at P. & S. Beechers store, sundry articles of the Estate of PHILLIP BAKER, deceased. Carpenter, cabinetmakers and printers tools and vessels.

Lancaster, April 15, 1818 JESSE BEECHER, Administrator

BARKER, JOHN H......1830-1850
Washington Courthouse, Fayette County

John H. Barker is listed in the 1850 Census of Ohio. He was born in 1809 in Virginia and worked as a cabinetmaker in Fayette County.

BARKER, JOSEPH......1789..D.1843
Marietta, Washington County

Information about Joseph Barker comes from the book, *Recollections of the First Settlement of Ohio*, edited with an introduction and notes by George Gordon Blazier. Joseph Barker's father was Deacon Ephraim Barker who was an important housewright and church builder in southern New Hampshire. Ephraim was also a cabinetmaker - the journal of Samuel Lane of Stratham, New Hampshire states, "I bo't my desk and bookcase of Eprhaim Barker 100 + old ten."

Joseph Barker was known for his athletic ability and ready sense of humor. At 14 years he became his father's apprentice. He acquired knowledge of architecture and he was later the carpenter on the meeting house in New Boston, New Hampshire. In 1789 he arrived in Marietta.

He had been educated at Exeter Acadamy in New England until the age of 15. He then apprenticed to his father and became a skilled architect in Ipswich; he also worked in New Boston, New Hampshire. In 1788 he married Elizabeth Dana, the daughter of William Dana. He left Amhurst, New Hampshire for Ohio in a wagon drawn by oxen to float on a flatboat to Marietta in 1789. He continued in the business of housewright and also built furniture. He built BLennerhassett Home on Blennerhassett Island. He died on September 21, 1843.

A chair attributed to Joseph Barker remains at Campus Martius Museum.

BARTLETT, WILLIAM D......1825
Athens, Athens County

William D. Bartlett advertised in the Athens Mirror & Literary Gazette of Saturday, December 17, 1825:

Cabinetmaking - The above business will be carried on by the Subscriber on College Street, one door north on James Street where his friends and customers are deserved to call.

William D. Bartlett
Athens, Dec. 12, 1825

William D. Bartlett and Isaac N. Norton were partners in the cabinetmaking business prior to December 16, 1825, and then they separated and went into business separately.

BARTON, WILLIAM M......1836 - 1840
Lebanon, Warren County

From the penitentiary records of Warren County:

WILLIAM M. BARTON, CABINETMAKER: born New York.
Sentenced in the county of Warren: Sentence for assault and intent to kill. Disposition: temperate, age 20; term; 7 years. Date of sentencing: 1836. Discharged: pardoned by Governor Stanton in 1840. His character: he has sunken eyes.

BEALL, W. N.......L. 1805-1890..W. 1841-1878
Point Isabel, Clermont County

The History of Clermont County states the W. N. Beall (born 1805) worked from 1841 to 1878 at cabinetmaking. He died in 1890.

BEEBEE, - 1817
Marietta, Washington County

The following advertisement appeared in the American Friend of October 24, 1817:

The subscriber commenced the Cabinetmaking Business on Ohio Street in the shop lately occupied by Mr. Haven as a bakery. Those who please to favor him with their custom, may depend on having their work done in the best manner and on the most reasonable terms- Most kinds of country produce will be received in payment.

Marietta October 23, 1817
Powers and Beebee

BEREMAN, JAMES......1823
West Union, Adams County

The West Union Register of December 2, 1823:

CHAIRS - The subscriber respectfully informs the public that he carries on the business of CHAIRMAKING in the town of West Union and solicits a share of their patronage. He warrants his chairs to be superior in point of workmanship to any ever offered for sale in this place and will sell cheap for cash. He also has on hand a quantity of spinning wheels which he will sell on reasonable terms for cash or country produce.

JAMES BEREMAN

BEREMAN, THOMAS......1824
West Union, Adams County

In the West Union Village Register of April 27, 1824 appears the notice:

ONE CENT REWARD - RAN AWAY from the subscriber on the 16th instant, GEORGE WELSH, an indentured apprentice to the Windsor chairmaking and painting business, 12 years old, light complexion, had on when he went away a new set of brown jeans, fur hat and a new shirt and shoes, being somewhat better clad than is usual for an apprentice to be. Whoever returns said GEORGE will be cooly treated and recieve no thanks, but shall have the above reward. All persons are cautioned against harboring him as I believe he was persuaded away.

West Union, April 23, 1824 THOMAS BEREMAN

This man had formally been in a stage coach line with Thomas McCague.

BERRY, JOHN L......1825-1830-1852
Springfield, Clark County

John L. Berry was in Springfield in 1825 for he was a fence viewer in that year. His shop was on South Street, later he was located on Main and Fisher as a cabinetmaker.

On Febuary 13, 1830, The Western Pioneer carried the following advertisement:

CARPENTER & CABINETMAKER'S TOOLS - The Subscriber has now on hand and will keep constantly for sale at his cabinet shop on South Street a general assortment of carpenter and cabinetmaker's tools, which will be disposed of at the Cincinnati prices. He will warrant them equal if not superior to any maker in the country, both for neatness and utility.

Springfield, Feb. 13, 1830 JOHN L. BERRY

In 1831 John Berry was allowed $3 for making a coffin for Isaac, a black man and pauper. He may have stayed in Springfield for a lifetime. He was still working in Springfield in 1852.

BINCKLEY, SAMUEL......1829
Xenia, Greene County

Ohio Farmers Records and Xenia Gazette, June 25, 1829:

HOUSEPAINTING & CHAIR MAKING:

The Subscriber wishes to inform the public generally that he has commenced the above business one door east of Mr. Hiveling's dwelling house and directly opposite Mr. Sander's grocery, where he intends keeping on hand an assortment of chairs and will be ready to do housepainting for all who may favor him with their custom; and from his experience in the business, hopes to merit a share of the public patronage.

SAMUEL BINCKLEY
Xenia, June 20, 1829

Samuel Binckley was not listed as working in Xenia in 1850 in the census.

BLACK, BENNINA......1826
Fairfield County

The following information comes from the Fairfield County Records of Indenture: 1814-1830, Dec. 7, 1824:

WILLIAM BLACK, age 17 years, 9 mos., son of Peter of Perry County, Ohio. Bound to Bennina Black of Fairfield County, carpenter and joiner and cabinetmaker, until age 21.

Nov. 2, 1826

BLAIR, BRICE R......1837-1850
Batavia, Clermont County

From the Clermont Courier of August 26, 1837:

ONE CENT REWARD - Runaway from the subscriber on the night of Wednesday last an indentured apprentice to the cabinetmaking business, of the name Joshua P. Jordan. All persons are forewarned not to harbor or employ said boy under the penalty of law. Any person

returning him will be entitled to the above reward, but no charges will be paid.
Batavia, Aug. 26, 1837 Brice R. Blair

Brice R. Blair was also named in *The History of Clermont County 1883* - William Lytle and Brice R. Blair - cabinetmakers. Brice R. Blair was in Brown County in 1850.

BLAIR, J. M.
Brown County

In the *History of Brown County* by W. H. Biers & Company (1883) J. M. Blair is listed as a cabinetmaker in Pleasant Township.

BOOTH,James M......1817-1825
Marietta, Washington County

Information from the Federal Manufacturer's Census 1820 for Washington County (Reprinted in the Tri-State Trader, 9 October 1971, p. 38)

James M. Booth - owner - Generally made cabinet ware. Used cherry, black walnut, poplar planks and scantling. 12,000 feet costing $100 - Employed one hand sometimes 2 men with apprentices. Operated tools, benches for 4 hands. Capital $550, wages $200 con't. expenses $175 (for locks, hinges, screws and nails) market sales $1,200 - Establishment has been rather improving lately, in demand for its manufacture but difficult to effect sales for cash. All articles are sold in this vicinity, a great portion of them for barter. It is about 3 years since it was commenced (1817)

He was still in operation in 1825.

BOPE, JACOB......1799-1889
Lancaster, Fairfield County

The following statement of Jacob Bope comes from the *History of Fairfield County*, courtesy of Mrs. Charles Drinkle.

Abraham Bope, father of General Jacob Bope of this county and Phillip Bopes of Lancaster, emigrated from Rockingham, Virginia in 1803 and located in Pleasant Township. A camp was erected and then a log cabin. Mr. Bope now in his 79th year. Indians, Wyandots and Delawares were all over the country in small hunting parties. There was a German Scool and English School before 1810. Money was seldom seen by anybody and it was exteremely difficult to pay what little tax there was. There was little that could be sold for cash. The price of a days work was 25 cents. Jacob Bope was a carpenter...He was also a Captain, Colonel and General in the Ohio Militia. He was born in 1799 and died in 1889. He is buried in Zeigler Lotham Church, 5 miles north of Lancaster on Route 37.

The following is from the Records of Indenture at the Ohio Historical Society, page 109:

BOPP JACOB - House carpenter and cabinetmaker in Pleasant Township, Fairfield County, Ohio - 28th of June 1828. Had CHRISTIAN SMITH, age 16, as an apprentice.

BOULWARE, C. H.......1820
Williamsburg, Clermont County

The *History of Clermont County*, Williamsburg Township states that there was a chair manufactory owned by C.H. Bolwear (Boulware) which employed 20 hands and was in Williamsburg, originally called Lytletown.

This splint chair manufactory was started in 1820 by Jacob and Andrew Boulware and was still in business in 1883 under Charles Boulware. Jacob and Andrew Boulware all manufactured by hand and sold to parties living in the place.

BOULWARE, JACOB & ANDREW......1820
Williamsburg, Clermont County

See BOULWARE, C. H.

Boulware, Andrew
Williamsburg Twp Cemetery
Died 17 October 1875 54y 2m
Estate Docket 5 p260 July 1876
Sale:

½	doz. rattan chairs	6.00
10	chairs	42.50
½	doz fancy rockers	3.87
½	doz childs rockers	2.75
1	set harnes	13.00
	Hise of wagon	2.25
2	large arm rockers	4.50
	wagon hise	1.30
200	com rocker	14.00
138	" child "	5.50
67	" large "	6.70
	A lot arm chair stuff	135.00
24	Dz ½ in chairs in white	78.00
9½	" ¼ in rockers	59.38
3	Dz ½ in chairs finished	12.00
1	Bay horse	40.00
7	dz ½ finish chairs	28.00
7½	dz ½ finish "	37.50
½	dz fancy chairs	5.50
160	posts for windsor chairs	2.00

continued on next page

1	spring wagon	16.00
8	cords oak timber	26.00
⅞	cords maple timber	2.89
	Walnut stuff for chairs	.75
1	Bay horse	50.00
1	Delaware chair	3.50
1	set cane chairs	5.00
14	cane chairs	35.00
⅓	dz Massa chairs	11.00

Boulware, Jacob
Administration Docket A p84
November 1842
Administrator: Emily Boulware
Inventory by: John Stevens
Sam McAdams
Sam L. Leffingwell
Inventory:

5	Pruning Gouger	.50
12	chizels	2.00
18	Spoke Shavy	3.00
17	Brass Bitts	2.00
2	Tenow Saws	2.00
1	Hand Saw	.75
2	©©©© 1 guage 1 bevel	1.50
3	wood files, 1 testor, & mallet	.50
2	Bung Augers, 2 pc compass	1.50
1	Drawing knife	.37
1	clamp ©©©© for bench	1.00
1	Lott squares & 2 rules	1.00
1	Adze & Bow Saw	1.75
1	Lott clamp, Ham with stone & Gemblit	.50
1	Glue Pot	.75
1	Work Bench	2.50
1	Mortering Bench	.25
1	Grindstone	1.00
1	Foot Lathe	2.00
2	Lott Scroll Chairs new	20.00
4	Lott Windsor "	28.00
1	Letter	6.00
9	small Childs Chairs	13.50
4	Rocking Chairs	5.00
1	Lott Chair stuff	2.50
1	Rocking Chair	1.25
1	Lott paints	3.25
1	Lott Lamp Black & Bottles	2.00
3	Bottles Paint	.75
1	Lott varnish, oil, spirits	12.00
1	Lott Glue	1.62
1	Box screws	1.50
1	Lott Brownz	10.50
1	Paint Box	.50
2	cows	20.00
1	sow & 5 pigs	5.50
2	Feather beds	40.00
1	Trundle Bed	2.00
2	Tables	5.00
1	Stand	2.00
1	Lott chair	7.00
1	Large spinning wheel	3.00

All inventories are printed as found without spelling corrections.

BOYD, ABRAM......1827
Butler County

Abram Boyd is mentioned in the *History of Butler County* edited by the Hon. Bert S. Bartlow, W. H. Todhunter, Stephen D. Cone and others. It is noted that he was a cabinetmaker but no specific date is cited. He probably worked about 1827.

BOYER, -......1825
Riley Village, Butler County

Riley Village (Township) was laid out by Pierson Konklin, Joseph M. Konklin and Samuel Grey on October 25, 1848. Years before the town was platted, it was a place of considerable importance to the township. Riley was a Post Office as early as 1825 and one of the first settlers was Mr. Boyer, furnituremaker. This information comes from the *History of Butler County, Ohio.*

BRADDOCK, WILLIAM A......1840-1844
Athens County

From the Athens County Penitentiary Records:

BRADDOCK, WILLIAM A. cabinetmaker, Born N.Y. Lived County of Athens. His crime was horse stealing, date: 1844.
Description - He was temperate, age 25, his prison term was 6 years. He was discharged at the end of his term in 1850. He had a wife living in New York City.

BRATTON, DAVID......1839-1840-1841
Xenia, Greene County

From the Xenia, Ohio, Torchlight of Thursday, September 12, 1839:

CHAIR FACTORY - The Subscriber would inform his friends and the public that he has commenced the chair making business in all of its various branches on Main Street, 2 doors west of Nieukirks Hat Shop, where he intends keeping on hand a general assortment of fancy Windsor chairs, all of which he warrants equal to any made in the Western county and will dispose of them on the most accomodating terms.

Persons wishing to purchase will find it to their advantage to call and examine for themselves as he is determined to sell low for cash or country produce.

Xenia, Aug. 15 David Bratton
Highest prices paid for chair stuffs.

He also advertised in the Ohio Peoples Press, Thursday, June 11, 1840:

CHAIR MANUFACTORY - South side of Main Street, west of Detroit Street, Xenia, Ohio.

Mar. 28, 1840 DAVID BRATTON

David Bratton's advertisement in the Greene County Torchlight of September 5, 1844 indicates that he apparently moved his shop.

CHAIRS, CHAIRS - from little chairs up to settees that weary person may have ease. THE SUBSCRIBER respectfully returns his thanks to the public for past patronage and solicits a continuance of the same. He has a large and splendid assortment of Windsor, cottage, and rocking chairs, settees, etc. which he will sell low for cash or approved country produce. Shop on Maxwell Street bet. Main and 2nd.

David Bratton

BRATTON, JAMES......1816-1840..D. 1867
Xenia, Greene County

James Bratton advertised in the Peoples Press, Xenia, Ohio, on July 16, 1840:

JAMES BRATTON, Chair manufactory - south side of Main Street, west of Detroit.
Xenia, May 29, 1840

Robinson's *History of Greene County* states that James Bratton came to Xenia in 1816 from South Carolina. He died on January 22, 1867 at age 75. He was buried at Woodlawn Cemetery.

BRINGHURST, T.H. 1818-1819-1843
Chillicothe, Ross County

T. H. Bringhurst was in Chillicothe before March 25, 1818 for in the Chillicothe Supporter of that date Peebles and Bringhurst advertised:

Cabinetmakers - Have moved their shop from Second to Water Street opposite McCoy and Culbertson's Store in the building on the corner of Bank Alley. From their acquaintence with the newest fashions and attention to business they hope to give general satisfaction to those who may favor them with their custom. They have on hand and intend keeping an assortment of mahogany of the best quality.

Two or three journeymen cabinetmakers and one or two apprentices wanted.
Chillicothe, March 17

They next advertised in Chillicothe on April 3, 1818.

This partnership was dissolved in 1819 when Peebles left Chillicothe and went to Gallipolis. It is not known whether Mr. Bringhurst stayed in Chillicothe or moved elsewhere. 25 years later a cabinetmaker named T. H. Bringhurst surfaced in Dayton. The following advertisement comes from the Dayton Journal & Advertiser of January 3, 1843, page 3, column 6:

NEW CABINETWARE ROOMS - Main Street, opposite the Market House, Sign of the Bedstead. T. H. Bringhurst respectfully informs the citizens of Dayton and vicinity that he has opened a wareroom at the above place, where he intends to make and keep furniture that will give satisfaction to all that may purchase. He is prepared to manufacture, to order, mahogany furniture of every description on moderate terms. Having received and being the constant receiver of mahogany veneers from Philadelphia, he is able to furnish superior articles upon very reasonable terms. He is also prepared to furnish coffins, etc. etc. Mattresses of all sizes made of and prepared from corn husks, moss and curled hair kept on hand and made to order.

BRODERICK, J. C. 1837
Columbus, Franklin County

From the Daily Ohio State Journal of Thursday, July 20, 1837, page 4:

J. C. Broderick - Chair Manufactory - Northeast corner of High and Town Streets in Columbus in 1837.

BROWN,-......1836
Batavia, Clermont County

See Lytle and Brown - Batavia, Clermont County

BROWN, THOMAS......1814
Zanesville, Muskingum County

The following advertisement appeared in the Zanesville Express & Republican Standard of May 4, 1814:

WOODEN CLOCKS - completely repaired and regulated. THOMAS BROWN - near Mr. James Reeves' Inn at the Sign of the Star, Main Street, Zanesville. AND CASES FURNISHED, if repaired. Said BROWN intends carrying on the usual business of cabinetmaking and chairmaking in a small way, together with sign, fancy and plain painting. Moderate prices to receive for share of public patronage.

Zanesville, May 3, 1814

N. B. He also accepts hog bristles.

BRUCE, EDWARD......1823
Leesburg, Highland County

Edward Bruce commenced making furniture for Samuel Saunder and John Henley on the 18th of November, 1823. Saunder and Henley were merchants or agents for several men who made the furniture, were paid for it and then the merchants sold it to others. This was a very unusual and rarely done practice.

The ledger book from Saunder and Henley indicates that Edward Bruce made one breakfast table - $2.25; one dining room table - $3.25; one cupboard - $5.00; making one dining table - $3.25; by making one chist (sic), making one cupboard - $5.00.

BRYANT, HAMILTON......1815
Bloomingburg, Fayette County

Hamilton Bryant was the first settler in Bloomingburg in 1815 and he was the first cabinetmaker there. He later went to Washington Courthouse. He was the father of Jesse Bryant. There was no will, estate or cemetery record for Hamilton Bryant in Fayette County. Information from the *Fayette County History*.

BRYANT, JESSE......L.1810-1880
Bloomingburg, Fayette County

Jesse Bryant of Paint Township was the son of Hamilton Bryant; he was born in 1810, he worked in Bloomingburg and his wife's name was Mary. A manuscript from the David Hankins Estate of Madison Township, Fayette County (O.H.S.) notes the following:

Paid Jesse Bryant for coffin.

BUNTON, JAMES......
Greene County

From the *History of Greene County* by R. S. Dills, 1881:

James Bunton was an early resident, an excellent carpenter and cabinetmaker.

CALDWELL, JAMES......
B.1791..1812-1813-1814-1815-1820-1823
Zanesville, Muskingum County

James Caldwell was born in Virginia in 1791 and probably began working as a cabinetmaker in Zanesville in 1812 at the age of 21. In November of 1813 he moved to a new home and bigger quarters for his shop for the Express and Republican Standard of November 3, 1813 notes on page 3, column 3:

REMOVED - JAMES CALDWELL - Cabinetmaker, informs his old customers that he has removed from his former stand to a house formerly occupied by Abel Lewis, Esq., next door to Dr. Moores. Anything in his line may be had on reasonable terms for cash or country product.

Zanesville, Nov. 3, 1813

He advertised again in the Muskingum Messenger of August 24, 1814:

WANTED IMMEDIATELY - One or two journeymen cabinetmakers to whom constant employment and liberal wages will be made. Application can be found.

JAMES CALDWELL

Generous price will be given on cabinetwork for cherry and walnut boards.

JAMES CALDWELL

His advertisement in the Muskingum Messenger of May 31, 1815 indicates that James Caldwell moved his shop once more:

JAMES CALDWELL - Cabinetmaker, removed to his new shop on the same street opposite his former stand. WANTED IMMEDIATELY - an apprentice boy of 16 years of age to whom good encouragement will be given.

IN NEW SHOP IN SAME STREET OPPOSITE HIS FORMER STAND...

Zanesville, May 22, 1815

In the 1820 Census, James Caldwell had 19 people in his home. He had a large factory for the times, since he was only 28 years old and couldn't have had so many children. Seven of those living in his home were apprentices and journeymen and listed as mechanics.

Another Caldwell ad appears in the Muskingum Messenger throughout 1820 and 1821:

FURNITURE:..THE SUBSCRIBER, after returning thanks for his general support, carries on the cabinetmaking business at his old stand and cabinet wareroom, Main street, in building formerly occupied by M.D. Brook. Furniture ready-made - Cherry, walnut and poplar wanted.

JAMES CALDWELL

In 1823, James Caldwell's brother or father,John, became an insolvent debtor. The following notice appeared in the Muskingum Messenger of July 23, 1823:

NOTICE...THE SUBSCRIBER has been appointed to the Court of Common Pleas, a Trustee for the purpose of receiving all the property of JOHN CALDWELL, insolvent debtor, on the 24th day of January next for the purpose of receiving all claims against the petitioner.

JAMES CALDWELL

At this time James Caldwell stopped advertising and went out of the cabinetmaking business. He was in a position whereby he had to pay off his brother's debt. This created a financial hardship for him to the point where he had to change jobs; it may have been more remunerative to be a merchant. In 1850 he was listed as a merchant; he was also 59 years of age. It is not known when he died.

CALDWELL, WILLIAM W.......1836
Chillicothe, Ross County

In the Scioto Gazette of April 13, 1836 there is an advertisement for turning by William W. Caldwell. The ad indicates he had a large lathe turned by horsepower.

CAMERON,STEPHEN......1840
Wheelersburg, Scioto County

In the *History of Scioto County* it is noted that Andrew Jackson Erislow learned the cabinetmaking business from Stephen Cameron in Wheelersburg.

CARMACK, EPHRAIM......
1794-1805-1806-1811-1820
Shandon, Butler County

Ephraim Carmack was working in Cincinnati very early in the history of the town. He came there in 1794 with Anthony Wayne's army. He was from Bourbon County, Kentucky. He went into business in 1805 in the yellow house belonging originally to Mr. Jeremiah Hunt. He went into partnership with Christopher Smith in June 1805. This partnership terminated on September 23, 1806. They both continued to work in Cincinnati. Carmack's wife Catherine died on June 23, 1806.

In 1811 he was a petty juror. By 1820 he had moved to Shandon, Butler County where he remained for 20 years or longer. He was a Justice of the Peace. Perhaps he continued in business or else he retired to farming; it is also possible that he could have done both.

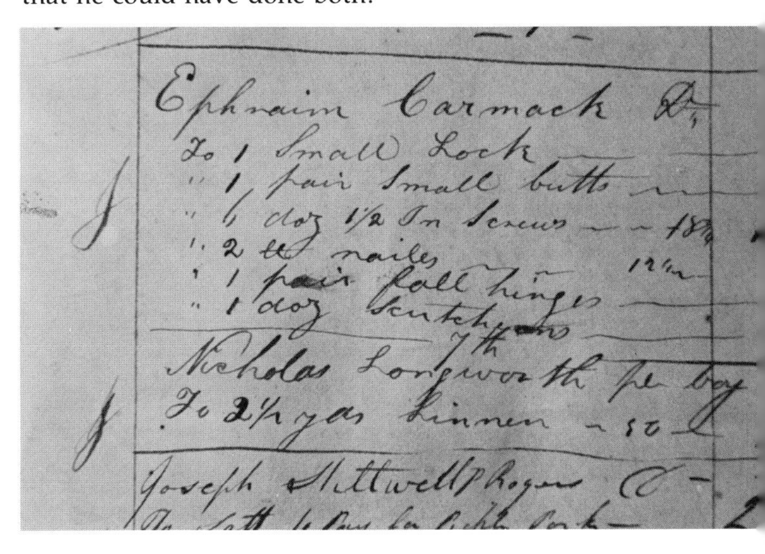
Ephraim Carmack Dr
To 1 Small Lock
" 1 pair Small butts
" 1/2 doz 1/2 In Screws
" 2 lb nails
" 1 pair fall hinges
" 1 doz Scutcheons
Nicholas Longworth

CAROLUS, JOHN......1824-1826-1827
Circleville, Pickaway County

From the Circleville Olive Branch of Saturday, October 30, 1824:

Cabinetmaker and Chairmakers

Wildbahn and Carolus

They have commenced the above business in all of its various branches in the shop formerly owned by Mr. McCrum (cabinetmaker) on North Main Street, three doors north of J. L. Lor and Company. Plain and fancy Windsors, sideboards, secretaries, bureaus, tables, bedsteads, sold very low for wheat, whiskey, oats or any other thing. Highest prices paid for cherry plank.

Circleville, October 9, 1824

The Circleville Olive Branch of September 23, 1826:

Dissolution

The co-partnership between Wildbahn and Carolus is dissolved by mutual consent. Those persons who have unsettled accounts with said firm are requested to call one of the subscribers and adjust the same without delay.

George Wildbahn and John Carolus

After September, 1826, John Carolus continued to advertise alone until July of 1827. It is not known how long after this date that he worked in Circleville.

CASSAT, DENNIS......L. 1804-1878
Higginsport, Brown County

Dennis Cassat was born in New York on June 5, 1804. At eight years old, he moved to Lebanon, Warren County, Ohio and then lived in Cincinnati in 1831. He came to Higginsport where he lived until he died on March 8, 1878. His occupation was cabinetmaker. His son, Edward Cassat, was a cabinetmaker in Higginsport also.

CASSAT, EDWARD
Higginsport, Brown County

See CASSAT, DENNIS

CAVETT, ANDREW M......1817
Fairfield County

The following notice appeared in the American Friend of July 11, 1817:

$50 reward - Stop the swindler - Made his escape from the constable of Hocking Township, Fairfield County, a presence by the name of ANDREW CAVETT, or A.M. CAVETT having been taken on capias for debt - He is a tall man, sandy complexion, red-haired, heavy eyebrowed, occupation, a cabinetmaker, though he generally follows gambling and defrauding for a livelihood, he is an arch-villian and well calculated for taking the unwary and the unsuspecting. He is a noted liar which is easily detected by his shortness of memory. The above reward will be given to any person to secure the said CAVETT in any jail in this state.
JOHN E BAKER

Columbus, June 26, 1817

CHARTERS, GEORGE......L.1775-1846
Xenia, Greene County

George Charters was born April 7, 1775 in Scotland. He came with his family to New York in 1784. George apprenticed to a piano maker there. In 1817 he came to Cincinnati where he worked with Adam Hurdus building the first church organ. It is said that these two men were pioneers in the music industry of Ohio. Charters played the piano in the Music Society of Appolonian and kept a circulating library on Main and Sycamore Streets. In the Western Spy and Literary Cadet, November 9, 1820 he advertised:

Pianoforte manufactory - Fifth between Main and Sycamore Streets.

THE SUBSCRIBER respectfully informs the inhabitants of Cincinnati & Vicinity that he has lately established his painoforte manufactory at the above place where he will make pianos of all descriptions to answer all climates. He has now on hand some of the best, which he invites amateurs and home manufacturers to call and examine. Instruments repaired and tuned in town and country.

N.B. The circulating library is open to subscribers as usual at the same place.

GEORGE CHARTERS

Charters moved from Cincinnati to Xenia after 1820 to join the Associate Reformed Presbyterian Church and became the first of a long line of Charters in Xenia. According to the book, *Ohio Town*, by Helen Hooven Santmeier: "In the beginning, he made whatever furniture that was needed and when there was a need for pianos, he returned to that. Not too many years ago, a few of these instruments stood in our parlours - grand square pianos of dark polished rosewood inlaid above the yellow keyboard with morning glory vines and mother of pearl."

He died in 1846 and was buried in Woodland Cemetery.

CHARTERS, JOHN......1817-1820-1825
Xenia, Greene County

John Charters was born in New York and came with his father, George, to Cincinnati in 1817. He worked with his father to make some of the earliest pianos in Ohio. John moved to Xenia to join the Associate Reformed Presbyterian Church in 1819 or 1820. He married Margaret Monroe in 1825 and they had 10 children. The family became very influential. A piano by John Charters still remains in the family. In 1918 it was owned by John Thorburn Charters.

In 1850 John Charters was listed as a silversmith. He owned 1200 acres of land.

CHILDS, JOHN.....1829
Dayton, Montgomery County

Childs advertised in the Dayton Journal and Advertiser of July 14, 1829:

CHAIRMAKING, PAINTING & GLAZING

The Subscriber respectfully informs the public that he has established himself for the purpose of carrying on the above business in the white shop one door north of STONE & BOSTWICK'S opposite the clerk's office, Main Street, where he will keep on hand chairs of every description, which will be sold for cash. Painting and glazing executed in the neatest manner, in the most reasonable terms.

JOHN CHILDS

CLARK, -......1823
West Union, Adams County

The West Union Village Register of December 15, 1823 announces:

Dissolution of Partnership

The partnership between Clark and Crumpton is this day dissolved. The business will be carried on by the subscriber in all of its various branches at the former stand of Clark and Crumpton.

William Crumpton

The partnership lasted only a month or two at the very most. The first name of this man is unknown at present.

CLARK, W.S.......1825
Marietta, Washington County

From the American Friend and Marietta Gazette of Friday, May 23, 1825:

W.S. CLARK - respectfully informs the citizens of Marietta and the vicinity that he has commenced the chairmaking business in the house formerly occupied by Sylvester and Brock - a few rods west of Esquire Booth's Cabinet Shop, where he will attend to all calls in his line of business. He wishes an apprentice of 15 or 16 years old to the above business, where he will also instruct in painting. He must be a boy of good habits. *May 17, 1825*

CLEVELAND, JEREMIAH......1810
Batavia, Clermont County

Jeremiah Cleveland worked in Batavia in 1810. He had been the apprentice to Aaron Chapin between 1799 and 1800 in Hartford, Connecticut.

CLUTCH, ALLEN
Warren County

The *History of Warren County* lists Allen Clutch as a cabinetmaker in Warren County before 1808.

COLBERT,JAMES H.......1850
Warren County

The 1850 Census mentions that James H. Colbert was a cabinetmaker working in Warren County in 1850. He was from New York and was probably the son of John W. Colbert.

COLBERT, JOHN W.......1818-1819-1820
Lebanon, Warren County

John W. Colbert was a cabinetmaker who worked in Cincinnati before 1814 with Christopher Smith. The partnership was dissolved November 15, 1814. He was in partnership in Lebanon, Ohio with William M. Wiles before 1818. In the Western Star of September 19, 1818 John W. Colbert and William M. Wiles dissolved their partnership. On the same date Colbert went into business for himself in Lebanon. His last notice was published in Lebanon, April 20, 1819. In 1820 John W. Colbert was listed in Clermont County, Ohio in the 4th Census as the head of a family.

COLES,WILLIAM......L.1803-1862
Springfield,Clark County

William Coles is mentioned in *Sketches of Springfield in 1856,* which presents views of Springfield's social, literary and religious institutions and business interests:

WILLIAM COLES - formerly of the City of New York, came to Springfield in 1833 and established a FURNITURE MANUFACTORY which was in business in 1856. It was considered in 1856 the oldest furniture manufactory in the city. He was in business with his sons with the annual income of $10,000 a year. His son, J.W. COLES, entered into business with him in 1852, and in 1854, H. COLES entered the business. The father retired in 1856. WILLIAM COLES is now in the undertaking business. The 2 sons, J.W. and H. COLES, having succeeded their father, will continue the reputation of the father "that in the longest period of 23 years he has been able to establish".

From *Yesteryear in Clark County, Ohio:*

My father, William Coles, Sr. who came to Springfield in 1832, lived in a little brick house on West Main Street. Later he bought property on the southwest corner of the alley between Fountain and Center. He was a cabinetmaker and an undertaker. His first place of business was 23 East Main Street.

Corn, flour, wood and everything was taken in trade for furniture and we would trade it off again as best we could. I frequently find about the country pieces of furniture turned out by my father 40 or 50 years ago.

These reminiscences are from interviews with aged citizens, which appeared in 1893 in the Springfield Sunday News; later they were copied by the W.P.A. and published in 1948. William Coles was still in the furniture business in 1852 with his residence on Main Street between Market and Center streets.

The following advertisements give testimony to Coles' work in Springfield:

From the Western Pioneer, Saturday, July 27, 1833:

Dissolution

The partnership heretofore existing under the firm of Spencer and Smith is dissolved by mutual consent. The business will be carried on under the firm of

Spencer and Coles

We are authorized to settle the business of the late firm

J.F. Spencer

James Smith

William Coles

Springfield, July 20, 1833

Wanted Immediately

Two Smart, Active Boys, as apprentices to the cabinet and chairmaking business. Good encouragement will be given to such on application to the subscribers.

Spencer and Coles

The next year in the (Ohio) Pioneer, August 30, 1834, page 3, column 4:

Dissolution

The partnership heretofore existing between the subscribers under the firm of

Spencer and Smith

in the cabinet and chairmaking business was dissolved on the 3rd of November, 1833 by mutual consent.

The business of chair and bedstead making will be carried under the firm of W. and G. Coles

Francis Spencer

William Coles

The above ad continued weekly for a year. On October 18, 1834, this ad appeared in the (Ohio) Pioneer:

Take Warning

Those persons indebted to the firm of Spencer and Smith and the firm of Spencer and Coles are requested to call and settle their accounts immediately, the former especially may expect an early official call should they not attend this notice.

Wm. Coles

The following entries are from the ledger book of the Mad River Mills at the Clark County Historical Society:

On Sept., 1837

William Coles Dr.
To 900 feet of sugarplank $9.00

On January 1838

William Coles Dr
To 625 Chair legs at 1 1/4 e $7.81 1/4

The Mad River Mills were planing lumber and turning an enormous number of chair legs for William Coles. Mr.Coles was still advertising in the Republic on Friday, September 13, 1839:

Chair and Cabinet Establishment

By W. Coles

The subscriber respectfully informs his friends that he continues the above manufactories in all their branches at the old stand opposite the Exchange Hotel.

He has such arrangements with regard to material and workmen as warrant him in assuring his friends that he can turn out durable work of the latest and most superior finish and on terms below the ordinary prices of furniture in neighboring towns. Thankful for the generous support already extended to him by the citizens of Clark County, he requests a continuation of public patronage.

The undertaking business will also receive the

30th John Craptree Dr
By Cash — $ 1.00 00

30th Baught of Samuel Drummond
One thousand bushels Corn @ 35 cts
to be Delivered til the first May next

1838
January 6th Baught of E. D. Baker
One thousand bush Corn @ 37½ cts
to be Deliv til the first May next

11th John Miller Dr
To 750 Laths @ 20 cts — $ 1 50

16th Wm Drummond Dr
To 500 feet 1 in @ 1.00 — $ 5 00

16th Ezra Baker Dr
To 233 feet 3/4 in @ 94 — $ 2 19

19th John Miller Dr
To 250 Laths — 50

20th Wm Coles Dr
To 625 Chair legs @ 1¼ cts — $ 7 81

23rd Humphrey Orance Dr
To 700 broom handles @ 1¼ — $ 8 75

25th Peter Heck Dr — [illegible] — 4 37
To 439 feet in @ 1.00 and [illegible] — 00

25th Joseph Cox Dr for plank — 50

attention of W. Coles, a HEARSE always in readiness and every preparation to insure prompt satisfactory arrangements for funeral occasions.

Sept.13, 1839

William Coles was successful. He continued in business with his sons, J.W. joined him in 1852 and H. Coles in 1854. Their business thrived. William Coles continued to work as an undertaker until his death in 1862.

CONKLIN, RICHARD......1815
Mt. Healthy, Hamilton County

HAMILTON AVENUE - Southwest corner and Compton Road, south of Peter LaBoiteau's home, at 7513 Hamilton Avenue, was the log workshop furniture factory of RICHARD CONKLIN. Machinery in his shop was powered by a horse or oxen treadmill. Next door was the house of the Conklins. He stayed only a few years and then went to Cincinnati to a factory making white lead. A RICHARD CONKLIN was working as a cabinetmaker in Cincinnati in 1829. He was the first trustee of the Mt. Pleasant Union Meeting House in 1825. It is believed he was working in his log workshop in Mt. Healthy about 1815.

CONREY, NATHANIEL......1816
Clermont County

The *History of Clermont County*, by Louis H. Evers lists Nathaniel Conrey as a cabinetmaker working in 1816.

CONWELL, JOHN D.......1844
Cincinnati, Hamilton

The Xenia Torchlight of March 7, 1844 announces the marriage of John D. Conwell to Susan M. Rich. Conwell was a prominent Cincinnati cabinetmaker who was originally from Delaware. When he came to Cincinnati he boarded in 1836, and later on, from 1839-1841, he was on the east side of Broadway between Columbia and Front streets, near the Public Landing.Even later, his establishment was called CONWELL & MCALPIN. He resided at the Broadway Hotel.

In 1841-1843, he was on the east side of Broadway, between Front and 2nd.

There is nothing known of Conwell after 1844. He was not listed in 1845 or after; it is believed he went to Xenia in Greene County after he married Susan Rich.

COOK, J. & DELL, A.......1838-1839
Athens, Athens County

From the Hocking Valley Gazette & Athens Journal, November 3, 1838:

J. COOK & A. DELL inform the public that they continue in the cabinetmaking business at the old market stand in the town of Athens. Have on hand and will sell or order fashionable sideboards, secretaries, bureaux, ladies dressing bureaux with glasses; ladies work and candle stands; Madison dining and breakfast tables; clock cases; sofas; bedsteads of all kinds.

A second advertisement concerning J. Cook was noted in the Hocking Valley Gazette and Athens Journal, Saturday, October 26, 1839:

Chair Shop, Athens - the undersigned would respectfully inform his friends and the public that he has commenced the chairmaking business in the town of Athens in the shop formerly occupied by J. Cook as a cabinet shop of High Street ---J.A. Murphy.

This advertisement began in June 1839. Therefore by 1839 Cook and Dell were no longer partners and Dell had left town or changed addresses. First names of these men are unknown.

CORNELIUS, JAMES......1840
Malta, Morgan County

The Pinkerton papers belonging to Robert Andrews note that JAMES CORNELIUS was a chairmaker who worked next door to ROBERT PINKERTON in Malta, Ohio.

CORWIN, ABNER......1817
Marietta, Washington County

The following information is from the American Friend, July 9, 1819:

ABNER CORWIN carried on the business of making little wheels, woolen wheels, chairs and screws for cider presses.
Shop in Marietta

COSGROVE, WILLIAM......B.1812..1833-1868
Cambridge, Guernsey County

The *History of Guernsey County, Ohio* by P.B. Sarchet notes:

William Cosgrove, a native of Mifflin County, Pennsylvania, was born in 1812 and in 1827 came to Ohio with his parents. They lived near Freeport, Harrison County, for three years, then went to Cambridge where he mastered the cabinetmakers trade. In 1833 he removed to Cumberland, Ohio where he engaged in chairmaking until 1868. Then, he took up the hotel business and became the proprietor of the Old Eagle Hotel.

CRAIG, JOHN......1819
Franklinton, Franklin County

This advertisement appeared in the Columbus Gazette of May 27, 1819:

READ THIS:
INHABITANTS OF THE COUNTY of FRANKLIN...that he commences the CABINETMAKING business - shop on the corner of Water and Main street in Franklinton. Furniture of the first quality and newest fashion from Baltimore.

May 10, 1818
JOHN CRAIG, Franklinton

This man had been an apprentice to A. Woods of Miami County and had run away. Woods also advertised in the Columbus Gazette - his ad of July 1, 1819 read as follows:

RUNAWAY FROM THE SUBSCRIBER - living in Charlestown, an apprentice to the CABINETMAKING business.
JOHN CRAIG - he had on a blue coat, brown cashmere pantaloons, yellow vest, etc. Find him and receive $1.00 reward.

A. WOODS, CABINETMAKER

After these advertisements appeared nothing more was heard from either of them.

CRETORS, -
Lebanon, Warren County

Hazel Spencer Phillips, in her book, *Traditional Architecture of Warren County*, mentions that the home of the Cretors, who were noted chairmakers in the early 1800's was on Mechanic Street at Silver Street.

CRUMPTON, WILLIAM......1823
West Union, Adams County

From the West Union Village Register of October 14, 1823:

CHAIRS, WHEELS, ETC. - THE Subscriber has removed his chair factory from Main street to his house near Peter Shultz' tanyard where he will keep on hand a constant supply of chairs and wheels for which he will receive country produce in payment.

Having employed experienced workmen, he warrants his work to equal any in the country. Orders from a distance will be punctually attended to. Persons wishing to purchase are respectfully requested to call and examine for themselves.

(N.B. House and sign painting done as above.)

West Union, October 14

WILLIAM CRUMPTON

Another Crumpton ad appeared in the Village Register of December 15, 1823:

DISSOLUTION OF PARTNERSHIP - The partnership between CLARK & CRUMPTON is this day dissolved. The business will be carried on by the subscriber in all of its varied branches at the former stand of CLARK & CRUMPTON.

WILLIAM CRUMPTON

DANIEL, J. GEORGE
Somerset, Perry County

The History of Fairfield and Perry County, by E.H. Colburn and A.A. Graham, notes that J. George Daniel carried on the carpenter trade in Somerset.

DAUGHTERS, TURPIN......1830-1840..D.1868
Neville, Clermont County

From *The History of Clermont County* we know that Turpin Daughters was working as a cabinetmaker around 1830-1840 in Neville. At the time of his death in 1868 his wife's name was Nancy. They had no children. He had a very lengthy will, and it sounds as though he was a wealthy landowner. It is not known whether he was in business at the time of his death since there is no recorded inventory of his assets.

DAVIS, ISACHER(IZAKER)......1802..D.1832
Georgetown, Brown County

According to the *History of Brown County* by W.H. Beers & Co. Isacher Davis was originally from Pennsylvania and directly from Kentucky. In 1802 he was in Brown County working as a cabinetmaker. He farmed, he was a carpenter, a millwright and an undertaker. He was in Georgetown or Pleasant Township for 30 years. He died and was buried in Wall cemetery.

There remains an interesting inventory of his household furniture and his shop tools. He was still following his trade at the end of his life.

Davis, Isachar (Izaker) Snr.
File #7641 30 October 1832
Executor: John Davis
wife Mary
sons Solomon
William
Samuel
Jno
Isaac
Issachar
grandson Anthony (son of Issachar)
children by first wife:
George
Sarah

Sale:

Chissles gouge & rasp	.62
2 chissles & 1 gimblet	.50
old irons & a bridle bit	.12½
1 oilstone	.40
four iron bolts	.06¼
1 wooden square	.19
2 plain stocks & guage	.25
1 saw	1.50
1 plough & groove	.75
1 handsaw	1.39
2 sash plains	.12½
three plains	.06¼
5 plains	.25
1 glue pot	.29
1 drawing knife	.50
1 auger	.14
1 box of tools	.25
1 pruning chissle	.20
1 grubbing hoe	1.51
1 saddle	1.18
1 saddle	.10¾
1 barrel	.18¾
1 barrel	.13
1 hogshead	.68¾
1 barrel	.06¼
1 pair streachers	1.00
1 grindstone	.41
1 table	2.75
1 bedstead & bedding	6.50
1 table	.50
1 cutting box	2.65
1 windmill	3.25
1 logchain	1.25

Most of tools were bought by John Davis. Isachar is buried in Wall Cemetery. Was probably in Bracken Co., Ky in 1799 and Bucks Co., Pa. in 1790.

DAY, DANIEL......1825
Xenia, Greene County

From the Interior Gazette, Xenia, Greene County, Ohio, Tue., Jan. 4, 1825:

FANCY & COMMON CHAIRMAKER

DANIEL DAY - Respectfully informs his friends he has taken a shop on lower end of Main Street. Fancy, half-fancy, mock-fancy and common rush bottom chairs made in the most fashionable style. He will also repair old chairs on shortest notice. His prices are: fancy chairs - $20.00; half-fancy - $12; mock-fancy - $9.00; and common chairs - $6.00.

Nothing more is known of this man except that he was working in Xenia, Ohio in 1825.

DELEPLANE, JOSHUA......L.1807-1886..W.1828-1865
Hamilton, Butler County

Joshua Deleplane came from Fredrick County, Maryland; he was born June 24, 1807. In 1819 he came to Hamilton where he farmed(and probably apprenticed to a cabinetmaker) until he was 21 years of age. Deleplane carried on the cabinetmaking and undertaking business for 45 years on D Street between Main and Ross in Hamiliton (Deleplane's Chair Factory). He began working in 1828 and he retired in 1865. He had five hands working for him. He died in 1886.

DENNISON, JOHN
Clermont County

The *History of Clermont County* lists John Dennison as a cabinetmaker. No more is known about the man.

DEVELLING & PATRICK......1838-1839
DEVELLING, PATRICK W.
PATRICK, MATTHEW
Athens, Athens County

From the Hocking Valley Gazette & Athens Journal, November 3, 1838:

Chairs, Chairs, DEVELLING & PATRICK have now, and will constantly keep on hand an assortment of Windsor chairs which they will sell low for cash and approved country produce.

This advertisement also comes from the Hocking Valley Gazette & Athens Journal:

Removal - DEVELLING & PATRICK have removed their goods to the old stand and well-known store immediately opposite H.R.

Gilmore's store, occupied formerly by MR. JEWETT & TANNER, and MR. WELSH and MCCABE, where they will continue to sell goods cheap.

PATRICK W. DEVELLING
MATTHEW PATRICK

From the Hocking Valley Gazette & Athens Journal, November 3, 1839:

DEVELLING & PATRICK

Chairs, chairs! Oct. 25 - DEVELLING & PATRICK sells lots of them.

DEVOL, JONATHON......L.1755-1823
Marietta, Washington County

Information from an interview by the author with Jerry DeVol concerning his ancestor, Jonathon DeVol. Jonathon was born in 1755; he arrived in Marietta in 1788 with the first group of settlers. He built a mill which ran by water power on the river; it had a 40' diameter beam. This mill was first used for a grist mill, later for planing and turning lumber for furniture in 1800. Nine years later it became a carding mill and a fulling mill. Jonathon DeVol was known as an ingenious builder of many inventions. The chances are that his water powered turning lathe was one of the first in the state.

DIEHL, HENRY......1827
Dayton, Montgomery County

Henry Diehl was born in Hagerstown, Maryland. He came to Dayton in 1806 and apprenticed as a coppersmith. But he was not happy as a coppersmith so he began making chairs in 1827. He had a shop on Main Street next to Mr. Henry Best and Co. where he made spinning wheels and reels. Mr. Diehl moved from Main Street in December 1828 and Elijah Githens stated in his ad that he was moving into Mr. Diehl's shop. It is not known at present where Henry Diehl moved but probably to another location in Dayton.

Source: *Pioneer Life in Dayton and Vicinity 1796-1840* by John F. Edger.

DIMMITS, EZEKIEL......1824
Batavia, Clermont County

This advertisement appeared in the Western Patriot, Clermont County, Saturday, December 4, 1824:

TAKE NOTICE; I wish to inform the public...(He is) selling Windsor chairs, clocks, and clock cases; likewise all kinds of cabinet work; shoes, boots and leather...Williamsburg and New Richmond.

EZEKIEL DIMMIT

DOGGETT, NEWTON......1810
Hillsboro, Highland County

Newton Doggett was an early cabinetmaker in Hillsboro, Ohio. His shop began in 1810 in the building where the first city building was located. He trained several workmen, including his son, Washington Doggett, in the art of woodworking. Washington Doggett became the first undertaker. This information comes from *The Hillsboro Story - Sesquicentennial year 1807 to 1857* by Mrs. Edwin B. Ayres.

DONOHOE, JOSEPH......1839
Eaton, Preble County

From the Eaton Register, Friday, March 1, 1839:

The Subscriber respectfully informs the public that they are now carrying on a chair shop in the town of Eaton, opposite the printing office - Flag-bottomed and Windsor chairs, settees etc. can be had at the best establishment of the best description and on moderate terms; having started a horse powered turning lathe; they also prepare to do fancy turning on the shortest notice. Also glazing, house, sign and ornamental painting. Imitation of the following wood and marbles can be seen at the paint shop: oak, mahogany, Sattan(sic), Rosewood, curl and Birdsye Maple, Egyptian, Italian, Irish and American Marbles etc. N.B. wheat, corn, oats, sugar, butter, will be taken in payment.

Sayres and Donohoe

Joseph Donohoe is mentioned often in Thomas Morgan's Probate Records, dated 1860.

DOPP, JOSEPH......1840
Columbus, Franklin County

From the Ohio Confederate, May 8, 1840:

CABINET MAKING - The subscriber takes this method of informing the public that he has furnished himself with an excellent supply of furniture: Centre tables of the best finish; dining, breakfast and other tables; bureaus, bedsteads, etc., etc.

Joseph Dopp - No. 63 High St., opposite Greenwood's Drug Store.

continued on next page

The Ohio Confederate, August 20, 1840:

RUNAWAY FROM THE SUBSCRIBER - on the 5th instant. Sweeley Leach, an indentured apprentice to the cabinetmaking business.

JOSEPH DOPP

DOWNEY, AMOS......1810-1820
Pioneers of Susannah, Clermont County

The *History of Clermont* lists Amos Downey as a cabinetmaker in Pioneers of Susannah which is a town in Ohio Township, 1810-1820.

DRUM, PHILLIP......pre 1847
Bethel, Clermont County

Clarence Grischy from Bethel, Ohio owns a chair marked PHILLIP DRUM, Bethel, Ohio 1847.

DRUMMOND, SAMUEL
Cambridge, Guernsey County

The Guernsey County 175th Celebration Booklet, containing the Carl Rech compilation of Cambridge lots notes that Samuel Drummond and Joseph C. Hunter came to town (Cambridge) as young men and started in the cabinetmaking business on the east end of lot 45.

DRYER, ISOBAN G.......1832-1837
Columbus, Franklin County

This ad appeared in the Daily Ohio State Journal of May 26, 1832:

Cabinet Wareroom

Isoban G. Dryer respectfully informs his friends and the public in general that he has removed to his New Establishment a few doors north of the national Hotel and nearly opposite the Court House where he intends keeping constantly on hand a general assortment of cabinetware among which will be sofas, sideboards, secretaries, together with every other article in his line - all orders for furniture thankfully received and promptly attended to

Lumber and most kinds of country produce received for payment.

This advertisement and one in the Columbus Sentinel continued for a year, and Isoban Dryer was still working in Columbus in 1837.

The Daily Ohio State Journal of Thursday, July 20, 1837 carried this notice:

I.G. Dryer - cabinetwarerooms and shop - East South High St. Below Rich Street.

Duffield, David
Estate #0203 — 24 July 1827
Appraisers — Matthew Richardson
Anthony Burns
Sam Kirkpatrick
Administrator — William Duffield
INVENTORY — 12 July 1827

Livestock	
1 dinning table	1.00
1 breakfast table	3.50
1 corner cupboard	4.00
1 silver watch	6.00
1 old bureau	2.00
6 old winsor chairs	1.50
6 old barrels	.37½
2 old tubs	.12½
1 old kitchen table	.50

Duffield, Robert E.
Estate #02146 — Will Record 1 p141
4 January 1855
Wife — Lucretia
Daughter — Mary Ann Patton
Ellen Roberts
Executor — Mark C. McMaken
INVENTORY

1 cupboard	12.00
1 stand	1.50
1 bureau	10.00
1 wardrobe	5.00
1 clock	4.00
1 watch	7.00
1 clock	4.00
1 wash stand	4.00
cabinet shop	200.00
1 bookcase & table	6.50

No record in estate packet of sale of cabinet shop.

DUFFIELD, DAVID......W.1811-1827..D.1827
Hamilton, Butler County

David L. Duffield worked as a cabinetmaker in Hamilton from 1811 until his death July 12, 1827. His will did not mention any tools. Perhaps his brother or son Robert E. Duffield carried on with his tools. He did have some furniture, probably made by himself.

DUFFIELD, ROBERT E.......W.1818-1855..D.1855
Hamilton, Butler County

It is not known exactly when Robert E. Duffield was born, but it is known that he married Jane Weaver on May 28, 1819 and he married Letitia Alston on June 30, 1842. He died January 4, 1855.

Robert Duffield went into the cabinetmaking business in 1818 in Hamilton, Ohio, and he continued in that business all of his life. He sold out his line of "coffins and stuff" to Harrison Watson, November 19, 1842, which would indicate that he declined the undertaking business to give full time to making furniture. In August 1844 his advertisement appeared in the Hamilton Intelligencer:

Cabinet Shop and Ware Rooms

R. E. Duffield

would inform his friends and the public in general that he has taken the shop formerly occupied by Mr. Richmond, opposite Smithman's Hotel (known as Sutherlands Corner) where he intends carrying on the cabinetmaking business in all of its different branches. A variety of finished work will be constantly on hand and for sale at the most reasonable prices - and work will be made to order at the shortest possible notice.

N.B. He is prepared to serve on funeral occasion with hearse at his former prices - Aug. 1, 1844.

His will indicates that his cabinet shop was worth $200; there is no indication that anyone bought the shop.

DUFFIELD, WILLIAM......1815
Lancaster, Fairfield County

William Duffield advertised in the Lancaster, Ohio Eagle, July 13, 1815:

A JOURNEYMAN CABINETMAKER to whom good wages in the above line will be executed in the neatest manner on the shortest notice, as I have a large quantity of seasoned planks on hand to execute any kind of cabinetwork. I solicit the custom of a generous public.

Lancaster, June 22, 1815

WILLIAM DUFFIELD

DURFEE, NATHAN......1834
Chillicothe, Ross County

Shortly after November 9, 1833 Henry Shepherd entered into a partnership with Nathan Durfee which did not last very long according to this notice in the Chillicothe Advertizer, April 5, 1834:

Dissolution of Partnership

The partnership heretofore existing between the subscribers in the Cabinetmaking business, has this day been dissolved by mutual consent. Those indebted to the late firm of Shepherd and Durfee are requested to make immediate payment to H. Shepherd who is alone authorized to settle accounts.

March 5, 1834

HENRY SHEPHERD
NATHAN DURFEE

EARHART, JOHN
Hennings Mills, Clermont County

The *History of Clermont County* indicates this man was an early carpenter in Hennings Mills, Washington Township. He might have also made furniture. No date cited.

EARHART, ROBERT......1816
New Richmond, Clermont County

Robert Earhart was working in New Richmond as a chairmaker in 1816. He was a member of the First Baptist Church. This information from the *History of Clermont County*.

EDWARDS, DANIEL......1820
Scioto County

The *History of Scioto County* mentions that Daniel Edwards was a chairmaker in 1820.

EDWARDS, JAMES......1815
Xenia, Greene County

An advertisement appeared in Xenia's Ohio Vehicle on Tues., Oct. 24, 1815:

CABINETMAKER - JAMES EDWARDS

EDWARDS, MILLS......1827
Xenia, Greene County

From Xenia's People's Press, May 31, 1827:

Has made an important improvement on the verticle spinner. Call at the subscriber's shop at the west end of Main Street, Xenia, Ohio where a few machines will be ready for sale.

An apprentice to the house joining and cabinetmaking business will be taken. A lad of 15 or 16 years of age will be accepted and meet with good encouragement.

MILLS EDWARDS......May 31, 1827

EGAN, GEORGE......1820
Piketon, Pike County

From the 1820 Federal Manufacturers Census, as published in the Tri-State Trader, Oct. 9, 1971:

GEORGE EGAN, Owner - made chairs and wheels. Used wood, paints, oils, $200. Employed 2 men operating a turning lathe - wages $130 annually. Extra expenses $100. Market sales 50 wheels and 200 chairs, bringing $600 per year.

ELAM, JAMES......1832
New Carlisle, Clark County

This item appeared in the Springfield paper, but concerns a cabinetmaker in New Carlisle, Ohio. From The Western Pioneer, Feb. 11, 1832:

ABSCONDED from the subscriber: living in New Carlisle, Clark County, Ohio - GARRY HOOVER, an indentured apprentice to the cabinetmaking business. All persons are forewarned not to employ or trust him.

Jan. 14, 1832 (s) James Elam, New Carlisle

ELLIOTT, JAMES
Dayton, Montgomery County

See HENDERSON, JAMES

ELMER, JACOB......1827-1829
Columbus, Franklin County

Elmer advertised in the Ohio State Journal on Nov. 2, 1827, pg. 4, col. 3:

Cabinet Furniture cheap for cash. The subscriber continues to manufacture and keep on hand all kinds of cabinet furniture and will sell cheap for cash in hand. Person's wishing good bargains will please call at his shop(nearly opposite the U.S. Courthouse) and examine for himself.

On June 22, 1829, in the Ohio State Journal he was advertising for a runaway apprentice to the cabinetmaking business - a 16 year old boy by the name of Charles Ogden.

EMMETT(EMMET), WILLIAM Y.......1824-1853
Chillicothe, Scioto County

William Y. Emmett came from Virginia. In June, 1824, the following notice appeared in the Scioto Supporter and Scioto Gazette:

HOUSE, SIGN, COACH AND ORNAMENTAL PAINTING AND GILDING

The Subscribers respectfully inform ____ and the public that for the greater facility in conducting the above business in all of its various branches, they have formed a connetion (sic) under the firm of MOORE & EMMETT, and taken the house formerly occupied by Mr. Henry Jack (coppersmith) on Water street, where all orders in their line will be thankfully received and attended to.

JOSEPH T. MOORE,
WILLIAM Y. EMMETT

This connection between Moore ad Emmett did not last long, for it appears that Joseph Moore returned to the Eastern seaboard where he painted more than 50 portraits in the towns of Freeport, Hollowell, Farmington, and Chesterville.

In 1826, Moore returned to Chillicothe and the following ad then appeared in the Scioto Supporter and Scioto Gazette, December 7, 1826:

FANCY SIGN & ORNAMENTAL PAINTER - continue to carry on the above business in all of its branches at their old stand where they are prepared to execute in the neatest manner signs of every description, military standards and plates, Masonic carpets and aprons. They also intend keeping constantly on hand the general assortment of Windsor and fancy chairs, finished in the very best style which they will sell on reasonable terms. All orders punctually attended to.

Nov. 28, 1826 MOORE & EMMETT

Also, in the same newspaper and date as above, the following:

J.T. MOORE, Portrait painter, has taken the upper room in the brick building on Water street, 2 doors above Mr. Hawks and Swifts hat store, and respectfully solicits the patronage of all the enlightened public. He invites his friends generally to call as above, where specimens of his work may be seen.

Nov. 28, 1826

This partnership was officially ended in the Scioto Gazette, June 21, 1827:

MOORE & EMMETT - The partnership heretofore existing under the above firm, has been dissolved by mutual consent.

J.T. MOORE and W.Y. EMMETT

The business will be carried on in all of its various branches at the old stand by William Y. Emmett.

Jun. 13, 1827

William Y. Emmett carried on the chairmaking business alone, for in the Scioto Gazette, March 3, 1830, the advertisement:

WANTED IMMEDIATELY - 3 apprentices to the painting and chairmaking business - Boys of steady and correct morals will only be taken.
WILLIAM Y. EMMETT - Mar. 3, 1830

By February 9, 1831, Emmett had moved his shop opposite the courthouse, 1 door south of the Scioto Gazette. He made chairs and was a coach, house, sign and ornamental painter.

In June, 1835, he was still advertising alone in the Chillicothe Advertiser:

FANCY & WINDSOR CHAIRS - CHAIR FACTORY - June 13, 1835.

This was the last ad - it had been running for several years. He had been working since 1824; but on July 6, 1836, the following notice was published in the Scioto Gazette:

Sheriffs Sale - Public sale at the shop of WILLIAM Y. EMMETT, in Chillicothe on the 9th day of July between 10 and 12 o'clock, the following property, to-wit;

A quantity of cabinet furniture levied upon as the property of William Y Emmett at the suit of Thomas Orr & Co. and others.

June 28, 1836
JOHN TARLETON, SHERIFF

Less than one month later this notice still appeared in the Scioto Gazette, July 6, 1836. This ad first ran September 23, 1835, before the sheriff's sale.

NEW FIRM - The Subscribers have entered into a co-partnership under the firm of EMMETT & MILLS in the chair and cabinetmaking business. House and sign painting, glazing and paperhanging business - all of which they are prepared to do on the shortest notice and in the best manner.

Their shop is at the old stand of WILLIAM Y. EMMETT on Paint street opposite the public square and next door to the office of the Scioto Gazette.

In 1839 William Y. Emmett moved to Circleville. This ad is from the Circleville Herald, May 9, 1840:

PAINTING, GLAZING & PAPERHANGING - W.Y. EMMET would especially inform this community that he has taken a shop on the west Main street, over the store of F. Crouse, for the prosecution of the above business, where he will be happy to receive orders for house, sign and ornamental painting which he will execute with dispatch, neatness and propriety. He also manufactures extensively Windsor, Fancy and common chairs made of the best materials and which he will warrant.
Circleville, Dec. 12, 1839

In 1850 Emmett was in Cincinnati's first ward with his wife Rachel; he was boarding and working as a universalist minister. In 1850 he was 51 years of age. He was in Cincinnati until 1853 and perhaps longer.

ENYEART, THOMAS......1831
Hamilton, Butler County

Thomas Enyeart of Hamilton was a cabinetmaker who worked with Isaac Falconer, 1812-1819, and alone in Hamilton in 1831. He may have continued until 1849 and he may have done other things in addition to cabinetwork.

ERISLOW, ANDREW JACKSON ......B.1824..W.1840-1846
Wheelersburg, Scioto County

From the *History of Scioto County:*

Andrew Jackson Erislow was born October 24, 1824 in Wheelersburg, Scioto County, Ohio. He learned the cabinetmaking business with Stephen Cameron in Wheelersburg. He became a school teacher, a bookkeeper, county commissioner and was in politics all of his life. In 1846 he was working but it is not known whether he was practicing cabinetmaking.

FALCONER, ISAAC......L.1780-1840
Hamilton, Butler County

Isaac Falconer and Thomas Enyeart were in the cabinetmaking business from 1812 to 1819 in Hamilton, Ohio. Source of information: George Cummins, Hamilton historian and the John Woods Papers.

Additional information about Isaac Falconer comes from the Memorial Record, Butler County, Ohio, which contains biographical sketches of Representative Citizens of the County.

Cyrus Falconer is the oldest surviving citizen (1894); when he came to this place a portion of the old Fort Hamilton built by Arthur St. Clair was still standing. He is respected and loved. His parents were Isaac and Nancy (Wilkins) Falconer who were born, reared and married in Washington County, Pennsylvania where their son Cyrus was born January 21, 1810. The father of the family was a cabinetmaker by trade but after coming to Ohio in April 1812 he kept a tavern in a hewn-log house where the suspension Bridge now stands. While being thus engaged he built a house on the corner of Main Street and B Street and there he kept in his home a cabinet shop. He also owned and operated a ferry. He resided there from 1818 until 1840 and there he died in the year last named (1840) at the age of 60 years. Buried in the Presbyterian Church Cemetery. He was a member of the Presbyterian Church. He was drafted in the War of 1812 but his marching orders being countermanded he did not serve. He was one of the most prominent men of Rossville, the 1st ward of Hamilton. His father was Abraham Falconer who came from England to Maryland and then to Washington County, Pa..

Hamilton in the Making by Alta Harvey Heiser also mentions Isaac Falconer:

The strongly constructed flatboats were built by Isaac Falconer and held in readiness for high water due to freshlets which was the busy time for making shipments by James Hough, James McBride and Isaac Falconer who were merchants. Mr. Falconer's cargoes were mostly furniture of his own manufacture.

Falconer, Isaac
Estate #0930
Bond $2000.00
Administrator Cyrus Falconer (son)
Security John H. Falconer
William Lefflor
Appraisers R.B. Milliken
Mark Boatman
Clement Clifton
Wife Nancy Falconer
INVENTORY 30 January 1841

6 winsor chairs	8.00
5 winsor chairs	2.50
4 winsor chairs	1.00
2 side tables	12.00
2 mahogany bureau	25.00
2 stands	2.00
1 mantle wood clock	5.00
1 brass clock & case	25.00

No tools

FIELDS, G.B.......1804
Springfield, Clark County

From the Springfield Directory, City of Springfield, 1852:

In 1799, not a house or a sign of a dwelling was anywhere visible. In 1800, David Loury built the first flatboat that navigated the Big Miami from Dayton down. Later the same man and a flatboat went from Springfield to New Orleans. In 1801 the town plat was laid out; 1804 12 log houses, one near the southeast corner of Main and Market in which G. B. Fields had a cabinet shop, the first of its kind in Springfield.

FORESMAN, ROBERT K.......1822..D.1823
Circleville, Pickaway County

Robert K. Foresman advertised in the Circleville Olive Branch on April 25, 1822:

WANTED IMMEDIATELY - A Journeyman Chairmaker, one who is a first-rate workman. Will meet with liberal encouragement by making immediate application to the subscriber.

ROBERT K. FORESMAN

From the Olive Branch of July, 1822, we know that he was administrator for the estate of Joseph C. Nixon.

Foresman may have been from Northumberland County, Pennsylvania. He died March, 1823, and his effects were sold, including much shop equipment.

FOWLER, JACOB......1839
Georgetown, Brown County

The *History of Brown County* lists Jacob Fowler as a cabinetmaker, formerly of Cincinnati.

Jacob Fowler was working in Cincinnati as a cabinetmaker on Gano Street between Vine and Walnut from 1830-1834, and perhaps longer. By 1839 he was in Georgetown, Ohio. He continued working there but may have moved back to Cincinnati later on, because an estate record is extant there for Jacob Fowler in 1849.

An advertisement appeared in the

Georgetown Democratic Standard, Brown County, Oct. 31, 1839:

JACOB FOWLER, cabinetmaker, formerly of Cincinnati, respectfully informs the citizens of Georgetown that he has taken the shop formerly occupied by DAY & MERRILL on the southwest corner of the town for the purpose of transacting the above business in all of its various branches, etc. Their orders will be promptly attended to.

Jan. 25, 1839

FROMM, SEBASTIAN......1782-1817
Hamilton, Butler County

Notes from Mr. George Cummins, the historian of Hamilton, indicate that Sebastion Fromm was a cabinetmaker and clockmaker between 1782-1817. He was the first Catholic resident as well.

GARNER, T......1835
Columbus, Franklin County

This ad appeared in the Ohio State Journal on Feb. 17, 1835:

Great Bargains. T. Garner begs leave to inform the citizens of Columbus and its vicinity that he continues to carry on the business of Bedstead Making, in its various branches at his shop on State Street directly opposite the State House and has now on hand and for sale a handsome assortment of fine fancy and common Bedsteads made of the best materials and warranted superior to any heretofore manufactured in this city for the price.

GEOGHAGEN, EDMUND......L.1799-1833
Lebanon, Warren County

Seen in the Western Star, June 7, 1823:

GEOGHAGEN, EDMUND
HAS ON HAND, and intends to keep in his shop on Mulberry Street, Windsor chairs inferior to none in the Western County, which he will sell cheap for cash, or approved country produce.

Foresman, Robert K.
Administrators Docket C #0-234
Administrator: Andrew Histon
SALE: 15 March 1823

Amanda Foresman	1 glue pot	.06¼
Erastus Webb	1 hammer	.18
John Barr	1 hand ax	.56 ¼
James Renick	1 sm chair	.12 ½
" "	1 kerg	"
William Britton	1 window sash	.06 ¼
" "	1 set paint brushes	.12 ½
Henry Sage	1 drawing knife "	
George Wolfley	1 grindstone & frame	
John Foresman	1 shaving horse	.15
Guyer Doan	1 whetstone	.06 ¼
Jonathon Foresman	1 file	.25
William Britton	1 vise "	
" "	1 file	.12 ½
Richard Tomlinson	1 chissel	.20
William Britton	1 gauge & 5 paint pots	.06¼
James Hedges	1 quart measure	.12½
George Wolfley	1 square	.37½
Alexander Forseman	1 saddlebags	2.16¼
Ebenezer Havens	2 pocket books	.18¾
Alexander Forseman	1 trunk	.75
John Forseman	1 foot adz	.80
Henry Sage	1 lot paint crocks	.07
Alexander Forseman	1 hold fast	.21
Peter Row	1 brace & bits	.56¼
Amos Hollenback	1 taper auger	.12½
Erastus Webb	1 pan shovel & tongs	1.12½

Will Book 1 August 1819
George Foresman came from Northumberland, Pa. Had a son Robert and a brother Robert.

From the Western Star & Gazette, Sat., June 7, 1823:

EDMUND GEOGHAGEN - WINDSOR CHAIRS FOR SALE:

An apprentice wanted who can make them in his shop.

Apprentice from 14 to 18 years of age.

continued on next page

Geoghagen continued to advertise at a much later date. The following is from the Western Star, August 8, 1829

CALL AND SEE - The subscriber having united in business, would inform their friends and the public that they now have on hand and intend keeping a general assortment of fancy and Windsor chairs inferior to none in the Western country, which they will sell very low for cash or approved country produce. Having procured the best quality of materials and experienced workmen, they hope by remitting assiduously to render general satisfaction to all who may favor them with their patronage. Their shop opposite Mr. Wood and Boyd's wollen factory on Mulberry Street where they earnestly invite ladies and gentlemen to call and examine their work and prices.

House and sign painting neatly executed and calls from a distance...promptly...attended to.

Lebanon, July 29, 1829
Sameul F. Yeoman & Edmund Geoghagen

Edmund Geoghagen died in 1833 at the age of 34. He was buried in the Methodist Burying Ground in Lebanon. His partner, Samuel F. Yeoman, carried on the business of chairmaking. Mr. Geoghagen's household inventory includes many interesting implements from his shop.

Geoghagen, Edmund
1833 Box 60 #1
INVENTORY: 17 May 1834

	Livestock	
1	brafast table plain	3.00
1	croscut saw	3.00
1	sword & scabbord, silver mounted	12.00
1	chest	1.00
1	square stand	1.00
1	mantle clock	16.00
5	winser chairs	3.00
1	diamond for cutting glass	3.00
1	spade	.50
1	meet barrel	.50
1	vinegar barrel	.37½
2	axes	1.62½
1	copper cittle	2.00
4	bench plains	2.00
1	brace & bits	1.50
1	hold fast	.7½
1	lote of chissels & gouges	7.00
	saws	2.50
1	paint stone with other utentuls to grind, paints & rowers for holding paints & brushes	5.00
6	winser chears, not finished	4.00
2	work benches & 2 old tables 2.00	
1	stove & pipe	10.00
1	tirning lathe	7.00
1	grindstone & crank	1.25
1	lot of stuff for making chars	1.00
1	shaving hore & rocker for bending chear slots	.50

GERENS, -
Clay Township, Ross County

This excerpt from the *History of Ross and Highland Counties, Ohio:*

The first mill in the township of Clay that we have a record of, was built by Mr. Gerens, on the banks of White Oak creek, in the southwest part of the township. The mill was made of logs, and the buhrs were made by Mr. Gerens, out of large granite boulders split in two, and worked to the proper shape. The wedges and tools necessary for these purposes, were also made by Mr. Gerens, who was not only a millwright, but a blacksmith and a worker in wood. A gearing for the sawing of logs was also a part of this mill, but unfortunately for Mr. Gerens, either he had not a sufficient head of water to propel his mill, or the machinery was not constructed so as to obtain the full advantage of the power. The latter is probably the truth. Not unfrequently this lack of power had to be supplied by Mr. Gerens himself, and he might then be seen standing on the log and pushing the saw up and pulling it down. Afterwards he added a horse-power to the mill, which enabled him to work when the water was low. The horse-power was ungeared from the water-power by knocking out a cog or two from the main wheel. Then he put in a turning-lathe, and made chairs and other furniture. This part of the establishment became quite extensive in time, and Mr. Gerens had the pleasure of supplying all the region about for many miles with chairs of an elegant pattern. They were of the splint-bottom variety. Mr. Gerens had a peculiarity: he would drop asleep at most unexpected times. He would fall asleep while standing at his lathe holding his chisel, and while putting his chairs together, and it is stated that sometimes at the dinner table he would reach out his fork for a potato and drop asleep before the fork could secure his prize.

GILLILAND, ADAM......1825-1839-1859
Shandon, Butler County

Adam Gilliland was a cabinetmaker and minister from the south. He preached in Bethel in 1825, in Venice, Ohio from 1839 until 1859; later he moved to Venice where he lived to be 90 years old.
Source: *Saga of Paddy's Run*(Shandon, Ohio) by Steven Riggs Williams.

GITHENS, ELIJAH......1828
Dayton, Montgomery County

From the Dayton Miami Herald & Dayton Republican Gazette, December 23, 1828:

ELIJAH GITHENS, Plain and fancy chair-maker, respectfully informs the citizens of Dayton and its vicinity that he continues to carry on his business in all of its various branches on Main street in the shop formerly occupied by Mr. Henry Diehl, where he has and intends to keep on hand a large assortment of palin and fancy chairs. Those who may be disposed to honor him with their custom, may depend upon his punctuality and the goodness of his work.

(Dayton, Dec. 13, 1828)

Further information from Betty Lawson Walters' *Cabinetmakers of Indiana:*

Elijah Githens was born in New Jersey; he worked in Dayton in 1828. He worked in Richmond, Indiana from 1833 until 1847 with his brother Griffith D. Githens. Later he became a grocer.

GLEARKEY, DAVID
Portsmouth, Scioto County

According to Portsmouth historian Elmer Sword, David Glearkey was a ferry boat man and a cabinetmaker in Portsmouth.

GLESSNER, WILLIAM ......L.1816-1894..W.1833-1855
Marietta, Washington County

Another chairmaker in Marietta was William Glessner, born in Somerset County, Pennsylvania, 1816. He died in Marietta in 1894. He made chairs in 1833 and later sold out to two men whose names were Mills and McCabe in 1855. This chair shop prospered and later became a well known factory called the Marietta Chair Factory which continued in business until 1940.
This information from Jerry DeVol of Devola, Ohio.

GORDON, CLARK
Fayette County

Clark Gordon is listed as a cabinetmaker in the Fayette County, Paint Township Pioneer Record & Reminiscences of Early Settlers of Fayette County, Ohio by Rufus Putnam of Chillicothe, Ohio. No date cited.

GORDON, WILLIAM......1806
Lebanon, Warren County
Xenia, Greene County

William Gordon worked in Lebanon before 1806. He moved from Lebanon to Xenia as a cabinetmaker in 1806. He advertised in Liberty Hall of September 23, 1806.

GRAHAM, WILLIS......1804-ca 1880
Buckskin, Ross County

Willis Graham emmigrated with his father George from Maryland in 1804 to Buckskin Township, Ross County, Ohio. He fought in the War of 1812. He was a carpenter and cabinet-maker there; he died at 84 years, 10 months.
He worked as a cabinetmaker for his entire life in Buckskin, Ohio.
The above information is from the Ross County - Pioneer Record by Isaac I. Findley and Rufus Putnam.

GRAVES, JACOB & CO......1817-1819
Zanesville, Muskingum County

Taken from the Zanesville, Muskingum Messenger, Apr. 3, 1817:

CABINETMAKING - JACOB GRAVES & CO., have established a cabinet shop and warehouse a few doors north of the court house. Highest price paid for cherry, black walnut and poplar. Also cherry and poplar bedstead scantling.

Zanesville, April 1, 1817

Jacob Graves bought out the cabinet business of James Reeves who began his shop in Zanesville in 1814 on Main Street. In 1817 it was owned by Jacob Graves & Co. and a short time after that the business became Graves and Reeves. In Aug. 18, 1819 as the depression set in, John Sheward bought out Graves and Reeves. The Shewards were still in the cabinet business in 1838.

continued on next page

GREGG, JOSEPH
Cambridge, Guernsey County

Guernsey County 175th Celebration Booklet 1973. The Carl Rech compilation of Cambridge lots:

On lot #48 the L shaped building occupied by John Gregg, cabinetmaker, later James Nelson as a cabinetmaker plied his trade in this building for more than 40 years. No date cited.

GRUBB, JOSEPH......1824-1831
Lancaster, Fairfield County

OSKER FURBUR - Age 14 years, six months, 21 days - Ward of Jacob Young, bound to Joseph Grubb, chairmaker of Lancaster for 6 years, 5 months, 10 days.

Source: Fairfield County Records of Indenture, Dec. 7, 1824.

Joseph Grubb was working as a chairmaker in Lancaster as early as December 1824 for in December he took an indentured apprentice whose name was Osker Furbur. This young man stayed with him because Joseph Grubb did not advertise until December 17, 1831, for three apprentices. This from the Lancaster, Ohio Eagle:

APPRENTICES WANTED: Three boys of good moral character about the age of 16 years will be taken as apprentices to CHAIRMAKING business. Boys from the country preferred.

Lancaster, Oct. 15, 1831 Joseph Grubb

GUTHRIE, STEPHEN......1794
Marietta, Washington County

Stephen and Truman Guthrie came from Washington, Connecticut with a share of the Ohio Company from their father Joseph. Stephen was buying table butts(hinges) and two brass knobs for cabinetmaking as early as 1793 in Marietta. He bought from Dudley Woodbridge, the merchant. In 1793 Stephen Guthrie had hardware delivered which was bought by Joseph Barker: 1 brass knob, 1 pair butt hinges. Perhaps Stephen Guthrie was working for Joseph Barker, a prolific architect and house builder. Barker undoubtedly knew how to make furniture.

GUTHRIE, TRUMAN
Marietta, Washington County

See GUTHRIE, STEPHEN

Catherine Remley's article for the Antiques Festival Catalogue, June 31, 1980 notes that Truman Guthrie built a tavern table while his bride cooked their wedding supper. This table was still in the family in 1902 and is mentioned in the *History of Belpre.* A photo appears in Chapter I of the Introduction.

GUTHRIE, WILLIAM......L.1769-1855..W.1803-1839
Chillicothe, Ross County

William Guthrie was born in York County, Pennsylvania (now Adams County) on November 11, 1769, the fifth child of William Guthrie, a veteran of the Revolution. According to the diary of Jacob Lehre, William Guthrie's father-in-law, William and his daughter (Kitty) Katherine Lehre, were married on June 8, 1797 at Mr. Henry Payne's place near the Anabaptist Meeting House on the road from Lexington to Frankfort, Kentucky four miles.

According to family tradition, William Guthrie was a wheelwright by trade, and while he played the fiddle, he was largely uneducated. He was known to have been in Chillicothe as early as September 1799 when he was an "Esquire Justice" at a Court of Common Pleas held in Chillicothe on the fourth Tuesday of that month. (Order Book of Territorial Court).

It was said by his descendants that Guthrie was not too much of a carpenter when he came to Chillicothe and worked on the construction of the old court house in 1801-1802. This old stone building became the Capitol Building in 1803 when Ohio became the seventeenth state.

Guthrie probably learned a lot on this job. The following story by Sam Doak, the family story-teller, seems pretty far-fetched:

William Guthrie has never built anything so complicated before as the new State House, with window frames, finished doors etc. So he built the windows for the whole building and when he tried to put them in, they would not fit the frames he had already installed. So, that night 'vandals' came in and broke up all the windows. That meant he had to make all new windows to fit the holes in the building. (This information from Mrs. Lloyd Lindsey of Paris, Ill. She is great-great granddaughter of William Guthrie.)

William Guthrie must have learned a lot in the next fifteen years as the date 1817 is carved on the front door step of the house he built for his family in Greene Township, Ross County. This old house is off Robinson Road facing the old abandoned Marietta Road. It is still in excellent condition. Guthrie is said to have made the brick himself on his "Sugar Loaf Farm". The front door is 6'6" high and is of the "Crusader" pattern. Every room of this large two-story house has a chair rail. The large cupboards beside the main fireplace are made of walnut.

Sometime after June 1839, the Guthrie family moved out west and settled on the north arm of the prairie in Edgar County, Illinois, at Baldwinsville, six miles northeast of Paris.

The most historic piece of furniture in Ohio, the Old Constitution Table, was constructed of black walnut by William Guthrie in 1802. It is of a very simple design and stands 27-3/4 inches high. The oval top is six feet long and 43 inches wide. The legs taper from 2 inches at the top to one inch at the foot.

It was around this table that members of the Constitutional Convention assembled in Chillicothe on the 29th of November, 1802, and framed the constitution of the new State of Ohio. Hon. Edward Tiffin was President of the convention and Hon. Thomas Scott was the Secretary.

The old Constitutional Table was long used in the Recorder's Office of the Court House of Ross County as a convenient place to lay books upon during examination of the records. It was once loaned to Henry Howe that he might obtain a photograph of it for his Historical Collections and he failed to return it to the Court House. It remained in the possession of Chillicothe photographer John H. Nugent so long that he claimed ownership. Finally in 1903, the County Commissioners took action and sent the Sheriff to Nugent's shop and returned the table. It was used in a special historical exhibit that year when the State Centennial was celebrated in Chillicothe.

Little did William Guthrie know that this simple table would become such a venerable piece of furniture. Since 1933 it has remained a prize possession of the Ross County Historical Society where it may be seen in the Museum Room dedicated to the four governors from Chillicothe.

The above information courtesy of John R. Grabb, Chillicothe, Ohio.

HALDERMAN,......
Shandon, Butler County

From *The Saga of Paddy's Run* (Shandon) by Stephen Riggs Williams:

Mr. Halderman, the father of Cyrus Halderman in Venice and Mr. Hawk, the great grandfather of Mrs. Alma Joyce Scott were early cabinetmakers.

HALSEY, WILLIAM......1816
Lebanon, Warren County

This man was a partner of the cabinetmaker William M. Wiles in 1816. When their partnership dissolved they sold off a great deal of furniture. It is not known whether William Halsey was a cabinetmaker or a merchant.

HAMPSHIR, JOSEPH......pre 1847
Highland County

This was found in the Highland County Penitentiary Records:

Name: JOSEPH HAMPSHIR, CABINET-MAKER. Born Ohio; lived in Highland County; crime - horsestealing; date: 1847. Description: temperate; age 25. Term 1 year. Discharge: expiration of sentence, 1848. Parents living in Pike County. He had lots of scars.

HANNAN, J.......1832
Marietta, Washington County

Seen in the Western Republican, March, 1832:

A NEW CHAIR FACTORY - J. HANNAN - on the corner above Mr. Withrow's saddle shop, Ohio Street. Fancy and Windsor chairs equal to any in the Western Country. Sign and ornamental painting done in the neatest style. Arm, writing, and rocking chairs.

Marietta, Mar. 1832.

HATCH, EBENEZER C.......1821
Ripley, Brown County

From *Ripley, Ohio: It's History and Families, 1965*, by Eliese Bamback Stivers:

PAINTER - CHAIR FACTORY - EBENEZER C. HATCH, Mar. 22, 1821.

HATFIELD, MOSES L.1780-1835 W. 1817-1835
Dayton, Montgomery County

Moses Hatfield was the son of Andrew and Christiana (Powell) Hatfield who were married in 1759. They lived in Montgomery County, Pennsylvania, and later moved to Montgomery County, Virginia, where they lived for twenty years. Then they moved to Cabell County, Virginia, near the Guyandott River near Parkersville(now Huntington, West Virginia). Moses Hatfield was their ninth child; he was born October 12, 1780 in Cabell County. He was married to Catherine John in Cabell County where he lived until he moved to Ohio in 1811. According to the *History of Preble County*, Moses Hatfield was the first settler in Bowers Mills(now Lanier), Preble County. He may have stayed there until 1817. *Early Dayton*,by Robert and Mary Steele, states that Moses Hatfield's ad first appeared in the Dayton Watchman in the Spring of 1817. Although family tradition has it that he was in Dayon in 1811, there is a possibility that Moses was in Preble County for a short while before moving to Dayton. However, he was certainly in Dayton by 1817. His advertisements of 1827 and 1832 are clear indications that he was doing very well. He had shops in Union, Montgomery County and Greenville, Darke County. Mr. Hatfield died Feb. 11, 1835 from an obstruction in the liver. He left many children, some also in the furniture business. The household and shop inventory taken at the time of his death is extremely interesting. He had an immense inventory, including 426 fancy front legs(for chairs), 1097 chair backs, 9100 legs and pillars and so forth. There are many pages of chair parts. It could be implied from this that he was selling extensively all over the area.

From the Dayton, Ohio & National Journal & Montgomery & Dayton Advertiser, October 1, 1827:

CHAIR & WHEELMAKING: MOSES HATFIELD respectfully informs the public that he produces common and flag-bottom windsor chairs and fancy chairs. Also spinning wheels. Has a shop in Union, Ohio, Montgomery County, and one at Greenville, Darke County. He has been engaged in business for a number of years.

Another ad from the Dayton Journal & Advertiser, December 25, 1832 reads:

MOSES HATFIELD - chairmaker and wheelwright offers his thanks to his customers...the public in general for the liberal patronage with which he has been favored. He has enlarged his establishment at his old stand adjoining Leyman's Tavern where he is now opening a large and general assortment of common and fancy flag bottom chairs & all kinds of Windsor chairs of the newest fashions; and fashioned in the newest, neatest style which makes his assortment superior to any yet offered in this market - All of which he will sell low for cash. All orders for work carefully and punctually attended to. WANTED - a boy of 17 years of age of strict habits, as an apprentice.

This ad began November 28, 1832.

Hatfield, Moses
Will Record #1296 13 March 1835
Executrix Catherine Hatfield
Bond: $2500
Appraisers Elisha Brabham
Aaron Richardson
Charles Snider
INVENTORY: 28 March 1835

2963	lumber	
9100	legs & pillars	29.63
426	fancy front legs	8.52
69	bent pillars	.75
1097	chair backs	8.25
186	fancy posts	5.58
1	stand little chair stuff	4.50
74	peices for hand screws	.75
131	wheel spokes	.98
1666	bucket & side handles	8.33
24	augar handles	.72
2	bench screws	.62½
26	scrowls sawed out	.58½
1	lot of wheel stuff	3.00
108½	common chairs	78.37½
33	slat backs	44.00
18	scroll top scroll sears	33.00
18	common scrolls	25.00
18	cottage chairs	21.00
3	slat back fancy	6.00
18	scroll top fancy	57.00
2	slat back arks	6.00
3½	scroll arks	12.25
1	writing chair	4.50
½	scroll settee	5.00
2½	slat settee	17.50
½	common sociable	1.50
3½	little chairs without arms	1.75
2	little chairs with arms	1.37½
1½	common rocking chairs	1.50
2½	cottage rocking chairs	5.00
72	slat backed primed	48.00
168	common primed	70.00
6	in the white	2.12½
26	fancy primed	41.20
30	slat backs finished	38.43¾
6	table chairs	6.00
2	cottage rocking chairs	4.00
3	common rocking chairs	3.00
1	sewing chair primed	.37½
4	cottage rocking chairs primed	5.00
52	little chairs unfinished	13.00
25	fancy frames	15.02½
2	foot stools finished	.75
3	foot stools primed	.56¼
81	bundles of flag	25.31¼
5	drawing knives ½ worn	2.50

3	new ones	3.00
3	small ½ worn	3.00
3	hand saws	2.25
3	tenant saws	2.25
4	new spoke halves	1.25
7	spoke haves ½ worn	1.31¼
10	large spoke haves	3.75
3	smoothing planes	1.87½
5	fore planes	3.75
3	jack planes	1.50
3	braces	1.50
21	chair bits ½ worn	2.10
31	odd bits ½ worn	1.00
5	large hammers	1.87½
6	small hammers	.75
1	lot of foils	2.00
5	morticing chissels	.50
6	small taper bits	.62½
1	lot of foils	2.00
5	morticing chissels	.50
9	pearing chissels	.87½
1	sweep saw	.50
6	small taper bits	.62½
2	large taper bits	2.50
6	augars - different sizes	1.12½
5	set screw tools	10.00
1	cross cut saw	1.50
2	hold forth	1.00
1	lot of squares	1.25
2	rules	.31¼
4	screw drivers	.75
4	pair compasses	.62¼
1	pair callipers	.37½
1	foot adz	1.25
1	hand ax	.68¾
1	fro	.25
6	turning chissels	1.00
6	turning gouges	1.00
2	oil stones	1.62½
2	glue kettles	2.00
1	varnive kettle	7.00
1	bending kettle	4.00
1	iron pot	.62½
2	iron wedges	.12½
1	compass saw	.12½
6	back racks	1.50
1	pillar racks	2.00
3	grindstones	2.50
5	work benches & iron vise	12.00
3	stoves & pipes	35.00
1	lot old tools worn out	1.00
1	pattent saw set	.62½
10	awls	.25
1	turning lathe	5.00
½	of a diamond in partnership	2.00
2	morticing benches	.62½
1	shaving horse	.12½
1	powder horn	.50
9	moulding planes	2.00
1	quarter sole leather	1.00
1	pr. scales & weights	1.00
1	rench	.18¾
2	patten heads	.62½
9	set wheel irons	1.68¾
5	beds, bedstead & bedding	50.00
1	clock	5.00
2	looking glass	2.00
2	set chairs	7.00
2	tables	4.00
2	stands	3.00
1	bureau	4.00
1	bookcase & desk	5.00
1	sugar chest	1.37½
3	carpets & stair carpets worn	20.00
8	blankets	10.00
4	coverlids	8.00
12	sheets	4.50
14	pr pilercases	1.40
5	quilts	10.00
1	lot of glasses & dishes	20.00
1	lot of barrels & cank	4.00
3	pr of shovel arm tongs	2.00
3	pr hand irons	2.00
3	dozen brooms	1.08
26	papers of lamp black	2.04
1	cow	7.00
28	gal oil	24.50
1	lot of sundry paints	6.00
1	lot of paint brushes	1.00
1	lot of oil cans	3.25
1	paint stone & muller	2.00
7	new paint brushes	3.75
1	lot kitchen furniture	11.00

HAYDEN, STEPHEN......1804
Shandon, Butler County

From *The Saga of Paddy's Run*, by Stephen Riggs Williams:

Clockcase owned by a descendent of Edward Bibb in Illinois made by Stephen Hayden in 1804. Made of cherry slabs; sawn by whipsaw, the clockworks are from Wales.

HAZEL, S.K.......1819-1827
Columbus, Franklin County

Mr. S.K. Hazel was working in Columbus before 1819; he advertised in the Columbus Gazette, June 21, 1819:

Have removed opposite the Auditor's office where I will attend to the CABINETMAKING business as usual. I continue to take country produce for furniture.

June 21, 1819 S.K. HAZEL

In the Columbus Gazette of October 14, 1820 Hazel indicates that he would take flax seed and will give any kind of cabinet furniture for the seed. He was farming also and raising flax. This was during the height of the depression and he was making ends meet as best he could. In 1821 he advertised in October in the Gazette that he carried on his business at his old stand and will take pork and flour for which he will give furniture of the highest fashion. This ad continues for a month. By February of 1822, he seemed to have weathered the economic storm and had so much business that he needed one or two journeymen immediately. By 1823 conditions were definitely better for Mr. Hazel moved into a new shop; this ad appeared in the Columbus Gazette, May 15, 1823:

KNOW ALL MEN; The Subscriber removed one door west of Judge Kerr on Broad street where he continues the cabinetmaking business.

Apr. 28, 1823 S.K. HAZEL

By 1825, he was again asking for flax seed in exchange for cabinet furniture. He was still working in 1827.

HEDGES, JOHN......L.1801-1850..W.1828-1850
Circleville, Pickaway County

John Hedges was born in the vicinity of Martinsburg, Berkley County, Virginia (now West Virginia) in 1801. He was the brother of Solomon Hedges.

John Hedges came to Circleville, Ohio in 1827, however his first advertisement in the Olive Branch & Pickaway Herald appears May 3, 1828:

Cabinetwork

JOHN HEDGES

Informs the citizens of this place and its vicinity that he has commenced the business of cabinetmaking in the brick building on West Main Street formerly occupied by William Black where he will prosecute the business in all of its branches. Those who may favor him with their custom may be assured they shall receive neat and substantial work from the best materials.

May 1, 1828

(An active lad, well recommended, from 14 to 16 years of age, is wanted, as an apprentice to the above business)

On May 19, 1837 in the Independent American and Circleville Herald he stated:

Removal

John Hedges has removed his establishment to house lately occupied as a hat store, nearly opposite Isaac Darst Store on Bastille Avenue where he will keep constantly on hand a beautiful assortment of mahogany and common furniture of every description and variety made of the best materials and substantial and workmanlike style.

He respectfully solicits his old friends and the public to call and examine his furniture and prices.

He has a quantity of good poplar weather boarding for sale.

April 14, 1837

In November 1840 Hedges advertised that he was on the circle west of the Court House. He said he would always be in the shop and that he would like to have some of the business of Mr. May (Michael), who was no longer in business. He says that he has been in business for 13 years, it sounds as though he probably was there longer than anyone else and may have had one of the most prestigious practices in the city.

He continued to live in Circleville and to work as a cabinetmaker until his death in May 1850. He was forty-nine and still working at his trade; he was probably at the peak of his career. The inventory of his estate lists many tools and unfinished furniture; this very long and extensive shop inventory would indicate that he died in the prime of his life and business career. He had 3 cherry breakfast tables, 2 cherry dining tables, 17 sets of unfinished bedposts, 3 pairs unfinished bedsteads. It is generally assumed that beds were not made in pairs, but John Hedges did. He had 5 work benches which would indicate that he had 4 apprentices and that would have been a good sized factory. His shop was heated by a stove and he turned by a foot lathe. He used poplar, walnut, cherry and maple wood for his furniture and veneered with mahogany.

His general home furniture inventory indicates that he had very nice furniture; he probably made most of it himself. He had glass waiters and candlesticks, much carpeting and 2 buggies. These are signs of affluency. His wife also had her $300 allotment of household goods.

John Hedges was an extremely successful man in his business and he was making and selling a great deal of furniture.

Hedges, John
High Street Cemetery, Circleville
Died: 31 July 1850 49 yrs.
INVENTORY:

1	Bureau	18.00
1	" "	
1	" "	11.00
1	" "	
1	" Mahogany front	12.00
1	pr tables - side	20.00
1	Table	10.00
3	Cherry Breakfast Tables	13.50
2	Cherry Dining Tables	14.00
1	Wash STand walnut	3.00
3	Walnut Breakfast Tables	12.00
2	" Dining Tables	12.00
2	Cherry stands	9.00
2	Posslers Sofas	12.00
3	" chests	9.00
5	Bedsteads	22.50
1	Trundle Bedstead	2.00
3	prs. unfinished bedsteads	9.00
12	sets unfinished bedposts	12.00
1	lot of turned stuff	2.00
1	old table & desk	2.00
1	lot of picture frames	2.25
2	work benches	3.00
5	gals varnish	10.00
1	work bench	1.50
2	work benches	5.00
1	lot of carpenters tools	5.00
1	lot of cabinet tools	5.00
10	hand screws, grindstone & clamps etc.	8.00
1	stove & pipe	7.00
1	" "	7.00
1	Turning lay & tools	3.00
1	lot of cuttings	1.50
1	Hearse frame	1.25
1	box bed pins	4.00
1	bureau frame (little)	1.00
1	hand saw	.50
1	wheel barrow	4.00
1	buggy	50.00
1	heavy buggy	80.00
1	bay mare	40.00
1	set single harness	5.00
4	hogs	10.00
1	saw buck & ax	1.00
4	barrels & a base	1.00
	contents of smoke house	4.00
1	brass clock	4.00
1	looking glass	.75
1	walnut desk	6.00
30	yds carpeting	10.50
20	yds rug "	5.00
14	" " "	2.80
1	lot " "	1.00
1	Looking glass	2.75
1	pair side tables	10.00
1	Bureau	10.00
1	Double drawer stand	1.75
1	lot winsor chairs	3.00
1	lot glass waie & waites & candlesticks	2.00
1	side table	5.00
1	Rocking chair	1.50
1	set common chairs	1.50
1	rocking chair	.50
1	lot ¾ inch board	19.18
1	" 1 " poplar	15.82
1	" 1 " walnut	9.93
1	" 1 " cherry	13.72
1	" 2 " maple	29.00
1	lot veneering	9.00
1	hogshead	.75

HEDGES, SOLOMON......1837-1840
Circleville, Pickaway County

Solomon Hedges was born in the area of Martinsburg, Berkley County, Virginia (now West Virginia). He began cabinetmaking in Martinsburg on June 7, 1832, for an ad in the Martinsburg Gazette of that date "informs the citizens of Martinsburg and surrounding country, that he is now prepared to execute all orders in the Cabinet-making Business." He continued in business in that town in 1835. By 1837, he had moved to Circleville, Ohio and on Saturday, July 8, he was advertising in the Independent American and Circleville Herald:

New Cabinet Shop

Solomon Hedges

Respectfully informs the public that he has permanently established his residence in Circleville and will prosecute the business of Cabinet Making

In all of its various branches. His shop is situated south of the Court House fronting on the Public Circle, one door from Diffenderfers Corner. He will keep on hand or make to order: Sideboards, secretaries, Bureaus, plain and fancy tables, Bedsteads of all kinds.

And - all articles in the line of his profession all of which shall be made of good materials and by the best of workmen.

All kind of lumber or country Produce taken in exchange for cabinetware.

Circleville, July7, 1837

And on May 9, 1840, he advertised in the Circleville Herald:

Removal

Solomon Hedges

has removed his Cabinet Shop to a room on West Main Street immediately opposite S. Swindel and Company's Tin, Copper and Sheet Iron Ware Manufactory where he has and intends keeping on hand a general assortment of Cabinet Ware

Bureaux, Bedsteads, tables etc.,etc.

His furniture is made of good materials and by the best of workmen. He invites those in want of furniture to call and examine his prices and quality. He keeps a hearse and is prepared to make coffins to order.

May 1, 1840

It is not known when or where Solomon Hedges died.

HENDERSON, JAMES and ELLIOTT, JAMES......1813
Dayton, Montgomery County

The following excerpt is from *Pioneer Life in Dayton and Vicinity 1796-1840* by John F. Edgar, Dayton, Ohio:

On February 23, 1813, Henderson & Elliott bought of D.C. Cooper the south half of lot 186 (where the Kuhns Building now stands), fifty feet, for fifty dollars, on which they built a one-story frame shop for their business as cabinetmakers. Mr. Henderson lived on Fourth Street near the shop. He afterwards sold his interest to Mr. Elliott and moved to Lafayette, Indiana. Mr. Elliott was a bachelor, and continued to keep the shop until his death. The last few years he did but little work, excepting to turn rolling-pins, on an old foot-lathe in the corner of the shop, as wedding presents for his bachelor friends...That shop was a great place for the boys of forty or more years to congregate at early candle-lighting to discuss politics and play practical jokes on each other...In 1862 it was partitioned into four small storerooms, and the wooden awning added. When this change was made, and the bunk occupied by James Elliott removed, it was found that quite an impression had been worn in the boards against which his head had rested for so many years. In 1882 the shop was taken down to make room for the present Kuhns Building.

HERR, SAMUEL......1815-1818..D.1858
Lancaster, Fairfield County

Samuel Herr was born in Hagerstown, Maryland and came with Jesse Woltz to Lancaster, Ohio in 1815. Herr and Woltz worked together until 1816 when Jesse Woltz began working alone. Samuel Herr advertised his wares in 1818 and also asked for an apprentice to apply. The following is from the Lancaster, Ohio Eagle, March 12, 1818:

CABINETMAKING

The Subscriber respectfully informs his friends and the public in general he continues to carry on the above business in all of its various branches at his old stand a few doors east of the printing office, Main street,Lancaster. He will keep a fresh supply of cherry and walnut suitable for making furniture. Furniture in the most approved fashions, such as secretary desks, wardrobes, bureaus, tables, stands, high and low post bedsteads, etc.,etc. He returns his sincere thanks to a generous public for the liberal patronage he received and hopes through unremitted exertions and assiduous attention to business to merit a continuance of their favors.

Lancaster, Mar. 12, 1818 SAMUEL HERR

N.B. A boy of 14 or 15 years of age will be taken as apprentice to the house joiner and cabinetmaking business, if immediate application be made.

This gentleman remained in Lancaster and probably continued in his profession until his death in 1858.

HIBBS, ADIN G.......1833-1837
Columbus, Franklin County

Adin G. Hibbs came from Pennsylvania to Columbus in 1832. He advertised in the Columbus Daily Advertiser in 1833:

Adin G. Hibbs - Chair Manufactory, sign of the Golden Chair, High Street, Columbus, Ohio - I take this method of informing my friends and the public in general that I have on hand, and for sale a large and handsome assortment of Windsor and Fancy chairs of every description made of the best materials and in the most fashionable and substantial manner.

This advertisement continued for 2 months. Hibbs remained in the chair business for he was still advertising in the Columbus Daily Ohio State Journal on July 20th, 1837.

Sometime after this date he joined with John and James Dalzell in the management of a saw mill called the Cottage Mills in the town of

Shadeville of which Mr. and Mrs. A.G. Hibbs were founders. Hibbs was a director of the turnpike company which built the Cottage Mills and Harrisburg Turnpike. Later Mr. Hibbs lived in Franklin township, Franklin County; he was a state senator in 1870 and a state representative in 1866. After he bought out the Dalzells in the Mill in 1851, he ammassed great wealth. He was married to Pamela Shade in Pennsylvania prior to 1830. There were no children.

HILDRETH, LOUIS A.......1832
Dayton,Montgomery County

This ad is from the Dayton Journal & Advertiser, December 18, 1832:

CABINETMAKING - The Subscriber continues to carry on the above business a few doors above Mr. Eaken's store on Second street. A large and general assortment of furniture which will be made in the most fashionable style of the best materials.

LOUIS A. HILDRETH

He will pay cash for 7,000 feet of good cherry plank. 4 or 5 good journeymen wanted to whom Cincinnati prices will be given.

HILL, ALEXANDER......L.1788-1841
Marietta, Washington County

From the *History of Marietta and Washington County:*

Captain Alexander Hill was of Scotch-Irish descent and was born February 28, 1777 in County Antrim, Ireland near Belfast and landed at Philadelphia in 1784. His parents were strict Scotch Presbyterians - "Force of circumstances put him in the way of learning the cabinetmaking trade, though his tastes strongly impelled him to a sea-faring life.

Captain Hill started from Pittsburg with an English emigrant named Alcock, in canoes lashed together, expecting to have gone to New Orleans; but on arriving at Marietta in 1798, he found it inadvisable to proceed further without more money. He therefore plied his trade at Marietta and soon found that the demand for furniture to supply the new settlers was increasing and offering opportunities for active and profitable business in that line. He established the first furniture factory in that county and the cabinetmaker of those days was also the undertaker. Captain Hill constructed the first coffin that was placed in Mound Cemetery.

In 1801 he married Sarah Foster, the daughter of Ephraim Foster.

In 1813 Alexander Hill received a commission as a Captain in the United States Infantry in the War of 1812 and in the fall of that year he was ordered to Zanesville and then to Detroit. Robert Wells Jr. went into the cabinetmaking business in Mr. Hill's shop in Marietta. In 1814, after his return from the war, Mr. Hill opened a tavern called the Sign of the Swan and became sheriff in 1815. He continued making furniture while keeping his tavern, for in 1816 he advertised in the American Friend for a 'competant workman at the Cabinet Making Business'. Therefore he was keeping a tavern and making furniture at the same time until 1837. He would fit up a boat with furniture to be shipped to New Orleans and the southern market and the outcome was uniformly profitable. In the fall of 1836, he entered into a contract with the state to build the dam and one half of the canal at Lowell, the state being engaged at that time in providing slack water navigation for the Muskingum River. Captain Hill died in February 1841, but his family profitted greatly from the dam and canal venture.

He had seven sons and two daughters of whom John, Hugh, Jessie, Hiram A., Daniel Y and Eliza lived to adulthood.

HILL, HUGH......1819-1823
Marietta, Washington County

Hugh Hill was the son of Alexander Hill of Marietta, Ohio and he joined his father in the cabinetmaking trade.

The following ad is from the American Friend, October 3, 1819:

---

6 CENTS REWARD for ASAHEL CLARK, an apprentice to the cabinetmaking business.

HUGH HILL

He also advertised in the American Friend,January 25, 1823 and although the ad does mention his occupation, it indicates that Hugh Hill had other talents as well:

Hugh Hill

Cabinetmaker

has commenced a dancing school at Major A. Hill's Assembly Rooms where he intends teaching for the term of 3 months, two evenings in each week. Those who wish to become acquainted with the refined life will be thankfully received.

Terms/dollar and 50 cents for each person

Hugh Hill

HILLHOUSE, -
Chillicothe, Ross County

Mrs A.W. Matlock has a card table made in Chilicothe, found by her grandmother in 1920. The name on the bottom is Hillhouse.

HILLS, REUBEN......1839
Oxford, Butler County

This excerpt is taken from a book called *Old Oxford Houses and People Who Lived in Them* by Mrs. William Ernst Smith:

At last the main part of the 'Mansion House' (so Romeo Lewis called it) must have been finished by November of 1839. In that month Romeo bought from Reuben Hills:

2 bureaus $14 . . . . $28.00
2 bedsteads $7 . . . . 14.00
1 table 5.50
2 dressing tables $3.50 . . . . 7.00
1 work stand 10.00
1 candle stand 2.50
1 French Bedstead 28.00
2 wash stands 8.00

In December, he bought from Hills:

1 kitchen cupboard and table united . $10.00
1 black walnut dressing bureau 55.00
1 painted wash stand 6.00
1 pr. footstools 1.50

HINES, E.A.
Point Isabel, Clermont County

The *History of Clermont County* indicates that E.A. Hines was in furniture making in 1847 and perhaps before.

HOFFMAN(HUFFMAN), GEORGE 1824-1866
Chillicothe, Ross County

George Hoffman came to Ohio in 1809 and settled in Chillicothe in 1812 when he was 14 years of age. He was bound as an apprentice to James Phillips and learned the cabinetmaking trade. In 1824, he set up in business for himself at the old barracks the corner of 2nd and Walnut street. Long known as Judge Hoffman because he was appointed Judge of Elections, he continued as a manufacturer and dealer of furniture for nearly 50 years on Walnut street or at his original location.

On October 2, 1845, he entered into a co-partnership with William Stewart as manufacturer of cabinetware and chairs. This partnership lasted for a year or more when on March 10, 1847 Hoffman announced that he still carried on the cabinet, sofa and chairmaking business. His stock includes a fine variety of the most...beautiful woods in use and his work is warranted to be strong, durable and fashionable.

In the Scioto Gazette, Chillicothe, June 26, 1866, a notice was given that James Hoffman & Co. have succeeded the old firm of George Hoffman in the cabinetmaking business, corner of 2nd and Walnut streets.

HOOD, JOHN PAGE......L.1813-1879
West Union, Adams County

From *A History of Adams County, Ohio from its Earliest Settlements until its Present Time* by Nelson W. Evans and Emmons B. Stivers:

John Page Hood, youngest child of John and Hanna Hood, was born in West Union, Adams County, Dec. 6, 1813. He learned the printing trade at 10 years old with the Village Register, edited by Ralph M. Voorhees. Later he learned the Cabinetmaking trade. He died of heart failure Oct. 8, 1879.

HOOKER, WILLIAM......pre 1843
Batavia, Clermont County

From the Ohio Sun, December 1, 1843

Cabinetmaking - William Hooker informs the public that he has removed to the south side of Main Street opposite the courthouse. He has hearses and transacts the business of funerals.

HOPKINS, JOSEPH......1801
South of Chillicothe, Ross County

This ad appeared in the Scioto Gazette, Saturday, December 12, 1801:

SPINNING WHEELS: The Subscriber being at the High Bank, 3 miles below PeePee Creek, has on hand a number of spinning wheels and means to continue an assortment of the same at the low rate of $3.20 for each.

JOSEPH HOPKINS, Dec. 12, 1801

HORSMANN, URIAH......1824
Leesburg, Highland County

Samuel Saunders and John Henley were merchants who had local cabinetmakers working for them. They in turn sold the furniture in their store.

Uriah Horsmann commenced work February 15, 1824. He was credited for one bureau for $5.00, credited for one stand for $1.00, and one stand for $1.00.

This information comes from the Leesburg, Ohio ledger book for Saunders and Henley.

HOWARD, JAMES......1812
HOWARD & YOUNG
Chillicothe, Ross County

From the Chillicothe Supporter, March 21, 1812:

CHAIRMAKING & WHEELWRIGHT BUSINESS

The partnership of HOWARD and YOUNG has been dissolved and the Subscriber intends to carry on at the business in all its branches in the North end of Mr. Joseph Shepherd's house on the corner of Mulberry and 2nd street, on the shortest notice and the reasonable terms.
JAMES HOWARD

HUEY, JAMES......1828-1851
Zanesville, Muskingum County

James Huey was born in 1805 in Pennsylvania. He moved to Zanesville and began advertising as a cabinetmaker there August 16, 1828.

Chair Factory

James Huey - respectfully informs the citizens of Zanesville that he has commenced chairmaking next door to Mr. George Hahn's gun shop where he keeps on hand a general assortment of Fancy Work, Fancy Flagseats, Fancy Windsors and common Chairs, with a variety of settees and sociables. He gives his own experience and expert workers from the East...

In 1829 he married Mary Ann Hahn, the daughter of George Hahn, the gunsmith and his next door neighbor. George Hahn was from Washington County, Pennsylvania. In 1836 J.H. Kilpatrick moved into J. Huey's chair wareroom. Mr. Huey's wareroom was now the first door east of his old stand.

The Zanesville Gazette of February 7, 1849 still carried advertisements from the "Chair and Cabinet Establishment of James Huey". In the 1850 Census James Huey was working in Muskingum County in Zanesville's 3rd ward and he was advertising in 1851. At present, no death record or will has been found for James Huey.

Antiques Magazine of December 1931 and Bjerkoe's *Cabinetmakers of America* both mention a desk of walnut and poplar with a note written on the bottom of a small drawer - "James Boyar - his desk made June 1808 by me J. Huey, Washington County, State of Pennsylvania - Desk for Mr. Boyar." Another drawer carried a 2nd inscription - "James Boyars Desk made of Walnut and Poplar, James Boyar of Peters Creek, Washington Co., Robert Jones, George Ross, Simon Snider, Gov. Dutch." The J. Huey who made this desk would have been an older relative of James Huey. In the *Made in Ohio Catalogue*, Columbus Art Museum, 1984, appears the note "John Huey lived in Washington Co., Pennsylvania in 1810 and John and James were in Zanesville, Ohio in 1820." Perhaps the Hueys came from Washington County, Pennsylvania; James' wife and family did also. Further research in Pennsylvania will substantiate this connection.

Chair Factory.
JAMES HUEY,

RESPECTFULLY informs the citizens of Zanesville and the public in general, that he has lately commenced the CHAIR MAKING business on Fifth st. next door to Mr. George Hahn's Gun smith shop, where he has and intends keeping on hand, a general assortment of common and

FANCY WORK,

Among which are Fancy Flag seats Fancy Windsor and common Chairs, with a variety of Settees, Sociables, &c all of which will be sold on the most reasonable and accommodating terms.

The subscriber will add, that all the above work will be warranted good to purchasers; and from his own experience and intention of keeping in employ the best workmen from the Eastern cities, he hopes to render general satisfaction (both for neatness and durability) to all those who may favor him with a call.

Zanesville, August 16, 18[illegible]8.—3m93

HULING, ISAAC
Point Pleasant, Clermont County

The History of Clermont County lists Isaac Huling as a cabinetmaker in Point Pleasant. No date cited.

HUNTER, JOSEPH C.
Cambridge, Guernsey County

The following information comes from the Guernsey County 175th Celebration Booklet, The Carl Rech compilation of Cambridge lots:

Samuel Drummond and Joseph C. Hunter came to town as young men and started in the cabinetmaking business on the east end of lot 45. (No date cited.)

HUSTON, JAMES W.......1831
Scioto County

These notes from the *Pioneer Record of the Scioto County,Ohio* by Nelson W. Evans:

James W. Huston was employed to repair the Court House. The cupola and railings were repaired and painted white, the roof painted Spanish brown, the door and frames painted white, the Venetian blinds painted green.

Knittle indicates that James Huston was a sign and ornamental painter and did fancy chairs and stenciling in 1831.

HUVEY, HENRY......1796
HUVEY, JOHN
Marietta, Washington County

John and Henry Huvey were cabinetmakers in 1796. They were also housewrights; they built the Lutheran Church in Marietta.

This information comes from William Reynolds, Campus Martius Museum, Marietta, Ohio.

IRWIN, JAMES......1827
Dayton, Montgomery County

From the Dayton National Journal & Montgomery & Dayton Advertiser, Oct. 1, 1827:

CABINETMAKING BUSINESS: JAMES IRWIN, south side of Main at Cross Street. One door east of the Methodist Meeting House, hopes to receive a fair share of the public patronage. Cherry, poplar, and walnut plank and country produce received in payment. Sign painting and lettering done in the neatest manner.

May 9, 1827.

ISENLORD, JAMES......pre 1841
Scioto County

It is noted in the Scioto County penitentiary records:

ISENLORD, JAMES, Cabinetmaker - born New York; sentenced in Scioto County for manslaughter; disposition - intemperate; Age; 29; term 1 year. Date of sentencing Dec. 1841. Pardoned by Governor Corwin 1842. Parents living in Dearbornville, Michigan.

JACKSON, TOTTEN......ca. 1820-1830
Nicholasville, Clermont County

From the *History of Clermont County:*

TOTTEN JACKSON, CABINETMAKER, also built shops and houses in that area.

JACOBS, WILLIAM & PIPER, GEORGE R......1826-1827
Circleville, Pickaway County

Seen in the Circleville-Olive Branch, July 24, 1826:

CABINETWORK - JACOBS & PIPER - respectfully informs the public that they have opened a shop on North Main Street in the new building of JAMES McCRUM where they will prosecute their business with the utmost fidelity. Persons favoring them with their patronage may rest assured of having furniture faithfully made from good materials and in neat style on reasonable terms. Plank, country produce, or each will be accepted in payment for work in their line.

June 10, 1826 (NOTE: This continued weekly for many weeks. It stopped Feb. 23, 1827.)

Also from the Circleville-Olive Branch of Sat., June 9, 1827:

JACOBS & PIPER - removed to new shop on North Main, directly opposite the old Tootine where they will be pleased to supply their customers with plain and fancy cabinetware on short notice, and accomodating terms.

They are grateful for their liberal encouragement already extended to them and will endeavor to merit continuance of same.

(NOTE: This ad went on into Sept. 1827.)

This also from the Circleville-Olive Branch, Sept. 6, 1827:

DISSOLUTION of this partnership by mutual consent - (S) WILLIAM JACOBS and GEORGE R. PIPER.

JEFFORDS, JOHN......1819..D.1821
Columbus, Franklin County

An advertisement appeared in the Columbus Gazette, Apr. 8, 1819:

JOHN JEFFORDS, CABINETMAKER, High Street, Columbus, Ohio, has on hand a handsome and elegant assortment of cabinet furniture: Sideboards; breakfast, dining and tea tables; candle and wash stands; French high post and common beds, with every other article in this line of business...all of which he offers cheap for cash, approved cash or country produce. He returns his sincere thanks to the public for their liberal patronage, and hopes to merit a continuance of their favors by having his work well done.

WANTED - AS AN APPRENTICE TO THE ABOVE BUSINESS - a boy from 14 to 16 years of age who can be well-recommended.

Columbus, April 8, 1819. (NOTE: This ad continued for a year and a half.)

John Jeffords died on Nov. 17, 1821. Sally Jeffords requested at that time for all those indebted to pay up. This advertisement appeared in the Columbus Gazette on Thur., June 12, 1822:

PUBLIC SALE - Saturday the 15th instant, at the house of Sally Jeffords in Columbus, all remaining personal property of JOHN JEFFORDS, deceased, consisting of all kinds of CABINETMAKING tools, ten thousand feet of seasoned lumber(of different descriptions), a variety of cabinet furniture viz: sideboards, secretaries, bureaus, desks, tables, etc., together with considerable other properties. Sale to commence 11 a.m.; 3 months credit for all sums owed him of $5.00 by giving notes with approved security.

John Jeffords was a fairly important man. His son, John E Jeffords was a cashier of the bank in 1843. They became an important family in Columbus. He didn't work very long, but he was prominent all the time he worked. He apparently was here before 1819.

Jeffords, John #0353
Administrator: Sally Jeffords 17 November 1821 Bond $2000
Securities David V. Deshler
Mahlon Northup
Will Book A missing
Sale: Saturday 19 January 1822

	Dressing Box	.12½
	for circular tables	13.50
	saddle	9.50
1	double barreled gun	16.50
1	tea table	5.25
	stand	1.12½
	craddle	3.12½
1	table	1.12½
1	table	1.12½
1	french bedstead	9.50
	trundle bedstead	1.50
1	chest	2.06½
5	chairs	1.62½
	cow & calf	11.62½
1	chest	1.62½
	circular bureau	15.25
	wheel barrow	2.12½
	bureau	9.50
	dinning table	9.25
1	wash stand	1.37½
1	candle stand	1.75
1	candle stand	1.75
1	clock case	10.50
1	spinning wheel	2.50
	irt	2.25
	reel	1.06¼
1	keg of nails	1.75
1	waggon & harness	40.00
1	shovel & tongs	2.37½
2	chests	1.56¼
	desk & bookcase	25.00
1	circular bureau	18.00
1	plain bureau	10.00
	bureau	16.00
	bedstead	6.00
1	bbl currant wine	6.50
	hay	8.00
	cupboard	10.00
47	bushel corn	8.00

JEFFERIES, JOHN C.......L.1769-1853
New Richmond, Clermont County
Georgetown, Brown County

The *History of Clermont County* indicates that John C. Jefferies was a cabinetmaker and wheelwright in New Richmond in 1816. In 1824 he was in partnership with A. Towner in Brown County, but he seemed to return to Clermont County for he died in New Richmond in 1853. He was buried in Green Mound Cemetery.

JEFFRIES, URIAH......1834
Cedarville, Greene County

The following information is from Broadstone, Vol. I, *History of Greene County:*

Uriah Jeffries, born in North Carolina; came to Cedarville, Ohio in 1830. The year of 1834 also witnessed the establishment of the first factory in town, although it could hardly have been called a factory at the time. The industry was that of furniture making or cabinetmaking, as it was usually called in those days, and the proprietor in this industry was one Uriah Jeffries. He started with nothing but a hand lathe, and in the course of time he added more machinery and introduced horse-power. When he decided to make these improvements, he moved his little shop to the west side of town near the site of the latter furniture factory. Business was good and by 1845 he felt the need of enlarging his shop. Accordingly he associated with James Jeffries, (his nephew) with him as partner and the new firm at once began the erection of a new plant, which was in use as long as the business was maintained. Uriah sold out to James Jeffries in 1855. He farmed for 2 years and returned to the firm in 1857. James ran the business until 1870, until Mason, Uriah's son continued in business until 1880 when it was closed down for good.

JESTER, THOMAS P.......pre 1842
Hamilton, Butler County

From the Western Telegraph, June 22, 1842:

CHAIRMAKER - THOMAS P. JESTER - Old stand east of the Post Office in Hamilton. Fancy chairs, settees, large and small rockers.

JOHN, LEMUEL......1821
Bethel, Clermont County

Lemuel John was the son of Captain James John who came to Kentucky in 1794 and then moved on to Clermont County, Ohio where he lived on Nine Mile Creek in 1796. The Clermont County History notes that Lemuel was a cabinetmaker in Cincinnati and a charter member of the Bethel Lodge in 1821. It is believed that Lemuel came to Cincinnati in 1816; he may have worked part time in Clermont County for he did not advertise until 1829 in Cincinnati, however he was not listed again until 1844. In 1850 he became general agent for the Intelligence Star. This man was in and out of the furniture making trade for a long time.

Lemuel John was the father of two important Cincinnati cabinetmakers - J.S. John and S.J. John (see *Furnituremakers of Cincinnati* by Jane E. Sikes.)

JONES & DINSMORE......1825
Wilmington, Clinton County

The following advertisement appeared in the Western Argus, January 13, 1825:

CHAIRS & WHEELS

The Subscriber respectfully informs the public that he has commenced the chair and wheel business in the shop formerly occupied by G.B. Moore, a chairmaker on South street where they intend keeping on hand an assortment of the above articles for which they will take in exchange - linen, woolsey, flax, tallow, beeswax, and almost any kind of country produce; and hope from their attention to business to share a part of the public patronage.

JONES & DINSMORE

Wilmington, Dec.23, 1824

The first names of these men are unknown.

JONES, SAMUEL G.......1826
Portsmouth, Scioto County

The Pioneer Record of Scioto County, Ohio by Nelson W. Evans notes that:

July 24, 1826

SAMUEL G. JONES - making two tables for the court, was allowed $6.75; and he was credited the bill of $9.00 for an old bar table.

JORDON, JOSHUA P.......1837
Batavia, Clermont County

From the Clermont Courier, August 26, 1837:

One Cent Reward

Run away from the subscriber on the night of Wednesday last an indentured apprentice to the Cabinetmaking Business of the name of Joshua P. Jordon. All persons are forewarned not to harbor or employ said boy under the penalty of law. Any person returning him will receive the above reward but no charges will be paid.

Brice R.Blair

Batavia, Aug.26, 1837

Long must have moved to Chillicothe for in the next year he was advertising in the Scioto Supporter, February 11, 1815:

WANTED IMMEDIATELY - a sober young man as a journeyman to the cabinetmaking business, constantly employed and good wages will be given.

DAVID LONG

Feb.14, 1815

LONGSHORE, JAMES (AND CO.)......1829
Lebanon, Warren County

This advertisement appeared in the Lebanon Western Star, February 7, 1829:

JAMES LONGSHORE & CO., cabinetmakers on Mulberry street nearly opposite Thomas P. Smith's tavern, Lebanon, will promptly attend to any business in their line and pledge themselves to furnish cabinetware as good and cheap as any in the country.

Country produce - boards and scantling will be taken in exchange for furniture.

Feb.6, 1829

LOTHRUP, SETH......1824
Marietta, Washington, County

From the American Friend & Marietta Gazette, May 6, 1824:

AN ABSCOUNDER - The Subscribers have been authorized by his creditors to caution the public against trusting or employing a person calling himself SETH LOTHRUP, by profession a cabinetmaker who absconded from Washington County, Ohio about the 15th day of April.

GEORGE BOWEN, EBENEZER BOWEN, ASLOM T. NEIGH, JAMES LEGGET, JOSEPH CHAMBERS

Waterford, Apr.26, 1824

LUCAS, JOHN......pre 1822
Waynesville, Warren County

The *History of Warren County* mentions that John Lucas was a cabinetmaker in Warren County, perhaps Waynesville, before 1822.

LYTLE & BROWN
Batavia, Clermont County

Lytle & Brown advertised in the Clermont County Courier on April 13, 1836 and the ad continued until June:

WANTED - The Subscriber wishes to employ two journeymen cabinetmakers and a turner.

LYTLE & BROWN

LYTLE, WILLIAM
Batavia, Clermont County

William Lytle is listed as a cabinetmaker in the *History of Clermont County.*

MACDONALD, WALTER......1818
Lancaster, Fairfield County

From the Ohio Eagle, April 23, 1818:

FANCY AND WINDSOR CHAIRS
CHAIRMAKING

The Subscriber respectfully informs his friends and the public that he has removed his shop next door west of the printing office, where he intends to carry on the above business in all its varying branches. He also makes high and low post bedsteads of superior quality, all of which he will sell as reasonable as any work in this line can be had in this state.

His work is all warranted and in case of any failure in the first 12 months, it is made good, free of charge. Approved country produce will be taken for chairs and bedsteads.

Lancaster, Apr.9, 1818

WALTER MacDONALD

MADDUX, JOHN
Brown County

The *History of Brown County* lists John Maddux as a cabinetmaker.

MAGEE, JOHN......1793-1819
Belpre, Washington County

John Magee was a farmer and furniture maker in Belpre, Ohio in 1793. According to *Made in Ohio*, Columbus Art Museum, Columbus, Ohio - "John Magee paid taxes on lands in Marietta township and in 1820 he is listed in a Federal Census as a resident of Salem township with the occupation of 'agriculture'".

In 1819 he made a desk of walnut and pine. In the skirt of this inlaid Hepplewhite desk with french feet is inlaid "John Magee 1819". It is a most graceful artistically built piece of furniture with beautiful vine and leaf inlay on the front of the fall front and also on each drawer front. The inlay is most graceful.

There is a miniature chest with a bonnet

drawer in the center which is closely associated with this desk. It has the vine and leaf inlay, it also has diagonal walnut and applewood geometric inlay with "J.M." inlaid in the skirt of the chest.

MANLY, WILLIAM T.S.......L.1813-1879
Springfield, Clark County

From *Cabinetmakers of Indiana* by Betty Lawson Walters:

WILLIAM T.S. MANLY - CABINETMAKER. He was born Apr. 10, 1813 near Poolsville, Maryland. Moved to Virginia and then to Springfield, Ohio, and then to Richmond, Indiana, Indianapolis to Logansport, Cass County. In 1838 with Isreal Neal he advertised at Logansport in the Logansport Telegraph. In 1840 he attached a power lathe. Manly died in 1879. Smith continued in the business.

This man was in Springfield, Ohio, probably in the early 1830's.

MARBLE,DANIEL......L.1793-1860..1839
Wilmington, Clinton County

Daniel Marble, who was the brother of David Marble, was born in Pennsylvania in 1793; he died in Fayette County November 23, 1860. His wife's name was Isabella. He was a cabinetmaker. There were a great many members of his family who were cabinetmakers also - H.L. Marble, Frank Marble and David Marble. There was a son Elliott who was listed as a silversmith in 1860.

Daniel Marble came to Wilmington,Ohio in 1839. The Marbles took over the cabinet business from Haines Moore when he moved to another part of Clinton County.

MARBLE, DAVID......L.1806-1888
Wilmington, Clinton County

David Marble was born in Pennsylvania, January 10, 1806; he married Elizabeth Vandervoort, May 26, 1844. He died May 5, 1888, at 82 years of age. He was buried in the Sugar Grove Cemetery.

In 1850 David Marble was in Green Township, which is New Antioch, so he had moved out of Wilmington by 1850. But he was still probably doing cabinetmaking work.

MASON, WILLIAM BOND SR.......L.1767-1813..W.1791-1813
Marietta, Washington County

William Mason Sr. was born in Lincoln Massachusetts, the twelfth child of Joseph and Grace (Bond) Mason on February 2, 1767. He came to Marietta in 1788 with the first group of 48 settlers. He married Susan Coburn of Brookfield, Massachusetts in 1790. They were married in Marietta. William was taken into the Society of Masons American Union Lodge I in 1791 with the profession of cabinetmaker noted. He was issued many commissions in the Ohio Militia of Washington County with his final rank of Captain. In 1796 William and Susan moved with their family to the town of Lowell, a few miles up the Muskingum River from Marietta and he lived on this farm until his death on September 26, 1813.

William Mason built the Rufus Putnam House and lived in the only other 2 story house in Campus Martius, it is thought that he probably built this house for himself. (information courtesy Bernice Graham, Marietta, Ohio: From the Mason Geneaological Record compiled by Mary Eliza Mason).

Mason lived in Adams township and was one of the earliest Baptist ministers at Rainbow settlement. He died in 1813 and on January 14, 1814 Susannah Mason announced in the American Friend:

Take Notice

All persons indebted to William Mason late of Adams tsp., Washington Co. deceased are hereby notified to pay their respective dues forthwith and all persons to whom said estate are indebted are requested to bring in the demand proven according to law for settlement.

Susannah Mason
Administratix

The desk in the Campus Martius Museum by William Mason was made for his own use and can be dated by the purchase of the hardware, i.e. desk lock, brass hinges and knobs bought in 1793. This would have to be one of the earliest pieces of documented Ohio furniture. It is cherry with poplar secondary wood. It stands tall with plain ends which are cut out, and has a simple construction similar to the earliest New England 6 board blanket chest. It also has graduated drawers with glass knobs.(These may be replacements.)

MAY, HENRY......1808-1814-1816
Chillicothe, Ross County

Henry May came to Chillicothe from Fredericksburg, Virginia in 1798,at the age of eleven, with his father and family. He is first noticed as a craftsman in 1808 when he advertises he "has commenced the wheelwright business on Second street, opposite Mr.

Winship' office, where he makes Cotton, and flax wheels, and split botomed (sic) chairs." (From the Scioto Gazette, January 11, 1808)

An ad in the Supporter and Scioto Gazette of July 23, 1814 indicates that May "removes his Chair-making and Wheelrights(sic) shop to Water street adjoining Drayton M. Curtis' store.

In 1816, this advertisement in the Scioto Gazette and Fredonian Chronicle, February 29, announces the beginning of a partnership between May and Thomas Renshaw:

FANCY CHAIR FACTORY
HENRY MAY & THOMAS RENSHAW

Respectfully inform the citizens and the public that they are commencing a co-partnership in the above chair business at the old stand of HENRY MAY on Water street, next door to D.M. Curtis. From the experience of the latter partner from Baltimore, they flatter themselves that they can finish work in a style equal to any imported. They have on hand a large assortment of gilt and plain chairs and intend on keeping an extensive collection of bent back, broad tops with landscapes, and plain chairs of every description which they will sell at the most reduced prices.

It is not known how long the May-Renshaw connection lasted. In the Scioto Gazette & Fredonian Chronicle, November 27, 1818, John M'Landburgh, a Chillicothe merchant, offered "on commission a few spinning wheels of Mr. May's make."

Henry May operated a tavern a mile and a half north of Chillicothe on the old stage road. In 1822 he sold his tavern and bought a farm in Pickaway County on the Ross County line. He made his home in Kingston, Ross County, where he continued his trade of wheelwright and chairmaker. This information from the *History of Ross and Highland Counties, Ohio.* Other information courtesy John Grabb, Chillicothe.

MAY, MICHAEL......L.1798-1869..W.1820
Circleville, Pickaway County

The following information comes from *Round Town Reminiscences, Illustrations & Notes of the History of Circleville* by Ned Harden and W.W. Wiggins:

EARLY CRAFTSMEN - MICHAEL MAY, 1798-1869, b. Maryland 1798, Scotch-Irish ancestry. Learned the trade of cabinetmaking in Louden County, Virginia; then came to Circleville in 1818. He was a cabinetmaker in the 1820s. He lived in 109 Mound street. He was a ruling elder of the Presbyterian Church for many years.

We know that Mr. May ceased making furniture by November 1840 for John Hedge's advertisement of that date stated so and asked that Michael May's customers should come to him.

The *Index of Inscriptions on Gravestones, Pickaway County, Ohio* compiled by the Daughters of the American Revolution notes that:

MICHAEL MAY - died Sept.27, 1869; age 71 years. He was buried in Forest Cemetery, Township of Circleville. His first wife was Lydia May Raynor; his second wife was Mary Leitz.

MCADAMS, SAMUEL......1820
Williamsburg Township, Clermont County

The *History of Clermont County* mentions that Samuel McAdams was a manufacturer of split bottom chairs in Williamsburg in 1820.

MCBURNEY, ANDREW......L.1817-1894
Lebanon, Warren County

Andrew McBurney was Lt. Governor of Ohio, a cabinetmaker, and he later studied law in Lebanon with Valandingham or Corwin. There is a sideboard attributed to him at Glendower State Memorial - Lebanon, Ohio.

MCCAMMON, THOMAS......ca 1823
Carthage, Hamilton County

Carthage Village was platted by James John and Perial Townsend who were coopers and carpenters. Thomas McCammon and Sons were the first cabinetmakers in Carthage. Thomas McCammon was in Cincinnati from 1817 to 1821; but he went to Carthage following the depression (ca 1823) and seemed to have stayed there.

MCCLELLAND, ISAAC......L.1805-1887
Shandon, Butler County

The Saga of Paddy's Run by Stephen Riggs Williams notes that Isaac McClelland 1805-1887 was born in Pennsylvania; his family moved to Crawfordsville, Indiana. Here he learned cabinetmaking by working with his older brother. He later lived in Richmond, Indiana and then moved to Shandon. He died at the age of 82 and is buried in Hamilton, Ohio.

About his chairs:

---

the rounds were turned out of well seasoned hickory, posts made out of green maple. Dry rounds with a supply of the finest glue in a depression as each end was driven into green maple posts. As the posts seasoned they drew totally around the rounds. Seat made of strips of swamp ash and since his supply was kept in a neighboring creek, the material was always flexible for weaving.

There are several of Mr. McClelland's chairs photographed in Mr. Riggs's publication - some full ladder back and some part ladder and part arrow back Windsors.

MCCLOSKEY, JOSEPH......1821-1837
Hamilton (Rossville), Butler County

Joseph McCloskey was a cabinetmaker in partnership with Deleplane. Information from the Alta Harvey Heiser Manuscript Directory.

MCCLOUD, H.H.......1821
Portsmouth, Scioto County

The *History of Scioto County* mentions that H.H. McCloud was a chairmaker in 1821 in Portsmouth, Ohio.

MCCONNELL, JAMES......1826
Hillsboro, Highland, County

From the Hillsboro Gazette,June 29, 1826:

Six Cents Reward
Run away from the subscriber in Greenfield, Highland Co. on the 4th Instant an indentured apprentice to the Cabinet and Joiners business, named John Hicks about 19 years of age. The above reward will be given for the apprehension of said boy but no charge paid - all persons forewarned from trusting or harboring him on my account.
James McConnell

MCCORMICK, GEORGE......1809
Chillicothe, Ross County

George McCormick came to Marietta in 1805 to be in charge of the construction of Adena, the home of Thomas Worthington. Tradition states that Adena was designed by Benjamin Latrobe and it was through this architect that Thomas Worthington became acquainted with McCormick.

George McCormick also built furniture for Adena. An 1809 extant receipt states that he made "2 dressing tables, 2 beaurows(sic), one sideboard, one knife box, 4 Windsor boards."(Manuscript - O.H.S.)

Other receipts describe other furniture made by George McCormick for Adena, such as 4 large bedstead high posts, 2 dressing tables (1 with drawer), 2 sideboards, 2 card tables-2 circles, 1 set of wide dining tables, 2 burias(sic), 3 washstands, 2 strong tables = $267.00. On the reverse side is:

Bill to George McCormick - Also 1808 Contra Credit
By one half of the bill done by you and C.C. (Conrad Christman)

	$ 1114.40
By am of your own account	*278.36*
By am of cabinet work not yet done	*267.00*
	$ 1659.76
255.41	
To additional acct	*39.00*
By cellar door	*5.00*
	221.41
May 4 to cash half of $22 paid Wilson	*–13.00*
May 13 cash	*30.00*

(Thomas Worthington Papers - Ohio Historical Society)

The Catalogue for *Made in Ohio*, Columbus Art Museum, Columbus, Ohio, 1984, states:

George McCormick, born near Battletown, Clarke County, Virginia, was apprenticed to the carpenters trade as a young man. He also became a cabinetmaker. In about 1802, McCormick went to Washington, D.C. to assist in the construction of the nations Capitol. While in Washington he became acquainted with Benjamin Henry Latrobe who had been appointed architect of the Capitol by Thomas Jefferson in 1803. Latrobe was commissioned by Thomas Worthington, then a senator from Ohio (1803-1807) to design and construct Worthington's home near Chillicothe. Latrobe chose McCormick to supervise the carpentry and cabinetwork for the building of the Federal style structure that was to be called "Adena".

The five pieces of furniture which remain in Adena today are of great refinement. The card tables and sideboards are of mahogany and walnut woods. The wide dining table is veneered with satin wood and other exotic woods. According to tradition, Hector Sanford is supposed to have made chairs for Adena but no chairs remain which can be attributed to him.

MCCRUM, JAMES......1821-1822-1825-1827
Circleville, Pickaway County

This man was in Circleville in June 1821, when he was credited in the newspaper as having made chairs for the Court House. His first

1809

1809 Thomas Wetherington 1605

to George McCormick Dr

to two Dressing tables ...... $7..00

to two beaurows ...... +20..00

to one Sideboard ...... 27..00

to one knifebox ...... 8..25

to four windowheads ...... 6..50

to fixing up two Glasses and two locks ...... 1..00

$93..75

+ This charge is 4$ too high according to bill furnish

+ This also is 7 higher than the bill

advertisement appeared in the Circleville Olive Branch, August 13, 1822:

CHAIRMAKER, PAINTER, GLAZIER -
JAMES MCCRUM

continues to carry on his business in all of its branches at his old stand, North Main street, Circleville, where he cheerfully accommadates his friends and customers on the shortest notice. Wheat, whiskey or pork will be received in payment at the market.

(N.B. An active, healthy lad wanted for apprentice to the above business)

August 13, 1822

On August 13, 1822 McCrum advertised that his apprentice Levi James had run away on August 8, 1822. And in the Circleville Olive Branch of November 6, 1825 appeared this ad:

JAMES MCCRUM

The Subscriber acknowledges his gratitude to his friends and customers and respectfully informs them that he has on hand and will constantly keep a supply of common and fancy chairs of a superior quality, manufactured from well-seasoned timber and by experienced workmen. The terms are as liberal as any shop in the country. Wheat, whiskey, flax and pork received in payment for debts or for work.

JAMES MCCRUM

He was still advertising in 1827 and noted in his usual ad that he would accommodate those who didn't have country produce "as he in the principle is opposed to refusing cash from his old friends." He was still in Circleville in August 1840 for his horse was stolen at "a camp meeting 4 miles west of Royalton on Sunday evening last about dark". (Circleville Herald and Olive Branch, August 14, 1840)

It is not known whether James McCrum died in Circleville.

MCDUGAL, LEVI
Portsmouth, Scioto County

The 1820 Federal Manufacturer's Census as reprinted in the Tri-State Trader notes the following:

LEVI MCDUGAL. Owner, made wheels, reels, chairs, bureaus, bedsteads and tables. Used cherry boards, pine and poplar boards, wheel timber, chairs - $300 in cost. Employed 5 men and a boy on 2 turning lathes. Turners and tools - Capital $1,000. Wages - $1,050 annually. Other expenditures - $50. Market sales $1,700.

MCGREGOR, ELI......L.1798-1876
Wilmington, Clinton County

Eli McGregor was born January 1, 1798 in Berkley or Frederick County, Virginia (These may have been the same county at the time). He was married to Moriah Sexton who was born May 5, 1798. Eli came to Ohio with his father John McGregor in 1802. John owned a tavern on the southwest corner of Main and Mulberry streets in Wilmington. Eli apprenticed to a cabinetmaker in Lebanon, Ohio, in 1813. He worked in New Paris, Bowling Green and Xenia for short periods of time but returned to Wilmington in 1821 or 1822 where he had a cabinet shop for his lifetime. He was elected Mayor of Wilmington in 1835 and was a member of the Wilmington library society. He was a member of the Hamilton Convention. He died July 23, 1876 and was buried in Sugar Grove Cemetery, Wilmington, Ohio.

MCKEE, PETER......1829
Fairfield County

The Records of Indenture, Fairfield County, December 16, 1829 note that Peter McKee, cabinetmaker, had Andrew Coffman, age 18, as an apprentice.

MCLAIN, WASHINGTON......1840
Circleville, Pickaway County

Washington McLain, a chairmaker, advertised in the Circleville Herald, May 10, 1840:

Look Out

Painting, Glazing, &c. &c.

Washington McLain respectfully informs this community, that he has established himself in this town, on Pinkney street, in a shop fronting the Market house, lately occupied by Emanuel Gephart, where he intends to prosecute the above business. He will be happy at all times to receive orders for

House, Sign, or

Ornamental Painting,

Which he will execute with neatness and dispatch. He also intends manufacturing
Windsor, Fancy and Common

CHAIRS

Made of the best materials, and warranted
Turning kept constantly on hand, or done to order on the shortest notice.
Thankful for past favors, he hopes to receive a share of public patronage.
Two Boys wanted as apprentices to the above.
Circleville, May 15, 1840

He probably continued in Circleville as a chairmaker for some time for he is mentioned in the town histories.

MCMASTER, JOHN......PRE 1840
Pomeroy, Miegs County

Ledderer in the *Drama of the Boot Shaped Bend, History of Pomeroy* mentions that John McMaster came and built a dwelling house on the east side of the tavern. He then began making furniture in his house. He was still there in 1840.

MCNEILL, JAMES & JOHN......pre 1843
MCNEILL, CHRISTOPHER
Batavia, Clermont County

From the Ohio Sun, Clermont County, September 8, 1843:

Dissolution of Partnership

JAMES & JOHN MCNEILL,

Cabinetmakers, was this day dissolved. All debts, etc...
The cabinetmaking business will be carried on by CHRISTOPHER MCNEILL to whom the said firm sold out.

JAMES MCNEILL and JOHN MCNEILL

McNeal, John
Buried in McNeal private cemetery
Docket 1 p222 31 July 1856
Administrators: Isaac Norton
James McNeil
Children: Francis Marion
Lovina
Harbson
and maybe others
Inventory:

1 small log chain	1.50
1 large log chain	2.00
1 lot of augers (4)	1.25
3 axes & 1 hand saw	2.25

3 iron wedges & mawls	1.50
1 set scales & hay hook	1.00
1 coopers adze	.25
1 meat tub	2.00
1 small meat tub	.50
4 old barrels	.50
1 large box	.50
2 Barrels	.30
2 Large spinning wheels	2.00
1 small " " & reel	.50
3 tight barrels	1.50
1 Large Keg	.37½
1 grain cradle	1.50
Farm tools	
1 Double tree	1.50
1 lot of single trees	.75
1 Two horse harrow	4.00
2 wagon wheels	4.00
1 two horse sleigh & 1 one horse sleigh	4.50
1 Bureau	4.00
1 rifle gun	5.00
1 Breakfast table & old cloth	2.50
1 lot of split bottom chairs	1.25
1 " of windsor " (6)	1.50
1 Safe	4.00
1 kitchen table	.50
1 Dinning table	5.00
kitchen dishes, etc.	
1 Family carriage & harness	6.00
1 Two horse wagon & wood bed	60.00
1 Three horse wagon & wood bed	50.00
1 lot of wagon tongue lumber	8.40
1 light wagon bed	2.00
1 lot of harnes	5.00
1 Side saddle	1.50
1 Man's saddle, bridle & martingales	4.00
1 waggon	2.00
1 windmill	10.00
cattle	
horses	
hogs	
1 Bureau	5.00
1 Stand	.75
1 looking glass	1.50
6 windsor chairs	3.00
1 Large rocking chair	1.25
1 settee & cushions	2.00
1 Brass clock	20.00
1 Breakfast table	3.00
1 Stand	.75
1 set split bottom chairs & rocker chairs	3.50
1 Bureau	5.00

MEDSKER, DANIEL......B.1808
Xenia, Greene County

Daniel Medsker was a cabinetmaker in Xenia and the brother of David Medsker. He was born in 1808 probably in Highland County. His wife's name was Elenor and he had many children. He had 2 apprentices - Samson Ferguson and James Knox.

MEDSKER, DAVID......L.1807-1879
Xenia, Greene County

David Medsker was born in Highland County, Ohio in 1807; he was the son of Joseph and Elizabeth (Templeton) Medsker. His wife was Elizabeth Williams who was the daughter of John Williams, the village smithy, and the grandaughter of Remembrance Williams (Source: Dills *History of Greene County*). He may have apprenticed in Highland County or Cincinnati. He was listed as working in Cincinnati in 1829, however, by November 6 of that year he was in Xenia. He did both cabinet-making and undertaking, but his business seemed to be more undertaking as time went on. He had a busy and prolific business. He was a founder of Woodland Cemetery and a member of the Methodist Church.

He advertised in the Greene County Torchlight, Xenia, Thursday, October 10, 1839:

D. Medsker

cabinetmaker and fancy turner; Green street, Xenia. All kinds of turning done in wood, iron, brass and ivory.

David Medsker may have still been working as late as 1876 for in the Xenia City Directory of that year D. Medsker and son were listed as undertakers at 14 East Market Street. Albert Medsker and A.W. Medsker were also in the undertaking business.

MEYERS, JOHN & FRYMAN, WILLIAM
Clermont County

According to the *History of Clermont County*, these men were cabinetmakers in Washington Township(Hennings Mills).

MIERS, GEORGE K.......1831
Lancaster, Fairfield County

This excerpt from the Lancaster Ohio Eagle, December 17, 1831:

WANTED - APPRENTICE between the ages of 15 and 17 years to the housejoiner and cabinetmaking business, of good moral habits, in such a good situation, may be obtained upon

immediate application in Lancaster.
GEORGE K. MIERS

MILLER, E.A.......1833
Zanesville, Muskingum County

From the Zanesville, Ohio Republican, February 9, 1833:

CABINETMAKING

Return to his former friends and customers, he still continues on Front street a few doors above Cushing Buckingham store in Putnam. He will supply them with substantial and cheap furniture. Give him a call.

Jan.5, 1833 E.A.MILLER, Putnam

MILLER, GEORGE......1807
Lebanon, Warren County

From the Western Star, February 13, 1807:

NOTICE: The Subscriber respectfully informs his friends and the public in general that he carries on the cabinetmaking business on Main street, near Mr. Seaman's tavern where all who will favor him with their custom shall be suited in the best manner and most workmanlike manner; and on the most reasonable terms.

GEORGE MILLER

MILLER, HENRY......1820
Lancaster, Fairfield County

Henry Miller advertised in the Lancaster, Ohio Eagle, September 7, 1820:

ONE CENT,a bundle of oats, straw and 25 lashes reward. RUNAWAY from the Subscriber June last: AN INDENTURED APPRENTICE to the cabinetmaking business. JOSEPH BIXLER. He is 5'9" sulky appearance; took with him a brown coat, calfskin shoes. Whoever will bring him back to Pleasant Township, Fairfield County, will receive the above reward.
HENRY MILLER

MILLER,HENRY B.......1828-1829
Lebanon,Warren County

The following advertisement appeared in the Western Star & Lebanon Gazette, June 7, 1828:

HENRY B. MILLER
takes this method of informing his old customers and the public generally that he now has and intends keeping on hand at his cabinet shop a general assortment of cabinet furniture. He carries on the planemaking business. He will take an apprentice to the cabinetmaking business, a boy of 14 or 16 from the country, of good morals. Will be received on good terms.

Lebanon, May 9, 1828

This ad continued March 28, 1829 and then on October 24,1829, Henry B. Miller again advertised in the Western Star and Lebanon Gazette:

CAUTION-RUNAWAY FROM THE SUBSCRIBER
on the 26th inst. an indentured apprentice to the cabinetmaking business by the name of ROBERT HAMILTON, by about 19 years of age. All persons are forewarned against harboring him on my account. A reasonable reward will be given to any person who will return him to the Subscriber.

HENRY B. MILLER

MILLS, JOHN E.......1836-1839-1840
MILLS & HUFFMAN
Chillicothe, Ross County

John E. Mills is first noted as working in Chillicothe in 1836. He advertised in the Scioto Gazette, July 6, 1836:

New Firm
The subscribers have entered into co-partnership under the firm of Emmett and Mills in the chair and cabinetmaking , House and Sign Painting, Glazing and Paper Hanging business all of which they are prepared to do at the shortest notice and the best manner. Their shop is at the old stand of William Y. Emmett on Paint street off of the Public Square and but one door to the office of the Scioto Gazette.
Wm. Y. Emmett
John E. Mills
Sept.23, 1835

By 1839 John E. Mills was in partnership with Joshua Seney for the Worthington Family Papers indicate that James Worthington had work done for his home by this firm. The receipt reads:

J.T. Worthington Dr. To Seney and Mills
April 8, 1839

To paper Hanging 10 pieces	*3.37 ½*
To 2 picture frames 5-3 each	*6.00*
one breakfast table	*5.00*
To Repairs on chair and stand	*.75*

This partnership lasted until 1844 when Joshua Seney went into the dry goods and grocery business.

In September 1844 John Mills was advertising alone as a chair maker. No more is known of John E. Mills at the present time.

MILLS, WILLIAM......1839
Chillicothe, Ross County

From the James T. Worthington Papers:

James Worthington to William Mills

1839	
April 9 To Painting Room white	*3.00*
To painting one mantle Black	*1.50*
To painting one mantle Black	*1.50*
To painting door & frame	*.75*
To 1 1/2 lbs. of lead paint	*.50*
To painting 2 fireplacesblack	*.25*
To Specting tapeline	*.50*
	7.50

Pd. Feb. 22, 1840 - Wm. Mills

MITTON, JOHN......1813
Dayton, Montgomery County

Mitton advertised in the Dayton, Ohio Sentinel, March 10, 1813:

RUNAWAY APPRENTICE

to the Windsor Chair making business. DAVID CONKLINTON, about 18 years of age.

March 2, 1813 JOHN MITTON

John Mitton later moved to Xenia for he is mentioned in *Dills History of Greene County*, Reminiscences by Mrs. David Medsker:

Ca 1817 - Mr. James Scott, bought some goods from James Gowdy's store..had them set aside and then drove his team over to John Mitton's chair factory.

MITCHELL, ALEXANDER......L.1783-1849..1814
Eaton,Preble County

The *History of Preble County* notes that "Alexander Mitchell who was born in 1783 was from Kentucky. His wife's name was Lovina (Lovena) and they were members of the Church of Christ(Disciples). The Second Church was built on ground sold them by Mitchell and his wife. He was a Trustee of the first school in 1807."

On May 16, 1814 he advertised in the Ohio Republican, a Dayton newspaper, that he was working in Eaton:

"By Mechanics is the Wealth and Grandeur of the State"

Immediately Wanted

Two Smart Apprentices
To the Cabinet Business

of about the age of sixteen, of ingenious minds and well recommended for industry, integrity and sobriety - Such will meet with liberal terms, good accommodations and find a commodious shop with good tools and plenty of work by applying to the subscriber in Eaton.

Also if they incline to inform themselves (as every youth should) in their leisure hours, they will have access to a variety of books, and the public news.

Alexander Mitchell

Eaton,May 5, 1814

In 1820, an unnamed cabinetmaker,thought to be A. Mitchell, was listed in the Federal Manufacturer's Census. In 1823 Mr. Mitchell kept a tavern which he sold in 1829, when times were getting better. Later he was in the hardware business selling countless varieties of hardware for the Cincinnati firm of Lyons & McKinnell. The business was not as prosperous as it could have been and Alexander Mitchell died in 1849 from the cholera with a huge inventory of hardware and many debts which were never paid.

Mitchell, Alexander
Administration #1403 roll 143
Bond $500.00
Administrator William J. Gilmore
SALE BILL:

4 old augers with handles	.65
1 lot of bench planers	2.75
1 lot of bench planers	1.75
2 gennow	.95
2 pruning saws	.57
1 square and brace	.50
5 thumle gauges & 1 mortice gauge	1.30
1 lot of old files	.50
2 screw drillers	.40
2 pair pincers	.37
1 compass	.12½
1 lot of chissels	2.88
1 mortice	1.40
3 gauges	.47
1 lot hand saw files	.80
1 lot brace awls	.35
1 oil stone	.75
1 iron square	.35
1 hand axe	.62½
1 drawing knife	.68
2 hand saws	2.05
1 saw set	.85
1 brace & bits	4.00

1	lot old planes	1.00
1	plain bits	1.25
1	cow bell	.65
1	2 feet rule	.35
1	lot whetstones	.50
1	lot military papers	.75
1	walnut stand with two drawers	.37½
1	work bench, screws and driver	1.50
1	pr dog cart iron rakes	.75
1	doz pr small strop iron hinges	1.25
11	pr long strop iron hinges	2.05
	Pair sheep shears	1.20
1	lot augers	.50
17	lots of augers, various sized 37	3.00
10	drawing knives, ea	.50
2	small braces	1.25
2	cleaners chissel, hammer & hoe	.37
1	broad axe	1.10
3	hand aces 62	1.00
1	cutting guage	.62
6	trimmer saws 57	1.27
5	large hoes .21	.25
9	gimlets	.46
7	padlocks	1.85
2	1¼ in chissels	.87
6	whip saws	1.50
	two foot rules	1.89
6	pr clips for x cut saws	.20
1	lot brass casting for plance	.56
2	iron bolts	.61
6	rabbit bits	.30
6	plough bits	.45
1	masons lines	.30
17	handsaw files	1.66
3	8 in flat files	.07
7	small flat files	.50
1	padlock hasper	.27
1	lot sandpaper	.80
3	axe handles	.82
1	woodsaw	1.00
1	woodsaw	.90
3	dz auger handles	1.25
4	wooden bowls	.50
16	scribing awls	1.37
2	flooring guages	.52
1	lot of rules & gauges	.10
5	shaving boxes	.20
1	doz cupboard locks	.33
1	7 ft mill saw	4.25
1	fire bucket	.16
1	box old iron	.10
1	stove & pipe	4.50
1	set trap hoops	.35

MITCHELL, JOHN......1822-1824
Lebanon, Warren County

John Mitchell and Abraham Delavere advertised as cabinetmakers in the Western Star,June 4, 1822.

By 1824, John Mitchell was working alone as evidenced by his ad in the Western Star, August 25,1824:

JOHN MITCHELL, CABINETMAKER
REMOVAL
Takes pleased(sic) to inform the public that he has removed from the shop that he lately occupied and has moved to Mechanics street, near Mr. Thomas Smith's tavern, where all orders of cabinetmaking furniture of every kind will be attended to.
August 25, 1824 JOHN MITCHELL

MONROE, DAVID......L.1783-1848
Xenia, Greene County

From *Greene County 1803 to 1908 - Xenia, Ohio:*

Mr. David Monroe, who had on his residence lot a shop, where he manufactured furniture, was called from his bed to receive a wagonload of what supposed to be furniture. In its stores were hidden members of the Underground.

David Monroe was born in 1783 in Scotland. He came to Xenia in 1819. He had on his residence lot in Xenia a shop where he manufactured furniture. He was one of the original proprietors of Old Town and he was the treasurer of the city of Xenia. It is said that his home was a station on the underground railroad. He died in November 1848 in Xenia.

MONROE, GEORGE......B.1811
Xenia, Greene County

Dills History of Greene County notes that George Monroe, the son of David Monroe of Xenia, Ohio was born in 1811 in Scotland. He was a chairmaker. He was married to Martha Cunningham, January 22, 1829. In 1850 he had apprentices in his home who were: George Galloway, 19 years old, chairmaker; James Knof, 19, Ohio chairmaker; William Keller, 21, Pennsylvania chairmaker; Warren Wright, 23, from New Hampshire,chairmaker. This would have been a small factory.

MONROE, JAMES......B.1825
Xenia, Greene County

James Monroe was the son of David Monroe of Xenia, Ohio. He was born in 1825 in Ohio, and he was a chairmaker. Perhaps he worked for his father or brother.

Source: *Dills History of Greene County.*

MONTJOY, THOMAS......1830
Springfield,Clark County

From the Western Pioneer,Saturday,April 17, 1830:

CABINETMAKING
THOMAS MONTJOY
respectfully informs the citizens of Springfield that he has commenced the above business on the west corner of the Public Square near the Court House. Has on hand well-seasoned mahogany and cherry.
Springfield, Apr.16, 1830

MOORE, GEORGE B.......1825
Wilmington, Clinton County

This ad appeared in the Western Argus, November 18, 1825:

CHAIRS
The Subscriber has taken this opportunity of informing his old customers and the public in general that he has on hand and intends keeping constantly, a supply of Windsor chairs and having employed the best workmen, can assure the public that he can furnish as good and elegant work as any shop in the western country and feels disposed to sell on as accommodating terms as any. He will receive in payment for the above articles corn, cork wheat, flour, linen, lincey(sic), flannel, or he will credit 9 months for cash, and those who will pay cash in hand may expect a bargain.
GEORGE B. MOORE
Wilmington, Nov. 18, 1825

MOORE, HAINES......1814-1815..D.1885
Wilmington, Clinton County

Haines Moore came to Wilmington in 1815 from Pennsylvania. He was the son of Thomas and Sarah Moore of Centre County, Pennsylvania and the brother of Joshua Moore. He worked in wood and was by trade a cabinetmaker. He lived on Main street in the former home of William Hobson, the gunsmith. His house later was inhabited by David Marble, who continued to build furniture at the same site. Mr. Moore did a large business; later he sold his business to Daniel Marble and went to Lytle Creek, which is known now as Ogden. The above information comes from the *History of Clinton County.*

The recorded date of Haines Moore's death was August 31, 1885, when his will was probated. His will was written on the 21st day of February, 1880. He was a dedicated Quaker.

MOORE, JOHN HAYNES......L.1818-1908
Springfield, Clark County

John Haynes Moore lived from 1818 until 1908. He lived at 568 Hadley Road, Clarksville, Ohio from 1852 until 1870. Then he moved to Wilmington, Ohio. He was the son of Joshua Moore and Nancy Stratton Moore. Joshua and Nancy Moore was the first marriage in Springfield Friend's meeting house in 1814. Joshua Moore was the son of Thomas and Sarah Moore of Centre County, Pennsylvania, he came to Ohio in 1811, bringing his woodworking tools with him. His brother, Haines, who married Elizabeth Antrim, also settled in Clinton County. Joshua was the father of John Haynes Moore, and was a cabinetmaker, carpenter and millwright; he was apprenticed in all 3 trades. He lived in Mino Creek, Adams Township.

John Haynes Moore married Ruth Lindley, who died in 1869. They lived on Handley Road. He was a teacher, a shop keeper in Sligo, a Justice of the Peace and Magistrate in Adams Township, a cabinetmaker and an active Quaker.

MOORE, JOSEPH THOITS......L.1796-1854
Chillicothe, Ross County

Joseph Moore was born near Yarmouth, Maine, March 8, 1796. He married Eleanor Blackstone in 1823. He came to Chillicothe in 1816 with his brother, Samuel, and later they advertised in the Scioto Supporter, June 28, 1823:

NOTICE
The partnership between J.T. and S. Moore in the chairmaking business has been dissolved by mutual consent.
JOSEPH T. MOORE and SAMUEL MOORE
All kinds of fancy and Windsor chairs for sale - House, sign, coach and ornamental painting and gilding.
J.T.MOORE - June 14, 1823

In June 1824, the following notice appeared in the Scioto Supporter and Scioto Gazette:

HOUSE, SIGN, COACH AND ORNAMENTAL PAINTING AND GILDING
The Subscriber respectfully informs his friends and the public that for the greater facility in conducting the above business in all of its various branches, they have formed a connetion(sic) under the firm of MOORE & EMMETT, and taken the house formerly

occupied by Mr. Henry Jack (coppersmith) on Water street, where all orders in their line will be thankfully received and attended to.
JOSEPH T. MOORE,
WILLIAM Y. EMMETT

The Moore-Emmett connection did not last long, however, for it appears that Joseph Moore returned to the Eastern seaboard where he painted portraits in Philadelphia in 1825. Moore then went to Maine where he painted more than 50 portraits in the town of Freeport, Hollowell, Farmington and Chesterville. By December 1826 Moore must have returned to Chillicothe for in the Scioto Supporter and Scioto Gazette of December 7, 1826, appeared this ad:

FANCY SIGN & ORNAMENTAL PAINTER continue to carry on the above business in all of its branches at their old stand where they are prepared to execute in the neatest manner signs of every description, military standards and plates, Masonic carpets and aprons. They also intend keeping constantly on hand the general assortment of Windsor and fancy chairs, finished in the very best style which they will sell on reasonable terms. All orders punctually attended to.

Nov.28, 1826

Also in the same newspaper and date as above, the following:

J.T.MOORE, Portrait painter, has taken the upper room in the brick building on Water street, 2 doors above Mr. Hawks and Swifts hat store, and respectfully solicits the patronage of all the enlightened public. He invites his friends generally to call as above, where specimens of his work may be seen.

Nov.28, 1826

In 1827, the Moore-Emmett partnership was dissolved and William Y. Emmett carried on the chairmaking business alone.

MOORE & EMMETT
The partnership heretofore existing under the above firm, has been dissolved by mutual consent.
J.T. MOORE and W.Y. EMMETT
The business will be carried on in all of its various branches at the old stand by William Y. Emmett.
Jun.13,1827

He was thought to have left Chillicothe after this and is known to have gone to Montgomery, Alabama where he painted over 400 portraits before his death in 1854. Information courtesy John Grabb, Chillicothe historian.

MOORE, JOSHUA......L.1794-1874
Wilmington, Clinton County

Joshua Moore was the son of Thomas and Sarah Moore of Centre (Chester) County, Pennsylvania. He came to Ohio in 1811 bringing his wordworking tools with him. His brother Haines also settled in Clinton County. Joshua was a worker in wood: a carpenter, and a millwright, who understood furniture making. He was married to Nancy Stratton which was the first marriage in Springfield Friends meeting house in 1814.

Their son, John Haines Moore was a cabinetmaker, carpenter and millwright.

At a later date, Joshua bought and operated a mill on land in the southwest corner of Clinton County. This mill and land he sold to his brother, Haines, who lived there until his death in 1885. It is not known where Joshua lived in his later years.

The Moores were very dedicated Quakers and were very active in their religion.

MOORE, WILLIAM......1827-1829
Lebanon, Warren County

William Moore advertised in the Western Star & Lebanon Gazette, July 7, 1827:

CHAIRMAKING
The Subscriber respectfully informs his friends and the public in general that he is commenced the chairmaking business on Mulberry street, one door west of Mr. D. Voorhis where he is prepared to make fancy and Windsor chairs on the shortest notice. From his experience in the above business, he hopes to receive a share of public patronage.
WILLIAM MOORE
Lebanon, July 2, 1827

N.B. An apprentice wanted to the above business - a boy from the country would be preferred.

From the Western Star and Lebanon Gazette, September 19, 1829:

GOOD BARGAINING
The Subscriber, thankful for the encouragement he has already met, wishes to inform his customers and the public in general that I still continue to carry on the fancy and Windsor chair making business 2 doors east of Henderson & Hardy's store on Mulberry street, and is now prepared to sell chairs of the best quality on one year's credit. Those who will favor him with a

call can examine for themselves.
WILLIAM MOORE
Lebanon, July 29, 1829

MORGAN, THOMAS
Portsmouth, Scioto County

The *History of Scioto County* lists Thomas Morgan as the first wheelwright in Portsmouth. The chances are that he made Windsor chairs also. No date cited.

MORGAN, THOMAS JR.......1820..D.1860
Eaton, Preble County

Thomas Morgan Jr. came from Washington County, Pennsylvania with his father Thomas Morgan Sr. to Eaton, Ohio in 1816.

Thomas Morgan Sr. may have been a skilled woodworker also. He was born in 1749 and died in Eaton in 1840. He was buried at Mound Hill Cemetery.

Thomas Morgan Jr. was born in Washington County, Pennsylvania, he married and had two children Robert W. Morgan and Julia Margan Foos.

According to the *History of Preble County*: "Thomas Morgan was a very ingenious mechanic and cabinetmaker whose handiwork is still (1881) seen in many of the old homes throughout Preble County. He settled in Eaton in 1816 and lived there all of his life. Before the church was built the Presbyterians assembled in Thomas Morgan's cabinet shop."

In the 1820 Federal Manufacturers Census he was listed as follows:

T. (THOMAS) MORGAN, OWNER
Made bureaus, desks, tables and cupboards, using 8,000 feet of plank and scantling; 3 men employed $150; operating a cabinetmaking shop and tools; capital of $500; market sales of $1,300. The shop, a commodious frame building having good tools and well used. sales not very ready. The complaint is want of cash, the Census Marshall reported.

Mr. Morgan kept the Eagle hotel from 1829 until 1839 when the Hotel burned. His cabinetmaking business prospered and he became a prominent member of the Eaton community. He was a skilled craftsman and a successful businessman. He died in 1860 and his will states that an unfinished bureau remained in his shop at the time of his death. His ledger book is extant and furniture made by him remains in the family.

Thomas Morgan.

Mrs. Thomas Morgan.

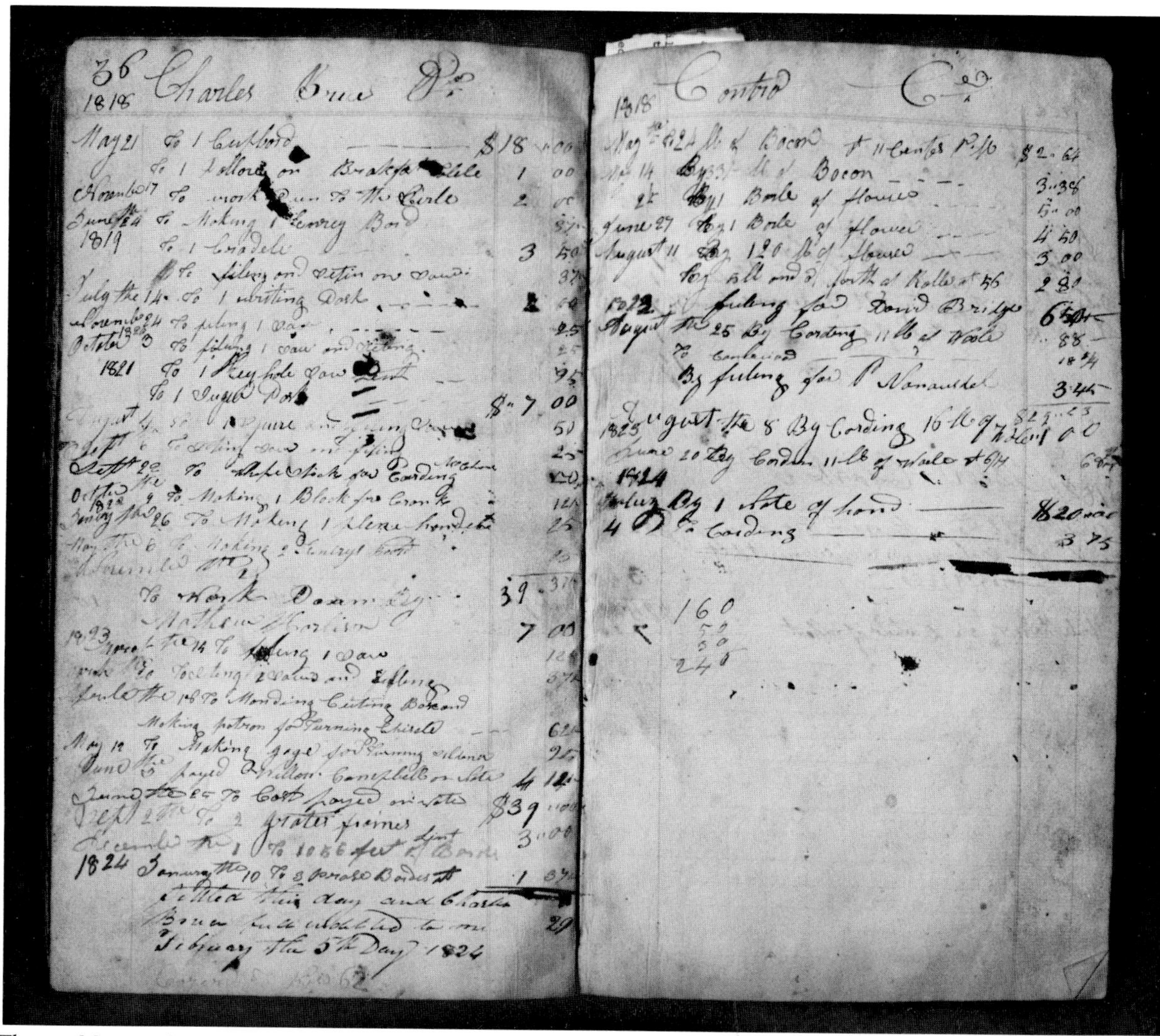

Thomas Morgan Account Book.

Portrait of Julia Morgan Foos.

Morgan, Thomas
Estate #3419 1868
Bond $1200.00 30 March 1868
Executrix: Abigail Morgan
Sureties Joseph Donahoe
Jacob H. Foos

INVENTORY

1 clock (36 hrs)	3.00
1 Secretary	10.00
1 stand	1.00
1 breakfast table	2.00
1 mantle glass	2.00
1 sofa	5.00
2 bedsteads	2.00
1 settee (small)	.75
1 rocking chair	1.00
½ doz. chairs	6.00
4 windsor chairs	3.00
1 kitchen safe	5.00
1 old ax	.20
1 unfinished bureau & mountings	15.00

MOUNT, S.D.......1820
Williamsburg, Clermont County

The *History of Clermont County* notes that S.D. Mount was a manufacturer of splint bottom chairs in Williamsburg in 1820. S.D. Mount was also mentioned in *Howes Historical Collections of Ohio*: "Williamsburg, Ohio (very early) Chair factory owned by S.D. Mount, 23 hands."

MURPHY, DANIEL......1825
Xenia, Greene County

From the Xenia Interior Gazette, April 30, 1825:

AN APPRENTICE TO THE CABINET-MAKING BUSINESS IS WANTED-
about 15 years of age.
My shop is at McFarland's Mill
March 22 DANIEL MURPHY

MUSSER, C. & STILER, W.......1819
Lancaster, Fairfield County

Musser and Stiler advertised in the Ohio Eagle, October 14, 1819:

CHAIRMAKING - C. MUSSER & W. STILER having commenced the chairmaking business in the shop formerly occupied by SAMUEL WILLET, near the corner of Columbia and Wheeling streets where they intend to carry on business in all of its varying branches. They will sell their work very low for cash or approved country produce, at market price. Persons favoring them with their custom may depend on having their work well done on the shortest notice. They hope by their strict attention to business to merit and receive a share of the public patronage.
October 14, 1819

MUSSER, CHRISTIAN......1821
Lancaster, Fairfield County

This ad appeared in the Ohio Eagle, April 26, 1821:

CHRISTIAN MUSSER, CHAIRMAKER, respectfully informs the public that he has removed to the above mentioned shop opposite Mr. Sturgeon's tavern and continued to solicit business.
Lancaster, Apr.18, 1821

Rhea Mansfield Knittle notes that a chair firm existed in Canton by the name of Goldburg and Musser. The first names of these men are unknown. This might have been Christian Musser.

MYERS, G.W. and F.......1830-1831
Circleville, Pickaway County

Reminiscences, a Description of Circleville, Ohio 1825-1840 notes that G.W. and F. Myers had a chair shop in Circleville about 1830. The following ad appeared in the Circleville Herald and Ohio Olive Branch, September 4, 1830:

G.W. and F. MYERS
Having established themselves as cabinetmakers in Circleville on West Main street in the house formerly occupied by William Martin as a shoe shop begs leave to inform their friends and the public generally, that they are prepared to furnish on the shortest notice in all articles manufactured in their line of business. They spared no pains in procuring the best mahogany to be found and flatter themselves from their mechanical experience that they will be able to please all who may favor them with their custom in plain and fancy work executed in the neatest and most durable manner, low for cash and approved country produce.

This advertisement ran for months. It terminated June 25, 1831. At the moment this is the only thing known about these men.

NARDIN, MONSIEUR P. FREDERICK......1821-1831-1835..D.1886
Hamilton, Butler Conty

Mr. P. F. Nardin was a native of Champey, France. He first advertised in 1831, in the Hamilton Intelligencer, February 1

Cabinet Making
Monsieur P.F. Nardin informs the citizens of Butler County and the public generally, that he has recently commenced his business in Hamilton on Basin Street, a few doors east of the Hamilton Intelligencer Office and south of the Court House.
Monsieur Nardin, having learned his trade with the best workmen in France, from which he has recently removed, feels no hesitancy saying that his work will be found equal to any heretofore offered to the public in the Western Country. He warrants his work to bear a polish that will stand washing equal to glassware. He feels a delicacy in speaking of his own manufacture well knowing that the work itself will pay a far greater compliment to him as a mechanic, than any eulogies he can publish. He therefore respectfully invites judges of good work and all who wish to furnish themselves with cabinetware to call and examine for themselves.

The ad continued until April 9, 1831. Then in the Hamilton Intelligencer of April 2, 1835 he announced that he had removed his cabinet shop and warerooms to his new brick house on the west side and fronting the Public Square where he intends keeping constantly on hand a general assortment of work in his line. He was happy with his abundance of business for "he returns the most sincere thanks...for the very liberal patronage he has received" and he hopes to receive more patronage by "his unremmitted attention to secure its continuance and give entire satisfaction in the beauty and neatness of his work." This advertisement continued until September 3, 1835.

Alta Harvey Heiser in *Hamilton in the Making* notes that Nardin made a coffin for Michael Delorac in 1821 and he was a vestry man in the Episcopalian Church in Hamilton in 1834; in 1836 he was paid $6 for repairing the fence around the graveyard. Nardin continued in the cabinetmaking and undertaking business until his death in 1886.

NELSON, JAMES
Cambridge, Guernsey County

From the Guernsey County 175th Celebration Booklet, The Carl Rech Compilation of Cambridge lots:

Lot #48 Joseph Gregg in L shaped building sold out to James Nelson as a cabinetmaker who plied his trade in this building for more than 40 years. (No date cited.)

NOEL, PETER......1826
Gallipolis, Gallia County

The *Pioneer Record of Scioto County, Ohio* by Nelson W. Evans credits Peter Noel with furnishing 9 chairs to the commissioners for the Court House in 1826 for $9.00. Peter Noel was in Gallipolis in 1826 but by 1839 Noel was noted as the Surplus Fund Commissioner. Perhaps he was making chairs and also involved in the politics of the city.

NORTON, ISAAC N.......1825-1826-1828
Athens, Athens County

From the Athens Mirror and Literary Gazette, December 17, 1825:

Cabinet & Chair Making
Isaac N. Norton wishes to inform his friends and the public that he is now carrying on the cabinet and chair making business at the shop formerly occupied by BARTLETT & NORTON, Washington Street, Athens. Will take country produce and wishes for cherry, walnut, poplar, and curled maple boards.

Athens, Dec.12, 1825

A later Norton ad appeared in the Athens Mirror & Literary Gazette of January 14, 1826:

ISAAC N.NORTON
Cabinet & Chair Making Business wishes to inform his friends at the shop formerly occupied by BARTLETT & NORTON on Washington Street in Athens, a liberal price will be given for cherry, walnut, poplar and curled maple lumber and boards.

Dec.12, 1825

This ad continued until April 1826. In March of 1828 Norton advertised at least twice for a journeyman chairmaker.

Norton, Isaac N.
File #218
Letter of Administration 20 March 1837
Cephas Carpenter
Appraisers: Isaac Taylor
H.R. Gilmore
John Brown

INVENTORY:

1	bureau	25.00
1	"	6.00
1	doz. shag bottomed chairs	24.00
1	rocking chair	2.00
1	doz common windsor chairs	9.00
1	stand	3.00
1	dinning table	4.00
1	breakfast table	3.00
1	looking glass, gilt	4.00
½	doz. silver table spoons	16.00
1	doz silver tea spoons	8.00
2	salt spoons	1.00
	china & other cupboard furniture	15.00
1	bookcase	3.00
1	mantle clock	10.00
1	kitchen cupboard & ware	10.00
	Iron ware in kitchen	6.00
1	large brass kettle	
1	small brass kettle	6.00
1	copper kettle	
	tin ware	2.00
1	bed, bedstead & bed clothes	15.00
1	wash stand, basin, & cracked ewer	3.00

2 looking glasses	1.25
2 beds & steads	10.00
2 small stands	1.50
1 high post bedstead, bed & bed clothes	16.00

NYE (NEIGH), SAMUEL......1828-1830
Lancaster, Fairfield County

Samuel Nye was a cabinetmaker in Lancaster in 1828 for in the Record of Indentures, Fairfield County he is listed as follows:

NEIGH, SAMUEL - cabinetmaker in Fairfield County

Dec.1, 1828 - Levi Dunbough, age 17 years, apprentice.

Nye left town and sold out in 1830. At that time this ad appeared in the Lancaster Ohio Eagle, February 20, 1830:

NEW FURNITURE AT AUCTION
The Subscriber will offer at public sale on Friday, the 19th day of March next, being the second day of Court in front of his shop at the house of C.Niebling and adjoining the office of Judge Dietrick, in the town of Lancaster - a variety of new cabinetwork, which he will warrant well made and of substantial material and which may be examined at any time prior to the sale. One cherry and two first rate mahogany sideboards; two mahogany secretaries; three mahogany and 12 cherry bureaus, full and half-columns; several dining and breakfast tables with a number of bedsteads, stands and other furniture. Also: a complete assortment of cabinet-maker's tools, consisting of planes and of all kinds of saws, chisels, carving tools, hand screws, work benches, one turning lathe and tools; also one road and two dandy waggons; three rifle guns; one 8-day clock; and two 30 hour clocks. At the same time and place he will sell his household and kitchen furniture which is too numerous to mention. 12 months credit will be given on all sums over $200 on giving notes with approved security.

Feb.20th, 1830
SAMUEL NYE

OSBORN, HIRAM......1825-1847
Oxford, Butler County

Hiram Osborn was born July 14, 1803 in New Jersey. On December 7, 1825 he married Abbey Harrison, who was born in 1805. He probably made furniture from 1825 until 1847. After that date he had a furniture store where he sold furniture made by others and also carried second hand furniture.

The Oxford Citizen Newspaper, March 22, 1856 carried this ad:

HIRAM OSBORN
I have just received large stock of furniture and chairs of the latest styles. Also secondhand furniture.
HIRAM OSBORN

OSGOOD, AARON & ISAAC
Oxford, Butler County

The *History of Oxford* by Ralph McGinnis mentions that Aaron and Isaac Osgood were chairmakers in Oxford, Ohio, in the brick building at the railroad crossing on South College Ave. They made bent back chairs, split seats of ash, slat back chairs. They turned out hundreds of plain chairs of the kitchen type - bent back with wood seats. A large 2 horse wagon delivered the chairs throughout the Oxford countryside as far west as Brookville. Sam Wray got his start in this factory where as a boy he painted chairs.

There is no exact date cited.

OYLER, ANDREW
Hamilton, Butler County

Hamilton, Ohio - Biographical and Historical Sketches by Stephen D. Cone notes that Andrew Oyler carried on furniture and undertaking and watch repair.

PAGE, JOSEPH......1824
West Union, Adams County

From the West Union Village Register, March 2, 1824:

SPINNING WHEELS - JOSEPH PAGE

---

continued on next page

PARKER, CHARLES F.......1836
Chillicothe, Ross County

Charles Parker advertised in the Scioto Gazette, December 7, 1836:

CABINETMAKING & TURNING
The Subscriber informs the citizens of Chillicothe and its vicinity that he has purchased the establishment of HENRY SHEPHERD on Market Square, one door West of Holler's Grove, where he is now prosecuting in all their various branches, cabinetmaking and turning. His apprentice for the latter trade of his business is in complete order, and he pledges himself to do the best in style unsurpassed by none. His prices reasonable and accomodating.

Nov.1, 1836 Charles F. Parker

PARKER, WILLIAM SR.......L.1745-1825
Salem Township, Miegs County

The *Pioneer History of Miegs County* states that William Parker Sr. was born in Malden, Massachusetts, June 5, 1745 and was married to Mary Warner on January 28, 1772. She was a daughter of Philomen Warner of Glouster, Massachusetts and was born in 1753. He was a cabinetmaker and exported furniture to the West Indies. In the 1800s, he moved his family to Salem Township, Meigs County where he lived and reared a large family. He died November 26, 1825.

PATTON, MATTHEW...L.1778-1856
Dayton, Montgomery County

Matthew Patton was born in Rockbridge County, Virginia, August 22, 1778. At the age of 16 he moved to Lexington, Kentucky, where he was apprenticed to a cabinetmaker and learned the trade. While living in Lexington he married Margaret Hamilton and they moved to Dayton in 1805.

The first newspaper published in Dayton, the Repository and Dayton Journal, carried this advertisement in September, 1808:

The Subscriber
Respectfully informs his friends and the public in general that he still continues to carry on the cabinetmaking business in all of its branches, he has and intends keeping a good assortment at Dayton and persons favoring him with their custom will expect to have work done in the neatest manner.

Merchandize Produce at Market price will be received for work done.

September 30, 1808

Margaret Hamilton had died shortly after their move to Dayton and on October 20, 1808 Mr. Patton married Elizabeth Ludlow, the niece of Isreal Ludlow, prominent early Ohio settler, surveyor and landowner.

The cabinet business was Patton's only profession. In the Ohio Centennial, November 14, 1811 he advertised for an apprentice, a boy of 16 or 17 years of age and in 1813, Luther Bruen, the shoemaker, moved into the house formerly occupied by Matthew Patton - Mr. and Mrs. Patton had moved from their cabin on the S.W. corner of 3rd and Main.

In 1820 the Federal Manufacturer's Census stated that Matthew Patton - owner - made "buorows (sic), tables, stands, desks and cupboards. 3 men employed, operating a turning lathe, 4 sets of brush planes, 3 sets of chissels, 3 sets of gauges and a set of turning tools. Capital $1000, Wages 700 annually. This establishment put into operation 1805".

A chest is known which was made in the Patton shop - on the drawer is a name almost illegible but thought to be - "W. Parker". The rest is very clearly read -

Made in Mr. Pattons Shop
January 9, 1828

Since this chest has been found many others have been found in the general vicinity of Dayton which are attributed to the Patton shop, most interestingly, a miniature of tiger maple. This is not surprising for Matthew Patton was known as the town cabinetmaker for his entire lifetime.

Besides his profession he was a contributing member of the Dayton community, a well respected citizen. He was President of the Select Council. In 1815, he was a manager of the Moral Society, and the first fire warden in 1827. He was an elder in the Presbyterian Church but later formed the Episcopalian Church. He died December 24, 1856, in his 78th year.

Matthew Patton is typical of the early Ohio maker of furniture who came to a town and stayed. He remained for several reasons: he was a fine craftsman in an affluent area where he could make a comfortable living, he was well connected with the Ludlow and Steele families who were leaders in the community and he too held positions of prominence.

Matthew Patton made other furniture but the pieces attributed to him are all bureaus. The interesting thing about these bureaus was the style - they were made with two large bonnet drawers on the top with two small rectangular drawers in between and three large drawers beneath. See photos - Montgomery County.

PEALE, JAMES A.......pre 1842
Lynchburg, Highland County

From the Hillsboro Gazette (Press Gazette), July 4, 1842:

Fancy and Windsor Chairs
James A. Peale of Lynchburg, Highland County, Ohio will continue to manufacture at moderate prices, every variety of Fancy and Windsor chairs, which he feels safe in warranting as to durability of structure - quality materials and beauty of finish. They will be kept on hand at his establishment in Lynchburg and by J.R. Emrie, Hillsboro, Ohio. Call at either place and examine the chairs and the prices before you purchase elsewhere.

PEALE, SAMUEL......1838
Lynchburg, Highland County

From the Hillsboro Gazette, August 17, 1838:

Chair Factory
The subscriber having located himself in Lynchburg, Highland County, Ohio would respectfully inform the citizens of Highland County that he will manufacture and keep on hand a general assortment of Fancy and Windsor chairs, settees and of superior workmanship and finished in the neatest and most fashionable style.

His terms will be accommodating. Approved country produce will at all times be taken in exchange for his work at the market prices.
Samuel Peale

This ad ran for 3 weeks.

PEEBLES, JOHN......L.1776-1846
Portsmouth, Scioto County
Alexandria, Scioto County
Chillicothe, Ross County
Gallipolis, Gallia County

The *History of the Lower Scioto Valley* states that John Peebles was born in Shippinsburg, Pennsylvania November 21, 1776 and was married to Margaret Rodgers, also a native of Shippinsburg, on November 17, 1795. He worked in the best shops in Philadelphia and came to Portsmouth, Ohio in the very early 1800s, worked there briefly and moved to Alexandria; he was in Chillicothe in 1808 and continued working there until 1818. From the Scioto Gazette, March 30, 1808:

JOHN PEEBLES, cabinet and chairmaker, informs the public that he has commenced business opposite the Court House in Chillicothe next door to the Lion and the Eagle Tavern. Having wrought in the best shops in Philadelphia and from his long experience in the business, he hopes to give satisfaction to those who might please to favor him with his custom. Rye, corn and young hogs will be received for his work.

N.B. two or three journeymen will meet with encouragement by applying above. Also, two apprentices who will be taken to learn the cabinet business.

Chillicothe, Mar.16, 1808

In 1819 Peebles went to Gallipolis where he continued the cabinetmaking business in connection with the hotel and commission business. It is not clear whether he worked until his death in Gallipolis or Portsmouth. He died October 22, 1846 in Hanging Rock, Lawrence County, and was buried at Greenlawn Cemetery, Portsmouth, Ohio.

See also PEEBLES & BRINGHURST.

PEEBLES & BRINGHURST......1818
Chillicothe, Ross County

Peebles & Bringhurst advertised in the Supporter, March 25, 1818:

PEEBLES & BRINGHURST
Cabinetmakers
have removed their shop from 2nd to Water street opposite McCOY & CULBERTSON. Mahogany of the best sort; two or three journeymen cabinetmakers and one or two apprentices are wanted.

Chillicothe, March 17, 1818

PEGGENS, JOSEPH......1820
Gratis, Preble County

Joseph Peggens is listed in the 1820 Federal Manufacturer's Census (as reprinted in the Tri-State Trader, September 18, 1971 by R.T. Mayhill) as working in Gratis, Preble County:

JOSEPH PEGGENS, owner, cabinetmaker made bureaus, desks, tables. He floored houses and ceilings. He used 6,000 feet of plank and scantlings: walnut, cherry and mahogany planks, costing $100. 2 men and a boy employed, $130 annually; operated house-joining and cabinetmaking tools; work well done - sales tolerable.

---

continued on next page

PHILLIPS, JAMES......1800-1802-1804-1815
Chillicothe, Ross County

James Phillips is first noted in Chillicothe as a defendant in a 1799 court case which was dismissed as the plaintiff did not appear.

He was working as a chairmaker when Chillicothe was the capital of the Northwest Territory. This advertisement in the Scioto Gazette & Chillicothe Advertiser, November 27, 1800, makes him the first artisan in the wood-crafts noted in the newspaper:

WANTED
A JOURNEYMAN
WINDSOR CHAIR MAKER
or a lad who understands turning and can produce good recommendations.
November 20, 1800 JAMES PHILLIPS

What was no doubt the largest order he ever received is revealed in the Scioto Gazette, March 13, 1802:

The General Assembly at their late session authorized the following accounts to be paid: (one such was) to James Phillips the sum of seventy-two dollars, for three dozen chairs furnished for the use of the Legislature.

The *Minute Book of the Quarter Sessions of the Peace* records at the June session 1802:

Ordered that James Phillips acc't be allowed to wit $48.00 per 24 winsor (sic) chairs & that he have an order on the Treasury accordingly.

These chairs were for the new courthouse which was nearing completion and which would be used as the Capitol Building of Ohio the following year.

It appears that Ross County got a bargain in its dealings with Phillips for chairs as evidenced by these "Wholesale prices current at New Orleans" as quoted in the Scioto Gazette, June 18, 1804 - "Chairs, Windsors for doz. 28 to $30.00."

In 1810, James Phillips took over Abner Meeker's tavern at the corner of Water and Mulberry streets and continued as host until sometime in 1813. He then again resumes his old trade and later was joined by John D. Cochran. Their card is found in the Scioto Gazette & Fredonian Chronicle, November 30, 1815, as follows:

CHAIR MAKING
JAMES PHILIPS & JOHN D. COCHRAN
Respectfully inform the public that they will keep constantly for sale, at their shop adjoining Mr. John McDougal's store in Chillicothe,
Windsor and Spindle Chairs,
of the best quality
Those who wish to purchase may be supplied for Cash or country produce upon as reasonable terms as elsewhere.

In 1818, he resumed "his old tavern stand on Mulberry street, sign of the SPREAD EAGLE" (Scioto Gazette & Fredonian Chronicle, April 3, 1818).

In 1820, he served as Captain of Hook, Ladder & Ax Co. as noted in *Early Settlers of Ross County*.

James Phillips later came on hard times and his property, including ten beds, five tables and two dozen chairs were to be sold at Sheriff's sale at the suit of the Bank of Chillicothe. (Scioto Gazette, Feb.18, 1829).

He died August 20, 1837 at the age of 60 years.

The above information courtesy of John Grabb, Chillicothe historian.

PINKERTON, ALEXANDER......L.1783-1837
THE PINKERTON FAMILY

Alexander Pinkerton was born in Allegheny County, Pennsylvania in 1783, a son of Alexander Pinkerton. He was raised on the family farm until his father was killed during an Indian skirmish, after which he accompanied his mother and the other children to Fort Pitt for safety. About 1797 Alexander Jr. was apprenticed to a cabinetmaker in Pittsburgh, completing his indenture in 1804. In January of the following year, he married Nancy Adams of Fayette, Pennsylvania, and the couple moved to Greersburg, Pennsylvania, where their first son, Robert, was born.

While in Greersburg, Alexander Pinkerton, along with his brother-in-law Alexander Adams, owned 400 acres of land, a saw mill, a grist mill, managed a general store, did watch repair and made furniture for the community. Documentation of these years can be found in account book manuscripts from 1805 and 1807. After 1811, because of a defective land title, Alexander Pinkerton lost title to all of his property, and left Greersburg to take up residence in New Castle, Pennsylvania, where he again made and repaired furniture for those in the area. Activity during this period can be verified from the 1811 account book manuscript.

By 1818, Pinkerton was considering a move to Ohio, according to a letter written to his wife from Chillicothe. By the next year, he had

Nancy Pinkerton.

Alexander Pinkerton.

enough business to share his shop with a partner, Andrew Stanley. However, by 1820, the country had slumped into a serious depression, causing many to look elsewhere for a living-the Pinkertons among them. With the thought that southeastern Ohio might be their destination, and having read a glowing account of McConnelsville in the Chillicothe Recorder, they came down the Ohio in a flatboat to Marietta and up the Muskingum in a keelboat hauled by the sons and father. Halfway to Zanesville, they stopped a lone man chopping wood to ask the way to the town of McConnelsville where they considered settling. James Larrison informed them that this uninhabitable forest was McConnelsville and that they might stay in his "tavern" called the Sign of the Buck, a structure "destitute of doors, windows and floors." It was in this place that Alexander settled. He built a loghouse on Centre and East Street, where his family lived and his cabinet shop produced much furniture. Among receipts in Pinkerton's account book for 1820 can be found one for a sale of Windsors to A.G. Spurgeon. The day books from this period also show that Alexander was doing a great deal of watch repair and that his son David, at thirteen years of age, was working with him. The likenesses of Alexander and Nancy are to be found in charming portraits painted by Sala Bosworth of Marietta in 1826, signed and dated

Robert Pinkerton.

Date	Item	$	cts
	Amt brot over	$222	07
Dec 27	To making 2 Br Table	3	50
1835 Jan 6	making Tablet Bu	6	00
" "	turning for Do		31¼
" 7	turning 2 Sett D Ta Legs		56¼
" 9	making Dining Table	3	00
" 10	turning Sett Com B. posts		18¾
" 13	making Dining Tab	[illegible]	[illegible]
" 20	making Varnish	"	25
" 21	work on Coffin (Tilkill)	"	75
" 24	making drop Bu 5 Dra	5	50
" "	turning for Do	"	18¾
Feb 1	making Tab Bu 5 Dr	6	50
" "	turning Colums for Do		12½
" 5	making drop Bu 5 Dr	5	[illegible]
" "	turning drops for Do	"	06¼
March 10	making Coffin (Conn)	2	00
" 11	turning Sett ½ Fr B posts		31¼
" 14	turning Shive block Pieces		25
" "	turning Sett Bed pins		6¼
" 16	making 9 Draw Bu	10	00
" "	Carving for Do	"	87½
" "	turning feet Do	"	31¼
" 24	making Cupboard	6	00
" 25	turning Sett ½ Fr B posts		31¼
" 26	making ½ Fr B stead	1	12½
" "	turning Shocks fiddledeene		12½
" 29	work on Coffin (Elliot)		25
April 1	making Br Table	1	75
" "	turning Legs for Do		18¾
" 2	turning 2 Sett F. B posts		88
" 3	turning 2 Sett Com B posts	"	37½
" 7	repairing boat pumps		12½
" 8	making Coffin (Rand)	1	00
" "	making boat pump	"	37½
" 10	making Br Table	1	75
" "	turning Legs for Do		18¾
" "	putting on Gaylords lock		12½
" "	turning 100 Bed pins		18¾
" "	turning Sett ½ Fr B posts	"	31¼
" 13	~~[illegible]~~	1	00
" 14	turning Chest feet	"	12½
" 15	making J. Pyles Table	"	12½
" "	turning Stand Legs	"	18¾
" 17	turning sett Com B posts	"	18¾
" 18	Discount with Clymer	2	50
		$228	43½

Date	Item	$	cts
1835	Amt Brot over	$288	43½
Ap 18	turning Pipers Bed posts	"	62½
" 20	making Coffin (Rogers)	1	00
" 21	making Richardsons Strait Edges	"	06¼
" "	making Robertsons Case	8	00
" 22	taking Bedstead Stuff out of the River Mayhew	"	25
" 23	turning Br feet Cundard	"	12½
" "	turning Laughlins door posts	1	50
" 25	making Br Table	1	75
" "	turning 2 Sett Ta Legs	"	37½
" 26	making Coffin (Vanhorn)	1	00
" 27	turning Sett French B posts	"	44
May 4	turning 43 Sett Bedposts	10	[illegible]
" 5	making Br Table	1	75
" "	turning Legs for Do	"	18¾
" "	work on Table frame	"	37½
" "	planeing board for Laughlin	"	06¼
" "	making Br Table	1	75
" 9	making 2 Br Tables	3	50
" "	turning legs for Do	"	37½
" 15	turning 2 Sett T. Legs J Palmer	"	37½
" "	turning iron for Griffith	"	62½
" 18	making Tablet Burea	6	00
" "	turning for Do	"	31¼
" 23	making 3 dinning Table	9	00
" "	turning 3 Sett Legs for Do	"	84
June	turning poppit heads	"	50
" 19	making pair Side Tables	10	00
" "	turning Legs for Do	"	46
" "	roping Do	1	25
July 3	Cash Lent	1	00
" 6	making Side Tables	10	00
" "	turning legs for Do	"	46
" 16	making 4 Br Tables	7	00
" "	turning legs for Do	"	75
" "	turning newell post (Bruce)	"	12½
" 21	making 2 [illegible] D Tables	5	00
" "	turning Legs for Do	"	56¼
" "	making 3 D Tables	9	00
" "	turning legs for Do	"	85
Aug 2	making Coffin (Roland)	1	00
	~~[illegible]~~	1	00
" 7	making Tablet Burea	6	00
	turning feet for Do	"	18¾
10	making Strait edges for R[illegible]	"	25
Sep 5	making Mahog. Bureau	12	00

on the reverse sides. The following year, Alexander sold his cabinet shop to his eldest son Robert, but continued repairing watches and did money cutting, which was quite remunerative. He died in 1837.

Robert Adams Pinkerton had been working with his father, and bought the business in 1827, as evidenced by the account book for that year. The Document of Sale indicates much about the shop and prices current: the stock, $20; cabinet tools, $20; boards, etc. to make shop of, $15; bureau, part made for the framing of shop, $12; bottles and jugs for shop, etc. This day book continues to mention "Bureaus for the Orleans trade," so it is evident that the furniture was not all made for the neighbors, but for outlying towns such as Bristol and Windsor, and points south. Among the furniture listed are dining tables, breakfast tables, cherry and walnut tables, desks, drop column and half column bureaus, plain bureaus, fancy stands, corner cupboards, French bedsteads and coffins. Bedposts and columns for mantels were turned on his lathe. By 1832, Robert employed a journeyman, N. Kennon, to work with him. Perhaps this allowed more time for him to build houses in McConnelsville, such as that for Mr. Mendenhall and the one for himself on Seventh street which is still standing and remains in the family. In 1840, Robert was elected mayor; ten years later he became sheriff and county commissioner.

An advertisement appeared in the Muskingum Valley newspaper October 22, 1840, that Robert A. and Henry Pinkerton would be opening a shop in Malta, a town directly opposite McConnelsville on the Muskingum. Apparently the two brothers continued in business together for the remainder of their lifetimes. Robert died in McConnelsville in 1891, a prominent pioneer leader in this community.

Child's chest by Pinkerton Family.

David Clendenin(1817-1894), fourth son of Alexander, was born in New Castle, Pennsylvania. He worked with his father and was apprenticed to George A. Jones of Zanesville in 1833. A sauce ladle was stamped with David's name and a spoon was made by George A. Jones for Lydia Ann Pinkerton at this time. At the end of his indenture, David returned home to take up business. An advertisement on October 22, 1840, in the Muskingum Valley newspaper announces that he is in the silversmith, clock, jewelry, and watchmaking business at the Sign of the Gilt Watch on Center street. He continued in this business for many years and also became involved in politics, as had his brother. He became a Probate Judge in 1861, and went to Washington, D.C., in 1876 to work in the first Comptrollers Office until his death in 1894. He is buried in Arlington National Cemetery.

The fifth son of Alexander was Henry (1820-1891). Born after his family's settlement in McConnelsville, he worked as apprentice to his brother Robert. A letter from their sister Eliza to Henry states, "and when you get your trade sufficient, I think here would be a good place to set up; that is Princeton or Petersburg (Indiana), for furniture is dear here. But, you must stick to it for some time yet." An advertisement in the Muskingum Valley newspaper in 1840 describes the new shop which they would open in Malta. Henry remained in the cabinetmaking business until his death. His will indicates that his real estate was valued at $7500 and his personal property at $150.

Although there are no identified examples of Pinkerton made furniture known to the writer, the ledger books have opened the door to the shops of this industrious and enterprising family of craftsmen that worked for ninety years. The rare and extensive collection of documents reveals the first known group of Ohio cabinetmakers ledger books to be discovered. The numerous receipts, accounts and letters describe in detail their shop enterprises, along with a peek into the joys and sorrows of Ohio frontier life.

The above information is from "The Pinkerton Family of Cabinetmakers and Silversmiths" by Jane E. Sikes and Robert M. Andrews, Ohio Antiques Review, February 1983.

PIPER, GEORGE......L.1805-1847..1826-1827
Circleville, Pickaway County

George R. Piper was born in Bedford, Pennsylvania in 1805. He married Angelina Williams who was born in Franklin County, Ohio, 1812. Piper began working in Circleville at the age of 21 as evidenced by this advertisement in the Circleville Olive Branch, July 24, 1826:

Cabinetwork
Jacobs and Piper
respectfully informs the public that they have opened a shop on North Main Street in the new building of James McCrum where they will prosecute their business with the utmost fidelity. Persons favoring them with their patronage may rest assured of having furniture faithfully made from good materials and in a great style on reasonable terms. Plank, country produce or each will be accepted in a payment for work in their line.

June 10, 1826

The above ad continued weekly until February 23, 1827.

And on Saturday, June 9, 1827 appeared the following in the Circleville Olive Branch:

Jacobs and Piper
removed to a new shop on North Main directly opposite the old tootine where they will be pleased to supply their customers with plain and fancy cabinetware on short notice and accomodating terms.

They are grateful for their liberal encouragement already extended to them and will endeavor to merit continuance of same.

This ad ended September, 1827 and in the Circleville Olive Branch of September 6, 1827 Jacobs and Piper announced the dissolution of their partnership.

Dissolution of this partnership by mutual consent
William Jacobs
George R. Piper

In 1830 George Piper may have moved away for he advertised in the Olive Branch, February 13:

For Rent
For one or more years, a neat and comfortable dwelling, now occupied by the subscriber in Circleville. The house consists of a new one story frame and is situated in the pleasantest part of

town. On the premise, a good garden, stable and other conveniences. Possession will be given on the first of April.
George R. Piper

If he left town he must have returned for he was buried in Forest Cemetery, Circleville, in 1847. His will was inventoried and settled July 30, 1848. From the tools, planes, plank etc. which were listed he was still in the furniture business at the time of his death, however he was in business alone or with one other person. It had been his shop and he was the master. He had a goodly amount of furniture so that he and Angelina were reasonably comfortable. It is not known whether or not they had children.

Piper, George
Forest Cemetery Circleville Twp.
Born in Bedford, Pa 1805 Died 1847
Wife Anna W.
Born in Franklin Co., OH 1812
Administrator: Jesse C. Thompson
Security: Marcus Brown
Henry Sage
Bond: $1000
Settled: 30 July 1848
INVENTORY: filed 5 June 1847

1	Rocking Chair	1.50
6	chairs	3.00
1	Table	3.00
2	stands	4.00
1	Side table	
1	Brass clock	5.00
1	wood clock	3.00
1	settee	4.00
1	Bureau unfinished	14.00
1	" "	20.00
1	Book case	4.00
1	safe	5.00
1	side board	30.00
1	Desk & book case	20.00
1	Desk	4.00
1	cabinet	3.00
1	washing machine	1.00
1	safe	6.00
1	lank settee	9.00
1	Bed stead	3.00
13	planes	5.00
1	oil stone	.25
1	hatchet	.37
4	augers	.25
1	drawing knife	.50
1	lot old plane bits	.25
1	lot carpenters tools	23.00
1	Tool chest	---
1	wash stand	1.00
1	small bureau	1.00
6	screw clamps	3.00
1	Pannell screw	.50
2	work benches	6.00
1	safe frame	1.40
1	pc dressed walnut lumber	.25
1	unfinished bedstead	2.00
1	lot scantling	1.25
1	lot sanded lumber	6.00
1	lot lumber	4.00
1	stran knife	1.00
500	shingles	2.50
1	lot walnut lumber	1.68
1	lot walnut lumber	5.00
1	lot thick lumber	3.75
1	lot 2" " "	4.25
1	lot walnut "	22.00
1	lot weatherboarding	4.00
1	keg copal varnish	9.00
1	lot vaneering	1.00

PLATT, WILLIAM......1824
Columbus, Franklin County

From the Columbus Gazette, March 11, 1824:

HOUSEHOLD FURNITURE FOR SALE
On the 27th of March, offer for sale at the shop of WILLIAM PLATT, the following: tables, chairs, stands, beds and bedding, together with almost any kind of furniture, wishing to exchange a horse for any of the furniture. Also two good clocks. Any indebted, please pay.
W.P.(WILLIAM PLATT)Merchant, in 1821

In 1821 William Platt was listed as a merchant.

PONTIUS, (PONTIOUS)MICHAEL......L.1804-1891
Circleville, Pickaway County

Michael Pontius was born in Northumberland County, Pennsylvania on July 1, 1804 and married Elizabeth Freeze in 1829. He began making furniture in Circleville before 1830 for on February 20, 1830 in the Circleville Herald and Olive Branch:

Michael Pontious
Informs the public that he continues to carry on the chair and bedstead making business on East Main street opposite Hedges Hotel where he will make in the neatest and most substantial manner
Chairs & Bedsteads
some of the latest and most approved fashions which will be warranted to stand. Persons wishing to purchase will please call and he will sell low for cash and approved country produce.

This ad continued until July 16, 1831 and then on July 16, 1831 a new ad began in the same paper:

M. Pontius
Chairmaker, Painter and Gilder
Informs the public that he keeps constantly on hand at his shop opp. Hedges Hotel a handsome variety of fancy and plain chairs, settees and bedsteads etc.
Job Painting
Executed in a neat style on the shortest notice. Wanted a journeyman turner and 2 apprentices to the above business to whom liberal terms are offered.

He was still working in 1840 for on Saturday, May 9th in the Circleville Herald:

M. Pontius
would inform his friends and customers that he has connected himself with D.D. Pontius in carrying on the business of _____chairs and cabinetmaking. He would therefore call on all such as are indebted to him to call and close their accounts by cash or otherwise as the business will hereafter be carried on under the firm of
M & D.D. Pontius
Sept. 20, 1839

Michael Pontius died at his home on Franklin Street in Circleville, Ohio, April 24, 1891. He and his wife had lived in the house in which he died for 51 years. Pontius left a wife and four children: George Pontius, Mrs. David Bennethun, Mrs. S.N. Smith and Mrs. Newton Harrick.

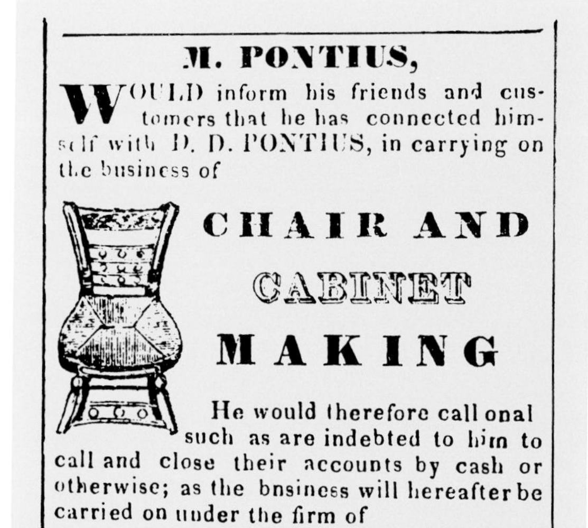

M. PONTIUS,

WOULD inform his friends and customers that he has connected himself with D. D. PONTIUS, in carrying on the business of

CHAIR AND CABINET MAKING

He would therefore call onal such as are indebted to him to call and close their accounts by cash or otherwise; as the bnsiness will hereafter be carried on under the firm of

M. & D. D. PONTIUS.

Sept. 20, 1839 20

POWERS & BEEBEE......1817
Marietta, Washington County

From the American Friend, October 24, 1817:

THE SUBSCRIBER commenced the cabinet-making business on Ohio street in the shop lately occupied by Mr. Haven as a bakery. Those who please to favor him with their custom, may depend on having their work done in the best manner and on the most reasonable terms. Most kinds of country produce will be received in payment.

Marietta, Oct.23, 1817
POWERS & BEEBEE

The first names of these men are unknown.

PRALL, WILLIAM
Pomeroy, Miegs County

In his book, *Drama of the Boot Shaped Bend, History of Pomeroy*, Ledderer notes that "William Prall made coffins. In 1845 Prall's cabinet and coffin shop was at Kerr's Run".

PROBST, JOHN......ca 1835-1836
Pomeroy, Miegs County

From the *Drama of the Boot Shaped Bend, History of Pomeroy:*

The cabinet shop of John Probst in the West end of the 2nd Ward had grown to John Probst and Company, chair factory and cabinetware house. Articles made to order. Also coffins, marble topped furniture, conversation chairs, reception chairs and ottomans.

PURCELL,BURGOYNE......1812
Wilmington, Clinton County

The *History of Clinton County* lists Burgoyne Purcell as a cabinetmaker and notes that "Burgoyne Purcell came to Wilmington in 1812. He had a workshop in log house and at that location for almost 50 years. Nothing more has been found about this man.

RADCLIFFE, DANIEL......1819
Wilmington, Clinton County

John Rogers bought back his unexpired contract of indenture and came to Wilmington, Ohio to work as a journeyman to Daniel Radcliffe in 1819. While working for Radcliffe, John Rodgers made the first bureau type desk ever seen in Wilmington for David Stratton, the Quaker merchant.

RAMSAY, ROBERT WARWICK
RAMSAY, THOMAS
Winchester, Adams County

The *History of Winchester, 1815-1965,* lists Robert Warwick Ramsay and Thomas Ramsay as early carpenters...possibly also cabinetmakers.

RAMSEY, T.
Marietta, Washington, County

At the Campus Martius Museum are two Windsor pieces marked "T. Ramsey": a Windsor bench with curved arms and a combed back Windsor. The only mention of T. Ramsey in Washington County is that he fought in the War of 1812, in the Washington County Militia.

A low backed Windsor cradle was sold at an Ohio auction house marked "T. Ramsey". (Courtesy Dr. and Mrs. James Sutherland) It is possible that these chairs and benches were made in Pittsburgh where Thomas Ramsey advertised in the late 1790s.

RANSOM, SAMUEL......1826
Portsmouth, Scioto County

From the Western Times, December 28, 1826:

CABINETMAKING
SAMUEL RANSOM
carries on the above business in all the various branches in Portsmouth; 3 doors east of Mr. John McDowell's store on Water street. From long acquaintance with this business, he will be able to give general satisfaction. His charges are reasonable. He will receive wood, pork, flour, cattle, corn, potatoes, meal, beeswax and, in short, almost any article of country produce. N.B. Steady, industrious boy 15 or 16 taken as an apprentice.

December 14, 1826

READ, EZRA......1809
Greene County

A clock case was made by Ezra Read for Melwyn Baker of Clark County in 1809 (Clark County history). The case remains in the family but the works and face have been removed.

The relationship of Ezra Read to Abner and Amassa is unknown, however, their names have been closely associated by clock collectors over the years. Ezra Read went to Champagne County, Ohio (See photo under Clark County).

READ, ABNER......L.1783-1858..W.1815-1858
Old Town, Greene County

Abner Read was born in 1783 in Northbridge, Massachusetts, originally Oxbridge (before that Mendenson); this town is 12 or 15 miles south of Wooster. His great, great grandfather had been clerk of the selectmen for 40 years. His father, Daniel Read Jr. married Mary Brown of Leichester, Massachusetts. Abner came to Ohio with his twin brother Amassa sometime before 1815 and went into partnership with Luman Watson, the clockmaker of Cincinnati. In the Ohio Republican, February 27, 1815,published in Dayton, Ohio appeared this ad:

Look Here - Wanted immediately - a number of good workmen at the cabinetmaking business, where good wages and constant employment will be given.
Reed(sic) and Watson
Waynesville, Warren County, Feb.27, 1815

This is the first ad found for Read and Watson and they were making furniture and clockcases in Waynesville near Lebanon.

On April 1, 1816, Abner returned to Northbridge, Massachusetts to marry Cynthia Adams.

In Dill's *History of Greene County,* there is an interesting description of the founding of Old Town, which is directly north of Xenia, and which is where the Reads lived:

The first house belonged to William Thorn from 1812 until 1815. The next one was built by Amassa Read in 1815. In 1817 Orrin North and Joseph Villard came from Connecticut and began blacksmithing and wagonmaking. Caleb West built in 1817 and was in connection with the Reads who are carrying on a cabinet shop on the premises now occupied by a barn formerly owned by William North.

This history also noted that Abner and Amassa Read, Caleb West and Orestes Roberts were Freemasons in 1818.

In the Warren County Historical Society is a Read and Watson clock with a note inside which says that the owner paid the bill to Read and North. Therefore, Orrin North was connected with the business, as was Caleb West.

An interesting receipt for a clock bought of Read and Watson by Elnathan Kemper on October 9, 1815 indicates that the partnership was still intact as of that date. The agreement was signed by Ephraim Downes, John D. Chamberlain for Luman Watson and Elnathan Kemper.

By 1816 Luman Watson was working alone in Cincinnati and Abner and Amassa Read were still making clockcases and selling clocks in Greene County. They were very busy and very active and a letter from Elijah T. Fisher to his parents in Wooster County, Massachusetts

(Ohio Historical Society manuscript) confirms this. His land was next to Mr. Read's house on the hill:

Wondrous height of ground...The way the Reads get hold of so much money, they have 8 hands working at cabinetwork, which is a cash article and they carry on the manufacturing of clocks. They carry that business so large that it keeps one business in collections, and one in peddling clocks, and one in selling cabinetwork and settling for timber.

This most interesting letter indicates that the Reads were making many clockcases and other furniture. The letter also indicates that they were making clocks and it is not known whether this relates to the works or the cases or both. Orestes Roberts, a clockmaker, may have taken the place of Luman Watson in the operation for he was associated with them in the Freemasons in 1818. He assembled and supplied clock works for the Reads - such work stamped "O.R." are extant.

By 1825, after the severe depression, the Reads were advertising in several newspapers including the Western Star, Cincinnait, Ohio, February 8, 1825:

The Subscribers have erected a woclen factory 2 1/2 miles north of Xenia on the Springfield Road. Abner Read, Amassa Read and Stephen Frothing

Xenia, May 27,1825

By this date the Reads seem to be no longer making clocks and cases. Abner Read continued to live in Greene County until his death on December 7, 1858.

READ, AMASSA......L.1783-1843
Old Town, Greene County

See READ, ABNER.

Amassa Read married Sarah Aldrick March 3, 1816 somewhere in Eastern Massachusetts. She died November 10, 1832. He married Jane Beard Henderson about 1836 and in the spring of 1838 they moved to Huntsville, Shuyler County, Illinois where he died in 1843 and she in 1890.

REAKIRT, JOHN......1816
New Richmond, Clermont County

The *Clermont County History* by Louis H. Evers notes that John Reakirt was a cabinetmaker in New Richmond in 1816.

REEVES, JAMES......1814-1815-1816
Zanesville, Muskingum County

James Reeves advertised in the Zanesville Express & Republican Standard, December 28, 1814:

FURNITURE FOR SALE
JAMES REEVES
The Subscriber informs the public that he has commenced the cabinetmaking business at the upper end of Main street, Zanesville, where furniture of all descriptions can be had at the shortest notice; executed in the most workmanlike manner; has on hand a large quantity of copperware.

Zanesville, Dec.27, 1814 JAMES REEVES

And again in the Zanesville Express, October 19, 1815:

JAMES REEVES
Cabinetmaker, informs the public that he continues his business at the old stand. A good assortment of furniture consisting of desks, tables, bedsteads, where he will sell for cash or country product. N.B. A boy wanted for apprentice - 12 to 15 years of age; also a good journeyman.

Zanesville, Oct.17, 1815

On February 22, 1816, this ad appeared in the Zanesville Express:

CABINETMAKER
JAMES REEVES
Auctioneer, selling all kinds of furniture in his house adjoining Mr. A. Read, adjoining J.C. Stockton's store, Main Street, selling bureaus, bedsteads, desks, tables, chairs, cupboards, clocks, and cases; watches, looking glasses, one large copper kettle, etc.

On March 23, 1816, James Reeves became a tavern keeper at the Sign of the Bear.

See REEVES, JAMES and GRAVES, JACOB.

REEVES, JAMES
GRAVES, JACOB
REEVES & GRAVES
Zanesville, Muskingum County

James Reeves became a tavern keeper in 1816 and sold out to Jacob Graves and Company on April 1, 1817; they had a cabinet shop and warehouse. Evidently in 1818 James Reeves went into partnership with Graves for in August 1819 John Sheward purchased the entire shop and stock of Reeves and Graves situated between the Court House and Post Office in Zanesville. These were years of difficult economic struggle for small businesses because of the serious depression. Perhaps James Reeves decided to help Graves out financially or he sold his hotel and went back into the cabinetmaking business. The vicissitudes of the various business partnerships were often so difficult to follow, constantly merging and dissolving for reasons known only to them.

RENSHAW, THOMAS S.......1816
Chillicothe, Ross County

Thomas S. Renshaw was another skilled craftsman who got his training in the Potomac region and who later was attracted to Chillicothe.

On August 31, 1801, Thomas S. Renshaw & Co. advertised in the Museum and Washington and Georgetown Advertiser that they have commenced a Windsor Chair Manufactory at Georgetown on the Potomic(sic)River City of Washington (Galavin, Anne C. *Cabinetmakers and Chairmakers of Washington, D.C., 1791-1841.* Antiques Magazine, May 1975)

In 1814 and 1815, Thomas S. Renshaw worked as a chairmaker in the city of Baltimore at No.37 S. Gay Street. A settee and a pair of side chairs by Thos. S. Renshaw, and painted by John Barnhart, Ornamenter, are prize possessions of The Baltimore Museum of Art. (Elder, William Voss, III. *Baltimore Painted Furniture 1800-1840.* Baltimore: Baltimore Museum of Art, 1972).

In the year 1816, Renshaw came to Chillicothe and entered into a co-partnership with Henry May, a Fancy Chair Factory. Their advertisement appears in the Scioto Gazette & Fredonian Chronicle, February 29, 1816. They announce that:

---

they have commenced the above business at the old stand of HENRY MAY on Water street...and from the experience of the latter partner (Renshaw) in the City of Baltimore, they flatter themselves they can finish work in a stile(sic) equal to any imported; they have on hand a neat assortment of gilt and plain chairs, and intend keeping an extensive variety of Bent Backs, Broad Tops with landscapes and plain chairs of every description...N.B. Orders from a distance will be promptly attended to and chairs put up so as to receive no injury from carriage...Feb.21.

The Renshaw and May co-partnership perhaps lasted until August 3, 1818 when according to records in the Minute Book of Quarter Sessions of the Peace for Ross County, Henry May obtained a license to "keep tavern" in Green Township.

Renshaw then seems to have faded from the pages of Chillicothe newspapers. No doubt he was going on his fine reputation as a chairmaker and perhaps felt he had all the business he could handle without advertising.

Nothing more is found on him until this notice appears in the Scioto Gazette, December 26, 1839:

William Cain - candlemaker...informs the inhabitants of this place he has removed his Candle Manufactory to the building on High street recently occupied by T.Renshaw, Chair-maker.

Ross County Recorder's deed records show that Wm. Cain purchased this property for $1200 - a sizeable sum for the times.

The above information courtesy of John Grabb, Chillicothe historian. For further information see "Thomas Renshaw: Search for Clues" by Mona Wilker Szente (Ohio Antiques Review, February, 1983).

REYNOLDS, JACOB......1834
Columbus, Franklin County

From the Western Hemisphere, January 1, 1834:

Cabinetmaking
Jacob Reynolds respectfully informs the public generally that he carries on the cabinetmaking business in all of its branches on the Mound, High street in Columbus where he intends keeping on hand a general assortment of Furniture viz: Sideboards, Sofas, Piec Tables, Ladies and Gentlemen's Dressing Tables, Centre Tables, Pillow and Claw Card Tables, Ladies Work Stands, Dressing and Common Bureaus, High Post, French and Common Bedsteads, Dining and Breakfast Tables and all other Furniture in his line, which shall be neatly executed on short notice. He will sell low for cash, or approved country produce. He will also exchange Furniture for all kinds of cherry lumber, such as scantling and boards. He also is preparing Hearse and suitable Biers for the burial of the dead. He tenders his thanks to all those who may favor him with their patronage.

REYNOLDS, WILLIAM B.......1817
St. Clairsville,Belmont County

This ad appeared in The Ohio Federalist, January 2, 1817:

CABINETMAKING: I wish to inform the public that I will carry on the cabinetmaking business at the east end of St. Clairsville. I can furnish any kind of furniture, at the shortest notice. I have coffin stuff; can finish a coffin in 4 hours and I am preparing a hearse to convey

coffins to the graveyard.
WILLIAM B. REYNOLDS, 1817

RICHARDSON, AARON S 1813-1818-1825-1829
Dayton, Montgomery County

We know that Aaron Richardson was in Dayton by 1813 for this advertisement appeared in the Dayton Republican, August 23, 1813:

NOTICE
My wife Deborah, having left my bed and board without any just cause. I therefore forewarn any person from trusting her on my account. I am determined not to pay any debts she may contract after this date.
Dayton, Aug.8, 1813 AARON RICHARDSON

From the Dayton, Ohio Watchman, June 11, 1818:

AARON S. RICHARDSON
CHAIRMAKER
informs the citizens of Dayton that he is commenced making chairs of every decription. N.B. Orders from a distance will be thankfully received.

And again in the Dayton Watchman, January 25, 1825:

AARON S. RICHARDSON, Wheelwright and chairmaking business; new shop, 2 doors west of the Courthouse, Main street, Dayton.

Richardson was still in Dayton in 1829 for he announced in the Dayton Journal & Advertiser, September 22, 1829:

A.S. RICHARDSON
Plain and fancy chairmaker
respectfully informs the public of Dayton and vicinity that he continues to carry on the chairmaking business in all of its branches, on Main street a few doors west of the court house, and immediately opposite Mr. Stanfair's Tobacco factory, where he intends keeping on hand common and fancy cane and rush bottom chairs inferior to none in Western County. Cheap for cash, whiskey, wood, wheat and chair plank. Cash always acceptable.

RICHEY, DAVID
Point Pleasant, Clermont County

The *History of Clermont County* lists David Richey as a cabinetmaker. No date cited.

ROBINSON, JAMES......1820
Chillicothe, Ross County

In Wm. R. Southward's *Reminiscences of Chillicothe,1866,* he states that in 1811, on the west side of Paint street in the block between Fourth and Fifth was the one-story frame shop and dwelling of James Robinson, cabinetmaker. Articles of furniture manufactured by him are still in use.

It was 1866 when Southward wrote the above story. While there are no notices of James Robinson in the Scioto Gazette, the Manufacturing Census for Ohio - 1820, gives this:

James Robinson a Chillicothe cabinet-maker has on hand 5,000 feet of cherry, walnut and poplar boards and employes three hands. Capital investment $500 and $600 paid out annually in wages. Production consists of bureaus, tables, secretaries, bedsteads, &c., at a market value of $2500 annually. Demand for product bad and no sales for cash.

James Robinson is listed as a Wheelwright in Finley and Putnam's *Pioneer Record and Reminiscences of Early Settlers of Ross County, Ohio*(Cincinnati, 1871). Above information courtesy John Grabb, Chillicothe historian.

ROBINSON, ROBERT......1812
Chillicothe, Ross County

From the Chillicothe Supporter, October 31, 1812:

The office of the Supporter has moved to Paint street in the house formerly occupied by ROBERT ROBINSON as a cabinetmaking shop at the Southwest corner of the Market House.

Apparently, Robert Robinson either moved or stopped making furniture in 1812. His brother, William, continued in the cabinetmaking business.

ROBINSON, SOLOMON......1830
Dye's Settlement (McConnelsville), Morgan County

In the Muskingum Valley News of March 16, 1830, Solomon Robinson is asking for 4 or 5 journeyman cabinetmakers at his shop in Dye's settlement, a few miles from McConnelsville. "If the workmen have families, houses will be provided. A lathe is propelled by waterpower."

ROBINSON, WILLIAM......1799-1844
Chillicothe, Ross County

According to the *Ross County, Scioto Township - Chillicothe - Pioneer Record,* William Robinson, cabinetmaker, came to the Scioto Valley in 1795 with his brother, Joshua Robinson, who was shot by the Indians. He was in Chillicothe as early as June 8, 1799 when he bought In-Lot #124 and Out-Lot #87 from Nathaniel Massie for 7b Kentucky money.

On June 19, 1809, Robinson announces that "he carries on the Cabinet Making Business in the shop formerly occupied by William Wallace, esq. on Paint street near the market house where he intends to be particular in having his stuff well seasoned, and will supply all those that will please to favor him with their custom...Furniture of every description finished in the best and neatest manner." He also wanted two or three apprentices from the age of 12 to 14. (Scioto Gazette, June 26, 1809)

Then on January 30, 1811, he informed his friends and customers that "he still carries on the Cabinet-Making Business, one door west of the Post Office, on Water street." At this time he also wanted one or two apprentices and one or two journeymen. (Scioto Gazette, February 11, 1811)

In the Scioto Gazette of March 13, 1815 he announced:

REMOVAL

WILLIAM ROBINSON, Cabinetmaker respectfully informs his friends and customers that he now carries on the cabinetmaking business two doors West of the Jail on Main street in the house formerly occupied by Joseph Thompson and nearly opposite to the cotton and wool making shop where he hopes to meet general satisfaction to all that favor him with their custom. He intends making furniture of the best quality and the newest fashions, and will sell low for cash, at his former price. N.B.: One or two good journeymen will meet with constant employment and two or three apprentices will be taken on advantageous application. Terms on immediate application to the above business.

March 6, 1815

William Robinson was in Chillicothe for a long time because he advertised again in the Scioto Gazette, May 26, 1842:

WILLIAM ROBINSON respectfully informs his friends and the public that he continues the cabinetmaking business at his old stand on Main street where he is prepared to execute in a neat and fashionable style every species of cabinet-work at short notice and for reasonable prices. He has furnished himself with a coffin __and likewise a hearse, so that he is ready to attend to orders in that line with dispatch.

May 26, 1842

William Robinson is last noted on October 3, 1844 when he advertised in the Scioto Gazette of that date:

The Subscriber has ascertained that there is a story in circulation that he has stopped making coffins; but such is not the case, as he is prepared to manufacture coffins at his old stand on Main street on the shortest notice and on more reasonable terms than heretofore.

He has generally a quantity of ready-made coffins on hand. He also has a good hearse which he will send to funerals when required.

WILLIAM ROBINSON

Oct.3, 1844

ROGERS, JOHN......B.1800..1819
Wilmington, Clinton County

Edna Whitley, in *Kentucky Cabinetmakers*, notes that "John Rogers was born in Clark County, Kentucky to Eziekiel and Rebecca Williamson Rogers, Dec. 6, 1800. He lived in Missouri until he was 10 years old. He returned to Carlisle, Kentucky and to Millersburg. He was bound to Henry and Moses Batterton, cabinetmakers, in Carlisle, Kentucky in 1816. He bought back his unexpired contract in 1819 and moved to Wilmington, Ohio to work as a journeyman for Daniel Radcliffe in 1819.

While working for Radcliffe, John Rogers made the first bureau type desk ever seen in Wilmington for David Stratton, a Quaker merchant. He was working in Richmond, Indiana by a later date."

ROLL, JACOB C.
Lebanon, Warren County

The R.M.K. Checklist notes that Jacob C. Roll made and decorated fancy sitting chairs, flag and rush bottoms. For further information see *Furniture Makers of Cincinnati* by Jane E. Sikes.

ROSENFIELD, C.E.
Paxton Township, Ross County

C.E. Rosenfield had a furniture and picture frame factory in Paxton Township.

SANDERS, JOHN M.......L.1823-1897
Samantha, Highland County

John Sanders was a farmer in Samantha, Highland County, Ohio. He was the son of Thomas M. Sanders and Judith Morman. He was born November 1, 1823, married Rachel Ann Banks in 1848 and remarried Lucinda Johnson September, 1856. He died in Highland County on April 13, 1897 at the age of 74. A chest was made by John M. Sanders in the early years of his life for his own use.

SANFORD, HECTOR......L.1780-1837
Chillicothe, Ross County

Hector Sanford was born September 1, 1780, the son of Angus Sanford, who came from England to Fairfax County, Virginia. Hector was orphaned at an early age and this record is found in the Court Order of Alexandria, made under the date of July 9, 1792. "Ordered that the overseers of the Poor for the town of Alexandria, or either of them, find Hector Sanford, 12 years old the 1st day of September next, apprentice to Ephraim Evans, who is taken to learn him the trade of Windsor chairmaker and to read and write as the law directs." This information is from E. Phillip Sanford, a descendant.

The Williams brothers' *History of Ross County and Highland County* notes that Hector Sanford emmigrated to Ohio in 1797 from the District of Columbia in a canoe with his slave, Thomas Watson. They landed at the big bend in the Scioto (River) above the mouth of Paint Creek (near Massie's settlement at Chillicothe). On page 142 of Williams History, it is stated, "Reverend Hector Sanford immigrated to the Sciota Valley in 1799 as one of the first ministers in Chillicothe."

Perhaps Sanford did come to Chillicothe in 1797 or 1799 to see what his chances might be to survive as a chairmaker in the then Northwest Territory. If he did, it is evident that he returned to Washington, for the next notice of him is found in the Washington Federalist,(Georgetown), November 3, 1802:

Windsor Chair Manufactory - HECTOR SANFORD begs leave to inform the public he has opened a Windsor manufactory on Bridge street a few doors below the Union Tavern. He will paint, gilt, and japan anew - Tea Urns, Waiters, &c. He will also Paint and Letter signs.

Sanford continued in business as a Windsor chairmaker for at least 2 years, "a few doors below Union Tavern". On November 19, 1804, he advertised in the National Intelligencer and Washington Advertiser:

...he has on hand a great variety of chairs - handsomely finished, among which are some Neatly gilt.

A fortnight after John L. Tabb's first advertisement was printed in the Scioto Gazette, Hector Sanford's introduction to the public as a chairmaker was made in the issue of December 26, 1805:

THE SUBSCRIBER
Begs leave to inform the
public that he has commenced a
CHAIR MANUFACTORY
At the upper end of Water street, nearly opposite the governor's at the sign of the WINDSOR CHAIR, where he intends to carry on the business in all its branches. He makes gilt ornamented chairs of various patterns, Windsor chairs, with round and square backs, settees, rocking chairs and children's chairs of various kinds and colours. He will also mend, paint, and varnish old chairs; draw, paint and letter signs of every description, in the neatest manner, on the shortest notice, and on terms that cannot fail to please all those who may favor him with their custom.
Hector Sanford
Chillicothe, December 11, 1805

In 1806, Hector Sanford entered into the lay ministry according to Methodist records, He also made chairs for the furnishing of the Thomas Worthington mansion, "Adena" which was nearing completion in 1806. (Thomas Worthington Papers).

In 1813, Hector Sanford built a 2-story stone house at the foot of Paint Street which still stands. At this location, he operated a cotton and wool carding mill for several years.

The last trace of Hector Sanford was in early 1837 when he was a circuit-riding preacher in Brown County, Ohio. He died May 10, 1837.

This information courtesy John Grabb, Chillicothe historian.

SARCHET, PETER
Cambridge, Guernsey County

Peter Sarchet is mentioned in the *Stories of Guernsey County, Ohio - The History of an Average Ohio County* by William G. Wolf. It is noted that Sarchet was ..." from the island of Guernsey - a carpenter, a skilled woodworker who made wooden hinges, latches and articles of furniture". No date cited.

SAYRES & DONOHOE......1839
Eaton, Preble County

This ad is from the Eaton Register, March 1, 1839:

THE SUBSCRIBER respectfully informs the public that they are now carrying on a chair shop in the town of Eaton, opposite the printing office.
Flag-bottom and Windsor chairs, settees, &tc, &tc, can be had at the best establishment of the best description and on moderate terms; having

started a horse-powered turning lathe, they prepare to do fancy turning at the shortest notice. Also glazing, house, sign and ornamental painting. Imitations of the following woods and marbles can be seen at the paint shop: oak, mahogany, sattan, rosewood, curl, and Birdseye maple, Egyptian, Italian, Irish and American marble, &tc.
N.B. Wheat, corn, oats, sugar butter will be taken in payment.
SAYRES & DONOHOE

Sayres' first name is unknown.

SCHAFER, SAMUEL......1842
Hamilton, Butler County

Samuel Schafer advertised as a chairmaker in the Western Telegraph, June 22, 1842. Among the items he offers for sale are "Windsors, fancies, settees and small rocking chairs". His shop was located at the corner of Front and Main, Rossville.

SCHLICH (SCHLEIGH), JOHN D.......1828
Lancaster, Fairfield County

The Records of Indenture (Ohio Historical Society) list John D. Schlich as a house joiner and cabinetmaker in Fairfield County, 17 March, 1828 with an 18 year old apprentice by the name of John Shull.

John Schlich is also mentioned in a letter to I.T. Frary from Mrs. Lella Trimble Dallow, whose great grandfather, William Trimble, was the surveyor who helped Ebenezer Zane lay out Lancaster. William Trimble's signature appears on "the first abstract of the lot on which house stands...lovely Reeves House". Mr. Schlich is listed formerly as a house carpenter and cabinetmaker and was the original architect for the Mumaugh House."

SCOTT, -
Shandon, Butler County

In *The Saga of Paddy's Run* by Stephen Riggs Williams a Mr. Scott is listed as a cabinetmaker.

SELTZER, S.Z.......1837
Columbus, Franklin County

The Ohio State Journal, August 31, 1837, carried this advertisement:

Furniture at Auction
There will be offered at Auction, on Sat., September 9th at S.Z. Seltzer's Cabinet Ware Rooms, Columbus, a variety of Furniture as follows: A Sofa, a Bookcase, Bedsteads, fancy and common, Bureaus, Mahogany and common, stands. Also the frame shop which stands on the rear of the lot, a quality of Lumber etc. and three stoves. Any of the articles may be purchased at private sale, presious to the day of the sale.
S.Z. Seltzer

SENEY, JOSHUA & MILLS, JOHN E.......1838-1839-1842
Chillicothe, Ross County

Joshua Seney was born in Dover, Kent County, Delaware. In 1834, when a young man, he became a cabinetmaker and he came to Chillicothe to follow his trade. His obituary in the Ross County Register, December 29, 1903 states: "He made a specialty of wooden chairs and made the first cane seated chairs ever used in Chillicothe".

He went into partnership with a man whose last name was Clark on Holler's Row in 1834. The partnership was terminated in 1837. Seney then went into partnership with John E. Mills in January, 1838; they were making cabinet work and chairs opposite the Court House. They had taken over the very prestigious shop of William Y. Emmett who had gone bankrupt and moved to Circleville. The following advertisement is from the Chillicothe Advertiser, January 6, 1838:

SENEY & MILLS,
Cabinet and Chair Manufacturers
Paint street, opposite the courthouse, in the shop formerly occupied by William Y. Emmett, Chillicothe, Ohio. All work from their shop warranted.
JOSHUA SENEY & JOHN E. MILLS

A receipt from the James Worthington Estate indicates that Seney and Mills did some work for the Worthingtons on April 8, 1839:

J.T. Worthington Dr. To Seney and Mills
April 8, 1839

To Paper Hanging 10 pieces	*$ 3.37½*
To 2 picture frames	*6.00*
To one breakfast table	*5.00*
To Repairs on chair and stand	*.75*
To Portrait frame and glass	*2.87½*
To Repairs on Bedstead	*.37½*
	$18.37½

Chillicothe Jan.4, 1842
Rec'd in full Seney and Mills

It is not clear but it is possible that William Mills may have joined this partnership briefly at some time. This partnership was still in operation in December, 1841, for they advertised in the Scioto Gazette:

Manufacturers of Furniture
No. 8 Paint Street - Opposite the Court House

The above ad began May 20, 1841. This concern was a stable one for Seney and Mills were together for 7 years. Then, John Mills advertised alone in the True Democrat, October 23, 1844:

Chair Manufactory - John Mills
(of the late firm of Seney and Mills)

Joshua Seney went into the dry goods and grocery business. He died in Ross County, December 29, 1903. Some of this information courtesy John Grabb, Chillicothe historian.

SHEARER, JOHN & SMEIGH, SAMUEL......1839
Xenia, Greene County

Shearer & Smeigh advertised in the Greene County Torchlight & Xenia Advertiser, May 23, 1839:

SHEARER & SMEIGH - Cabinetmaker and turner on the southwest corner of Detroit and 2nd street

No further ad has been found for these two cabinetmakers. They were both in Xenia in 1850 working as cabinetmakers.

Samuel Smeigh was a cabinetmaker from Maryland. His wife's name was Isabella and he had a lot of children. He had an apprentice and journeyman whose name was Lewis Hammer.

John Shearer was a cabinetmaker from Pennsylvania and his wife's name was Mary. In 1850, Shearer was 38 years old and he had apprentices by the names of Christian Hosteller, 23 - cabinetmaker, and William Lillie, 23 - cabinetmaker.

John Shearer probably died in Xenia because his son was mentioned in Dills History as having become an attorney and a very prominent man.

SHELL, JONAS
Bainbridge, Ross County

The N. Smith Ledger Book (Ohio Historical Society) contains the following excerpt:

Oct. 1826 - Credited to JONAS SHELL, Jan. 20th, by 6 days work - bedstead, clock, bedtick, painting.

SHEPHERD, HENRY......1833-1835
Chillicothe, Ross County

Henry Shepherd's introduction is found in this notice in the Chillicothe Advertiser, May 18, 1833:

Cabinet Making
HENRY SHEPHERD respectfully informs the citizens of Chillicothe and the public generally that he has commenced the above business in all of its branches in the building in Holler's Row, one door north of the building recently occupied by the late Judge Swearingen as a store, and two doors South of Mr. Taggart's store, where he will execute all orders in his line in the most workmanlike manner and with the utmost dispatch. His terms will be as advantageous as any other shop in this place.

N.B. An apprentice, between the ages of 14 and 16, will be taken to learn the above business; one from the country would be preferred.

Chillicothe, May 18th, 1833

As evidence of Henry Shepherd's skill as a wood worker, he was awarded a premium at Ross County's Agricultural Fair in 1833:

To H. Shepherd, for best specimen of cabinet work -- $3.00 (Chillicothe Advertiser, Nov. 9, 1833)

The show and fair were held under the direction of the Ross County Agricultural Society, and according to the Chillicothe Advertiser, Nov. 9, 1833 "took place on Friday and Saturday last; the former at Harley's Grove (note: this was John H. Harley's Sugartree Grove and pasture in West end near Honey Creek, out at the end of Arch street) and the latter at the Paint street Market House." A long list of premiums follow, the last of which is Mr. H. Shepherd's.

Shortly afterward, Henry Shephard entered into a partnership with Nathan Durfee which did not last very long, according to this notice in the Chillicothe Advertiser, April 5, 1834:

DISSOLUTION OF PARTNERSHIP
THE partnership heretofore existing between the subscribers, in the Cabinet making business, has been this day dissolved by mutual consent. Those indebted to the late firm of Shepherd & Durfee are requested to make immediate payment to H. Shepherd, who is alone authorized to settle the accounts.

Henry Shepherd
Nathan Durfee *March 5th, 1834*

Henry Shepherd continued on in business alone as evidenced by this advertisement in the Chillicothe Advertiser, April 5, 1834:

CABINET AND CHAIR WAREHOUSE

The subscriber respectfully informs the citizens of Chillicothe and the public generally, that he will continue business at the old stand in Holler's Row, three doors north of the Market-house, and that in addition to Cabinet Making, he has added the manufacture of

FANCY & WINDSOR CHAIRS

Having the very best materials and the most experienced workmen, he will warrant both his cabinet and chair work not to be inferior to any in the Western Country; which will be sold on very reasonable terms.

April 5, 1834 Henry Shepherd

The Chillicothe Advertiser of November 8, 1834 notes that among the premiums awarded at the recent fair by the Ross County Agricultural Society was "Mr. Henry Shepherd, pr. of tables ($)3.00".

As these were the hard times of the 1830's and Shepherd's business was not immune, the August 1, 1835 issue of the Chillicothe Advertiser gives this:

Notice is hereby given,

To all persons interested, at my instance a writ of Attachment was this day issued by James Miller, a Justice of the Peace of Scioto township, Ross county, against the goods, chattels, rights, credits, moneys and effects of Henry Shepherd, an absconding debtor.

July 24, 1835 R.Stewart

This information courtesy John Grabb, Chillicothe historian.

SHEPHERD, JOHN B.......pre 1855

Gallipolis, Gallia County

John B. Shepherd may have been in Gallipolis in the 1840s.

From the Scioto Gazette, May 14, 1855:

A fire in Gallipolis a few days since, which destroyed the chair factory owned by MR. JOHN B. SHEPHARD in the block between 2nd and 3rd streets below the Public Square.

John B. Shephard died September 15, 1866 at the age of 61 and was buried in Pine Street Cemetery, Gallipolis. Information courtesy of John Grabb, Chillicothe historian.

SHEPHERD, JOSEPH

Chillicothe, Ross County

Joseph Shepherd Sr. came to Chillicothe in 1805 when he was about twenty years old. He came from Shepherstown, Virginia and was a grandson of Thomas Shepherd, the founder of that town. In 1809 he was married in Chillicothe to Mary(Polly) Betz the daughter of Adam Betz. The latter was the doorkeeper of the Statehouse at the first seating of the Legislature in 1803 in Chillicothe.

Joseph Shepherd, Sr. died in Chillicothe on the 2nd of August, 1858 in the 73rd year of his age. There is a close connection between Joseph Shepherd and John L. Tabb since they both came from the Shepherdstown, Virginia area, and it is thought that they came together to Chillicothe in 1805. They both married Betz girls (probably sisters) in Chillicothe.

While no mention of Joseph Shepherd is found in the newspapers, as a cabinetmaker before 1820, he could have been working in John L. Tabb's shop and continued the business after Tabb shot a man and left Chillicothe in 1813.

The following, found in the Scioto Gazette, November 28, 1820, is the first notice of Shepherd as a cabinetmaker:

Joseph Shepherd of this town will carry on his business of cabinetmaker at his old stand on Mulberry street where all kinds of work in his line will be executed with neatness and dispatch. He has lately purchased a neat and convenient hearse, with which he will attend the funerals of those persons, coffins for whom may have been made at his shop, without additional charge.

In a list of expenditures, for the County of Ross, for the year ending March 6, 1822, is this:

Paid Joseph Shepherd, book case for Clerk's office --25.00

Paid Joseph Shepherd, for coffin for George Hill (colored man) -- 5.00

(The Supporter & Scioto Gazette, May 15, 1822)

The Scioto Gazette, September 22, 1830, contained several items about:

BELL'S PATENT BEDSTEAD. A specimen of this valuable bedstead, is now in this place, and may be seen at Madeira's Hotel. Its advantages over the common bedstead are, in its being constructed so as that the posts are put together without screws, it is stronger and less liable to get out of order, it affords no refuge for bugs and it can be taken down and put up in a few minutes. The sacking bottom is so constructed as to be tightened in a quarter of a minute by turning a screw, without removing the clothes. It promises to be very useful to large families and to gentlemen keeping public houses. The Agent here is authorized to dispose of patent rights for counties, or for a less extent of territory.

The same newspaper contained this notice:

BELL'S PATENT BEDSTEAD
The Subscriber has been employed to make a number of these bedsteads for the market in this place; and will be ready in a few days to fill orders. He invites those who wish to purchase these bedsteads, to call and examine them at his shop, under the Masonic Hall, on Second street.

Sept.22 JOSEPH SHEPHERD

The last advertisement of Joseph Shepherd appeared in the Scioto Gazette under the date of October 17, 1844:

CABINETMAKING AND UNDERTAKING
The Subscriber respectfully informs his old friends and customers that he has removed his shop to Second Street, near Wm. Welsh's Foundery (sic) opposite the residence of James Howard, where he offers his services to the public in the business of Cabinet Making and Undertaking. At the instance of a number of his friends he has supplied himself with a fine lot of Mohogany (sic) Wood, for the manufacture of Coffins, and continuing to keep a hearse, he is ready to attend funerals on reasonable terms and short notice.

October 17, 1844 JOSEPH SHEPHERD

While Joseph Shepherd died in 1858, he kept active in his business as late as 1857, when according to an account filed against his estate, he had purchased various items including these:

To D.A. Schutte,, Dr. (Hardware Dealer)
Oct.5,1857 - 2 pr. Coffin Handles 1.00 2.00
Oct.5,1857 - 1 doz. Silver screws - 10 2.10

One week after Joseph Shepherd's death it was announced in the Scioto Gazette, August 10, 1858:

James M. Woltz & Joseph Shepherd, Jr.
(Successors to Jos. Shepherd & Son, dec'd.)
Coffin Makers and Undertakers
Second St., one door East of Welsh's Foundry

This old Shepherd residence still stands at #146 East Second Street, Chillicothe.

The above information courtesy John Grabb,

SHEPHERD, WILLIAM......1835-1839
Chillicothe Ross County

From the Chillicothe Advertiser, August 29, 1835:

CABINETMAKING
WILLIAM SHEPHERD respectfully informs his friends and the public generally that he has taken a shop on Holler's Row recently occupied by Mr. Henry Shepherd, having the very best of materials and the most experienced workmen. He will warrant his cabinetwork not to be inferior to any in the Western Country and which will be sold in the most reasonable terms.
Chillicothe, Aug.29, 1835

Shepherd's advertisements ceased on March 5, 1836; he began advertising again in the Scioto Gazette, January 13, 1839:

THE FLORIDA WAR...The undersigned respectfully notifies the public that they have entered into co-partnership for the transaction of cabinetmaking business and have taken the shop formerly occupied by Joseph Shepherd under the Masonic Hall on Second street where they are prepared to receive orders to any extent for all articles in the line of business. A portion of public patronage is solicited.

Chillicothe, __16, 1837
William Shepherd, James Willett

The above information courtesy of John Grabb, Chillicothe historian.

SHERMAN, GEORGE
Waynesville, Warren County

According to the *History of Warren County* George Sherman was a cabinetmaker in Warren County, perhaps Waynesville, before 1830.

SHEWARD, JOHN......1819-1820-1838
Zanesville, Muskingum County

The Muskingum Messenger of August 18, 1819 carried this notice:

CABINETMAKING
THE SUBSCRIBER, having purchased the shop and stock under the late firm of REEVES AND GRAVES, situated between the court house and post office, carry on the various branches; long acquaintance with the above business, and working in principal shops in the Eastward. He requires the public patronage.
JOHN SHEWARD
A quantity of curled maple scantling and boards wanted. Zanesville, July 20, 1819

John Sheward bought the stock and shop of the late firm of Reeves and Graves. Reeves had commenced in 1814; then Reeves became a tavern keeper in 1816; so Jacob Graves & Co. in 1817 became Reeves & Graves in 1819. They went out of business and sold out to John Sheward. Sheward advertised again in the Zanesville Express & Republican Advertiser, September 12, 1820:

Cabinet Making

The subscriber, grateful for past favors, and the liberal patronage so generally extended towards him, now informs the public that he continues to carry on the

CABINET MAKING BUSINESS,

At his old stand opposite the engine house and nearly opposite the post office, where he hopes by making use of none but the best materials, and employing none but the best of workmen, to give general satisfaction.

August 14, 1820 JOHN SHEWARD

From the Zanesville Aurora, September 7, 1838:

Cabinetmaker - JOHN SHEWARD & JAMES SHEWARD

(This is just the beginning of a long ad which continued until September 28, 1838.)

Norris Schneider, Zanesville historian, believes that John Sheward went to New York City some time later.

SHIVELEY, CHRISTIAN......L.1770-1836..W.1805-1836

Madison Township, Montgomery County

The following excerpt is from the *History of Montgomery County*, published by W.H. Beers and Co., 1882, Book III. (Courtesy of the Montgomery County Public Library, Dayton, Ohio)

The year 1805 witnessed additions to the settlement (Wolf Creek settlement) in the persons of the Shivelys, embracing several families - Christian and Susannah with seven children, Christian, Jacob, Daniel, John, David, Elizabeth and Susannah, the boys all being married except David and John. They left their Pennsylvania homes with high hopes of finding beyond the Ohio their share of the unquestioned wealth slumbering in the wilds of that land. Going by wagon from Huntingdon County (Pennsylvania) to McKeesport where they boarded a flatboat called a "broad-horn" thence to Cincinnati and by wagon to Wolf Creek settlement, where they were hailed with joy and with their families, clustered around the little nucleus already formed, adding to its strength and social comfort, as well as facilitating labor. They were industrious and of that hardy class coming from the Keystone state - large of stature and well developed physically and equal to the occasion of surmounting the many obstacles and braving the dangers incumbent upon those destined to be the people of a new country.

Christian Jr. married Susan Gripe and upon their arrival the family was composed of four. He entered the southeast quarter of Section 27 and there built his cabin....He was a very useful man among the colonists; his strength and activity were excelled by none, giving him precedence over all at log rollings and raisings, on which occasions he was generally chosen Captain. He was of an ingenious turn, being a "jack of all trades" and serving as the cabinet-maker and undertaker of the neighborhood; also as the physician, being a natural bone-setter.

Christian Jr. resided in his rudely built cabin until 1811 when he contracted with David Baker of Dayton to build him a two-story stone house for the sum of $100. It was war times and mechanics had little to do, hence the exceedingly low price. There was a good cellar dug and a fine house erected covered with lap shingles, the stone was taken from quarry in Section 28.

Christian Shively died in 1836 at the age of 66. Charles Muller, in his article "The Extraordinary Cupboards of Christian Shively" (Ohio Antiques Review, June 1983) notes the following:

The 'accurate Inventory of the goods and Chattles of the Estate of Christian Shively Deceased' was prepared on February 27, 1838, and included a sack of screws valued at $1.00 and '1 Lot of plank' valued at $4.00. The furniture listed '1 Clock and Case - 30.00', '1 Table & dish - 4.00', '1 Bet and beting' at $6.00, another at $15.00, yet another at $10.00 and then '2 bet and betsteads' at $17.00. The two rifles were given a value of $15.00 and the one cupboard was appraised at $12.00. Except for the 16 acres of corn, the 'Lot of Carrepenter tools' was given the highest appraised value...$50, the same amount as designated for a wagon, one gray mare, or 25 head of hogs.

According to the will, the carpenter tools were to be divided among the sons: John, David, Samuel, William and Owen. There were also three daughters: Christine, Elizabeth and Susan. A faint inscription on the back of a drawer of one cupboard could be read as Susan Shively, either the daughter or the wife.

There are five cupboards made by Christian Shively Jr., all found in Montgomery County, Ohio in the general vicinity of the Wolf Creek settlement, namely New Lebanon and Johnsville area. They are of massive proportion and excellent workmanship. Most are distinctively executed of cherry, walnut and maple - two doors with six glass panes with a center partition of 3 glass panes, an open shelf, 4 drawers across and 2 blind doors below.

The example illustrated remained in the Shively family until recently. It was acquired from Noah H. Shively, a grandson of Christian Jr., the cabinetmaker.

The Shivelys originated in Switzerland, lived for a time in Hagerstown, Maryland where Christian Jr. was born, but later moved to Huntingdon County, Pennsylvania. The influence of the cupboards would be a combination of Swiss and German. It is not known whether Christian Shively Jr. was apprenticed in Hagerstown or Huntingdon, which is in the vicinity of Altoona, Pennsylvania.

SIFFORD, DANIEL......1828
Lancaster, Fairfield County

The Record of Indentures for Fairfield County notes that Daniel Sifford was a house carpenter and cabinetmaker in Hocking township, Fairfield County in 1828.

Mr. Sifford is also mentioned in a letter to I.T. Frary from Mrs. Zella Trimble Dallow. In speaking of the homes in Lancaster, such as the Reeves house and the Mumaugh house, she says "...Daniel Sifford...builder and contractor in as much as he did practically all of the real old homes".

SLOAN, BENJAMIN......1813
Zanesville, Muskingum County

This notice appeared in the Zanesville Express & Republican Standard, October 27, 1813 and indicates that Benjamin Sloan could have been a cabinetmaker:

PUBLIC VENDUE
In dwelling house of BENJAMIN SLOAN of Springfield, Nov.19, 1813, a handsome desk; 2 card tables; clock and case; a complete set of cabinet and joiner's tools; a quantity of boards and scantling; shop stove.

SMEIGH, SAMUEL......1839
Xenia, Greene County

See SHEARER, JOHN & SMEIGH, SAMUEL

Samuel Smeigh was born in Maryland in 1808. His wife's name was Isabella and they had many children. He had an apprentice in his home whose name was Lewis Hammer.

From the Xenia, Ohio Greene County Torchlight and Xenia Advertiser, May 23, 1839:

Shearer and Smeigh - Cabinetmaker and Turner on the Southwest corner of Detroit and 2nd street.

The author did not find another ad for these two gentlemen but guesses that they stayed together as partners. They both were in Xenia in 1850 working in the cabinetmaking business.

SMITH, ANDREW......1820..D.1868
Williamsburg, Clermont County

The *Clermont County History* lists Andrew Smith as a manufacturer of splint bottom chairs in 1820 in Williamsburg.

Andrew Smith died March 27, 1868 and was buried in Williamsburg Cemetery.

SMITH, JEREMIAH
Felicity, Clermont County

According to the *History of Clermont & Brown County* by Byron Williams, Jeremiah Smith came to Felicity where he had the first chair shop. No date was recorded.

SMITH, JOHN......1804
Waynesville, Warren County

The List of Letters in Cincinnati Post Office, October 3, 1804 lists John Smith as a chairmaker at Waynesville.

SMITH, JOHN......1837
Columbus, Franklin County

John Smith advertised his cabinet shop on "High street opposite Hughes Tavern" in the Daily Ohio State Journal, July 20, 1837.

SMITH, NATHANIEL......1815..D.1817
Marietta, Washington County

The following ad is from the American Friend, December 15, 1815:

HELP THE POOR - THE SUBSCRIBER being anxious to settle his business and to close the year, requests those persons who are indebted to him to make payment on or beyond the first day of January next to there, will be put into an officer's hands for collection. Windsor chairs made in the newest fashion and most substantial manner for sale at his shop on moderate terms.

Dec.15, 1815
NATHANIEL SMITH

And then this sad notice appeared in the American Friend, April 25, 1817:

DIED IN THIS TOWN - Sunday evening last of a long and intensive illness which he bore with patience and resignation - CAPTAIN NATHANIEL SMITH, age 25. On Tuesday morning, an infant son of Captain Smith; both interred in one grave.

SPENCER, J. FRANCIS & SMITH, JAMES
Springfield, Clark County

J. Francis Spencer and James Smith had been partners in the cabinetmaking business before January 10, 1833, but on this date they announced their move to new warerooms in the Farmers Chronicle and Clark County Advertiser:

CABINET AND WAREROOMS
SPENCER & SMITH
that they have taken large and commodius rooms one door west of Green's Hotel, South street, Springfield. Cabinet furniture: chairs, secretaries, sofas, sideboards, bureaus, tables, stands, field and common bedsteads, cane seat, fancy and plain chairs and settees.

Springfield, Jan. 1, 1833

This appears to be a most elegant business, however, by July 20, 1833, only 6 months later, the partnership was dissolved. Mr. Smith departed and J.F. Spencer went into business with William Coles of New York City. On that same date in the Western Pioneer, Saturday, July 20, 1833 Spencer & Coles were advertising for two smart active boys as apprentices to the cabinetmaking business. "Good encouragement will be given to such on application to the Subscribers."

Spencer and Coles

A year later, in 1834, Francis Spencer and William Coles dissolved their cabinet and chair making business. This notice is from the Springfield (Ohio) Pioneer, August 30, 1834:

Dissolution
The partnership heretofore existing between the subscribers under the firm of
Spencer & Smith
in the cabinet and chair making business was dissolved on the 3rd of November 1833 by mutual consent.
The business of chair and bedstead making will be carried on under the firm of W. & G. Coles.
Francis Spencer
William Coles

The above ad ran until the paper stopped, July 3, 1835.

SPRAGUE, JONATHON......L.1767-1840
Waterford(Marietta), Washington County

Jonathon Sprague was the son of Joshua Sprague(1767-1840). He came to Ohio in the spring of 1788 and was a farmer by trade, although he did build furniture for his own home.(See Sprague cupboard under Washington County in the photo section.)

SPRAGUE, NATHANIEL......L.1795-1845
McConnelsville, Morgan County

Nathaniel Sprague advertised in the Muskingum Messenger, March 19, 1823:

FANCY CHAIRS, SIGN & ORNAMENTAL PAINTER
He has recommenced in the shop he formerly occupied opposite the market.

Zanesville, Mar.12, 1823 N.W. SPRAGUE

The following information about Nathaniel Sprague is provided courtesy of Mrs. Sarah E. Rusk:

Nathaniel Sprague (1795-1845) wheelwright and chairmaker of McConnelsville, Ohio and the third generation of his family in America, was born in Philadelphia where his grandfather William Peter Sprague was the founder of the first carpet factory in America. About 1805 Nathaniel and his parents, William and Leonora Sprague, migrated to Pittsburgh where his father and his uncle Peter Strickland were jointly engaged in building flatboats for the growing river trade and where another uncle Samuel Sprague was a gilder. The Peter Stricklands in 1816 came in one of these boats with a group bound for Zanesville by making their way down the Ohio to Marietta and thence up the Muskingum River. They were followed soon after by their nephew, Nathaniel Sprague, who had apprenticed as a wheelwright.

In 1827 Nathaniel and his wife Ann Silvey moved down river to a farm near Malta in Morgan County. By this time he had apparently added cabinet making to his trade of wheelwright. He opened a shop across the river in McConnelsville and according to family tradition one of the chairs he made was hung over the entrance to his shop to show passersby what he could do. The pride he took in his work was that of an artist as well as a craftsman and he always painted and decorated these chairs of his own well-proportioned arrowback design and graceful line. The family still have a number of the chairs he made for himself and rare few have turned up at auctions of old homes in the area.

continued on next page

How much training he had is unknown, but his interest in things artistic is attested by a small self-portrait in watercolor done about the time he was married in 1820. He appears as a young man, well dressed and confident of his own abilities. He was undoubtedly well aware of the high esteem in which his grandfather was held in England and America.

His grandfather, William Peter Sprague, had learned the trade of weaving at Kidderminster in Worcestershire, England and from there went to apprentice under Thomas Whitty at the famous center of fine carpet making in Axminster, Devonshire and became a member of the firm. There Sprague met and married Mary Whitty a young relative of Thomas Whitty. The Whitty carpets were very wide Turkey-type, hand-knotted rugs and were in demand by members of the Royal family for several generations. The Axminster rugs of that day must not be confused with the very cheap machine woven carpets that came to be known as Axminster at a much later date.

About 1783 William Peter Sprague migrated to America and settled first in Burlington, N.J. and later in Philadelphia where he founded his own carpet factory and made a carpet for Congress Hall in 1790 and one for George Washington's home. He died in 1808. After his death his widow followed her three children to Pittsburgh and made that her home until her death in 1815.

STEELE, WILLIAM......pre 1819
Eaton, Preble County

In the *History of Preble County* it is noted that "William Steele, a cabinetmaker, lived in the log house in the rear of the Presbyterian Church. He removed to Indiana in 1819 and after a few years, represented his county in the Legislature".

STEVENS, VINCENT......1820
Williamsburg, Clermont County

The *Clermont County History* lists Vincent Stevens as a manufacturer of splint bottom chairs in Williamsburg in 1820.

STEVENSON, WILLIAM......1836
Norwich, Muskingum County

From the Zanesville Gazette, January 27, 1836:

---

6 CENTS REWARD
The above will be rewarded without thanks or charges will be given for returning to me JAMES GUTHRIE, an indentured apprentice to the chairmaking business. He absconded the 10th instant at 16 years of age, with clothing.
WILLIAM STEVENSON, NORWICH, 1836

STIBBENS, EBENEZER......1817-1818
Dayton, Montgomery County

Ebenezer Stibbens was born in New Jersey in 1788. At the age of 28 he came to Dayton and went into partnership with ___Hall in the cabinetmaking business. They advertised in the Dayton, Ohio Watchman, October 16, 1817:

STIBBENS AND HALL,
CABINETMAKERS
VERY respectfully inform their friends and the public, that they intend keeping at their FURNITURE ROOM, opposite the courthouse
A GENERAL ASSORTMENT OF FASHIONABLE FURNITURE
which they will sell remarkably low, either for CASH or COUNTRY PRODUCE. Cherry, walnut and Poplar planks or Scantling will also be received in payment for any article in their line. Customers and others may depend on their punctual attention to their directions
Dayton, June 19, 1817

In 1818, the partnership ended, as per this ad in the Dayton, Ohio Watchman, March 19, 1818:

DISSOLUTION - The co-partnership heretofore established between STIBBINS & HALL is hereby dissolved by mutual consent. EBENEZER STIBBINS continues to carry on the cabinetmaking business at the old stand in all of its various branches, and solicits the continuance of the public patronage. He, at the same time, returns his grateful acknowledgement for the very liberal encouragement he has received since his establishment here.
March 18, 1818

In the late 1820's Ebenezer Stibbens was the Justice of the Peace and also was the Sheriff of Montgomery County. The following notice is from the Watchman & Farmers & Mechanics Journal, April 20, 1824:

---

10 Reward
Where as there are sundry mischievous persons disturbing the peacable inhabitants of this town, during midnight hours in taking and removing Signs from one door to another & other improper practices: The above reward will be paid to any person giving information for an act of that kind committed on Sunday night the 11th instant that they may be brought to conviction.
April 19, 1824 E. Stibbens, Marshall

In the Montgomery County 1820 Census Stibbens is listed as:

EBENEZER STEBINS (sic), owner, made sideboards, seckratureys, tables,stands; employed 4 men at the annual wage of $460; market sales, $2,000.

He was still residing in Montgomery County in 1850, at the time he was 62 years old, his wife Hannah was 46 and they had a nine year old son. Stibbens was not given a profession in 1850; he was probably retired and farming. There was no will or estate found for him.

STICKNEY, DANIEL......1816
Putnam, Muskingum County

From the Zanesville Express, February 15, 1816:

Chairmaking - A journeyman cabinetmaker wanted by DANIEL STICKNEY of Putnam.

Feb.14, 1816

STILER, W.......1819
Lancaster, Fairfield County

From the Lancaster, Ohio Eagle, October 14, 1819:

Chairmaking
C. Musser and W. Stiler
having commenced the chairmaking business in the shop formerly occupied by Samuel Willet, near the corner of Columbia and Wheeling Streets where they intend to carry on the business in all of its varying branches. They will sell their work low for cash or approved country produce, at market prices. Persons favoring them with their custom may depend on having their work well done on the shortest notice. They hope by their strict attention to business to merit and receive a share of the public patronage.

It is not known how long W. Stiler worked in Lancaster.

STINE, GEORGE......1811
Chillicothe, Ross County

This notice appeared in the Scioto Gazette, March 13, 1811:

ONE CENT AND A BASKET OF SHAVENS REWARD
Ran away on the night of the 5 instant, HENRY JOHNSON, an apprentice to the cabinetmaking trade: about 5 feet 6 inches high, 20 years old, talks English and German. Whoever takes up said apprentice and brings him to his master shall have the above reward, but no thanks.
GEORGE STINE

STOCKTON, DOUGHTY
Williamsburg, Clermont County

The Stocktons were from Williamsburg, Clermont County. The family originally came from New Jersey and Doughty might be the brother of Job Stockton. His will indicates that he was a cabinetmaker, for it lists cabinet tools, planes, beading planes, etc., one desk lock, 8 damaged bureau handles and one unfinished bureau.

STOCKTON, JOB......1821..D.1837
Hennings Mills, Clermont County

In the *History of Clermont County* it is noted that Job Stockton from New Jersey was a cabinetmaker in Hennings Mills before 1821. Further evidence of his trade is supplied by this notice which appeared in the Farmers Friend, Williamsburg, Ohio, July 21, 1821:

DIRECTORS - MARSHALL'S SALE: Directed by the U.S. District Court for Ohio for Public Sale at JOB STOCKTON - 1 secretary; 5 bureaus; 2 bookcases; 1 clockcase; 2 tables; 5 candlesticks; 3 cupboards; 1 high post bedstead; 1 yoke of oxen; taken in execution as the property of JOB STOCKTON on the suit of the U.S. to be sold without appraisement.

The Clermont Courier, January 6, 1838, carried this notice:

EXECUTOR'S NOTICE: All persons having claims against the Estate of Job Stockton, deceased, late of Williamsburg, Clermont County, submit them within one year of this date.
Azel Bryan
Jan.6, 1838

STOCKTON, VOLNEY......L.1821-1877
Williamsburg, Clermont County

Volney Stockton was born in Williamsburg April 24, 1821. The *History of Clermont County* says that "Volney Stockton - made 10 to 12 dozen chairs per week". He was the son of Job Stockton and he was a prolific producer of chairs in his day. Volney Stockton seemed to have retired from chairmaking by the time of his death since there were no tools listed in his will, but he may have been doing some coopers work. He apparently was comfortably fixed in his old age for he had up-to-date furniture, a looking glass and a carriage and buggy.

Inventory of the Goods and Chattles of Doughty Stockton deceased with the appraised value thereof viz

One Secretary valued at	50.00
One Corner Cupboard	10.00
One Table	1.00
Two Chairs	1.00
One fine Shovel	1.00
One Smoothing Iron	.50
3 Cups & Saucers & 3 Plates Teapots 3 bottles	1.50
1 Tin Bucket	.62 1/2
1 Valisse	2.00
1 Handsaw	2.00
2 Sash Saws	4.00
1 Compass Saw	.75
1 Bow Saw	.75
2 Match planes	2.00
4 Jack Planes	2.50
3 fore planes	6.25
1 sash plane	2.00
2 cock planes	
1 Beading plane	.50
1 Reeding plane	.75
2 Round planes	.75
2 match planes	2.00
1 Hollow plane	.50
2 Smoothing planes & 1 Stock	3.50
1 Rabbet plane	.75
1 Small Hollow plane	.25
6 Gages	.75
1 Small drawing knife	.50
19 Gouges	4.25
4 Large Chisels	1.87
3 Small Do without handles	.75
7 paring Chissels	1.50
5 files & 1 rasp	1.00
2 doz. Screws	.25
1 lot of brads	.25
1 Desk lock	.37 1/2
1 Punch and Whetstone	.37 1/2
1.2feet rule & 2 small Squares	3.00
8 Damaged bureau handles	.50
3 pr small brass hinges	.56 1/4
1 Glue pot & 2 Paint brushes	.25
17 Handscrews	5.00
1 Harp	.25
2 Clamps	1.00
1 Ruding box	.75
1 Bench screw	.75
3 Work Benches	4.00
1 piece of pummice Stone	.12 1/2
1 broken bottle and a gage	.12 1/2
1 Cupboard	.50
1 Tool Chest	2.50
1 axe	1.50
1 Hatchet	.75
1 Lot boards & Scantling	10.00

STRODE, GEORGE HAMILTON......L.1799-1876
Lancaster, Fairfield County

According to Mrs. George Utley there is a sideboard and dining table in the Georgean by George Hamilton Strode. He married Rebecca Arnold in 1810 and their portraits are in Lancaster. The sideboard made ca. 1825-1830 is made of applewood root, it has acanthus leaf carving, a walnut top with sides of cherry and the full turned columns are mahogany. The table which may be by his hand has sunburst medallions, roped legs and crotched cherry veneering on the skirt.

TABB, JOHN L.......1805-1813
Chillicothe, Ross County

John L. Tabb was the first cabinetmaker to advertise in the Chillicothe newspapers. His original notice which appeared in the Scioto Gazette,December 12, 1805, stated: "...he has commenced business in the town of Chillicothe, in Water street, opposite Mr. John Mantle's tanyard,...he will execute his work to the newest fashion, and most durable manner. He will also exchange furniture for good seasoned inch and half inch cherry and walnut plank."

In 1806 he "returns thanks for the encouragement he has been given by his friends and customers. He also informs the public in general he has rented that commodious brick house on Water street opposite Mr. George Hanes(sic) smith shop. He will exchange furniture for good plank or country produce, or even cash." (Scioto Gazette, August 7, 1806)

Then, this notice appeared in the Scioto Gazette, May 16, 1808:

Troop Orders

The members of the Chillicothe Light Dragoons, are requested to attend at the court-house, on Friday the 27th inst. at 10 o'clock A.M. in compleat(sic) uniform.

May 16, 1808 John L. Tabb, Capt.

John L Tabb was "...MARRIED - On Wednesday evening last...to the amiable MISS HANNAH BETZ, both of this place". (Scioto Gazette, August 9, 1808)

Tabb's business must have continued to flourish, for this ad appeared in the Scioto Gazette, May 29, 1809:

WANTED IMMEDIATELY

AN APPRENTICE for the Cabinet-Making Business; one from twelve to fourteen years of age, will be preferred. He must come well recommended. JOHN L. TABB

John L. Tabb was one of the original Chillicothe craftsmen who met on the 30th November, 1809 at Buchanon's Tavern and organized the Chillicothe Mechanic Society. As a member of this Society Tabb participated in the 4th of July Celebration in 1811, where he gave the following toast:

James Madison; smoothed by the plane of republicanism, Fastened together with the glue of his country's love, and polished with the wax of science; may he long shine as the first piece of furniture in the American drawing room.

William R. Southward, in his *Reminiscences*, wrote: "JOHN L. TABB, cabinet maker, occupied a large two-story brick on Water street, just west of Nathan Reeves' tan yard on the river bank at the head of Walnut Street." Southward recalled that "Tabb shot a man and then ran off to Virginia." The Tabb family lived near Shepherdstown and were related to Joseph, William and Henry Shepherd who were Chillicothe cabinetmakers who came from Shepherdstown, Virginia.

Notice of this unfortunate incident was printed in The Fredonian, July 28, 1813:

Yesterday afternoon, Mr. Shaw, a respectable young man was shot dead nearly opposite Mr. Wood's tavern on Water street, by a citizen of this town...A coroners jury sat on the body last evening and returned a verdict of wilful murder against JOHN L. TABB. We are also concerned to state that the murderer has effected his escape.

Information concerning John L. Tabb is printed courtesy of John Grabb, Chillicothe historian

TAYLOR, JOSEPH......1836
Zanesville, Muskingum County

According to the Zanesville Gazette, July 27, 1836, Joseph Taylor "WANTED IMMEDIATELY - 2 journeymen cabinetmakers. Apply to JOSEPH TAYLOR, Zanesville."

THOMPSON, DANIEL......1831
Wilkesville, Gallia County

A fascinating letter from Daniel Thompson to his brother in Massachusets (from the manuscript collection of Joseph Thompson, Ohio Historical Society) describes the town of Wilkesville in 1831, and how it was 4 years previous when Thompson first arrived. He describes his farm with three houses on it - "one I use for a shop...my work has been cabinetmaking principly, since I have been here except finished one small organ the first summer that I lived here at Gallipolis and now I have just begun a small organ..."

THOMPSON, WILLIAM......1834
Wilkesville, Gallia County

On November 3, 1834, William Thompson wrote a letter to his grandmother in Bellingham, Massachusetts (Joseph Thompson Manuscript Collection, Ohio Historical Society) telling her that he is well and working in the shop with his father, at his trade of cabinetmaking. "I have been to work in the shop two years next January, father is now making a cupboard for uncle Ziba."

TOMKINS, JAMES
Laurel, Clermont County

The *History of Clermont County* says that in Laurel, Monroe Township, a chair factory was carried on by James Tomkins and others having steam power. Tomkins was formerly in Cincinnati. According to the 1850 Census, he was living in Clermont County although no will, estate or burial record has been found for him.

TOWNER, A.......1824
Brown County

J.C. Jeffries and A. Towner were partners in the cabinet and wheelwright business in Brown County in 1824.

VAN TRUMP, -
Winchester, Preble County

An Ohio Historical Society manuscript about the history of Gratis (Winchester was renamed Gratis in 1902) notes that in this town there was a tinshop and a cabinetshop, and the cabinet shop's man was named Mr. Van Trump.

VORYS (VORIS), ISAIAH......1828
Lancaster, Fairfield County

Isaiah Vorys Sr. was a housewright and furniture maker. He was born in Virginia and went to Columbus with his family in 1823. He moved to Lancaster in 1828 for it is recorded that he had an indentured apprentice in his employ by the name of Robert Cochran. He lived the rest of his life in Lancaster and built many of the fine homes in that town, one of which is the house known as the Garaghty-Mumaugh house with its elliptical fan, light, lovely woodwork.

A beautiful cherry candle stand is still privately owned and remains in the family. (See photo - Fairfield County)

WADMAN, JAMES......1826
Hillsboro, Highland County

James Wadman advertised in the Hillsboro Gazette & Highland Advertiser, August 17, 1826:

NOTICE; The Subscriber will offer for sale Mon. 21 instant at his residence, 4 miles south of Hillsboro, great variety of cabinet and carpenter tools in excellent quality. The sale will commence at 10:00 a.m. and the terms made known. Persons desirous of bargains are requested to attend.
JAMES WADMAN

WAITE, JOHN......1820
Adams County

The 1820 Federal Manufacturer's Census as published in the Tri-State Trader by R.T. Mayhill, October 9, 1971 lists the following:

JOHN WAITE, Owner, made Windsor chairs, used 200 worth of wood, paints, and oils, and 1 man employed. Market sales, $200.

WALTON, SOLOMON......1823
Leesburg, Highland County

Solomon Walton made furniture for Samuel Saunder and John Henley, merchants in Leesburg, Ohio. The Saunder and Henley Ledger book commenced on the 18th of November, 1823. Walton made one secretary, three bureaux, one cupboard, one stand, one bureau, one small coffin, one cupboard, another cupboard, one breakfast table, one dresser and one stand. The total bill amounted to $7.25.

The Saunder and Henley Ledger book is at the Ohio Historical Society.

WARE, JACOB......1820-1840
Frankfort, Ross County

According to John Grabb, Chillicothe historian, Jacob Ware was a cabinetmaker and an undertaker in Frankfort, Ross County. Ware retired from business in or about 1830 or 1840. A large sideboard, made by Jacob Ware is exhibited in the Ross County Museum; it is made of cherry, mahogany and butternut. It was part of the furnishings of Duncan MacArthur's home at Fruithill.

WARE, THOMAS ALLEN......1830-1840
Frankfort (Franklin), Ross County

Thomas Allen Ware, son of Jacob Ware, followed his father in cabinetmaking trade in 1830 or 1840.

See WARE, JACOB.

WATSON, HARRISON......pre 1842
Hamilton, Butler County

Harrison Watson came to Hamilton in 1840 and worked as a cabinetmaker. His notice in the Western Telegraph, June 22, 1842, advertised his services as a cabinetmaker and coffin maker and informed the public that his shop was opposite C. Schmidman's, Hamilton.

He advertised again in the Western Telegraph, November 19, 1842:

Cabinet Changes
Harrison Watson, cabinet maker, undertaker etc. informs his friends that he has purchased the entire stock of coffins and stuff and hearse of Robert E. Duffield and will attend to all calls in that line with promptness and on reasonable terms.

He also continues his regular business as a cabinet maker, as formerly at his shop on the Market Square where furniture of all kinds may be purchased lower than anywhere else in town.

N.B. He will keep on hand a stock of chairs of superior finish on moderate terms.

WEAKLY, JAMES A.......1828
Fairfield County

The Fairfield County Record of Indentures notes that James A. Weakly, a house joiner and cabinetmaker in Fairfield County, May 16, 1828, had an apprentice named Joel Searle (Hearls), age 15.

WELLS, ROBERT......1813
Marietta, Washington County

From the American Friend, October 23, 1813:

ROBERT WELLS - CABINETMAKING
The Subscriber respectfully informs the citizens of Marietta that he has commenced the above business in the shop lately occupied by Major Alexander Hill; and he flatters himself that from the quality of good boards and other materials, general satisfaction will be given.
ROBERT WELL, JR.

WHITEMORE, SAMUEL......D.1823
Gallipolis, Gallia County

A household inventory from Samuel Whitemore indicates that he was a cabinetmaker. He worked before 1823 in Gallipolis.

WILDBAHN, GEORGE......1824-1830
WILDBAHN, GEORGE & CAROLUS, JOHN
Circleville, Pickaway County

This advertisement is from the Circleville Olive Branch, October 30, 1824:

CABINET & CHAIRMAKERS
WILDBAHN & CAROLUS - They have commenced above business in all of its various branches in the shop formerly owned by Mr. McCrum on North Main street, three doors north of J.L. Lor & Co. Plain and fancy Windsors, sideboards, secretaries, bureaus, tables, bedsteads sold very low for wheat, whiskey, oats, or any other thing. Highest prices for cherry plank.
Circleville, October 9, 1824

The Wildbahn - Carolus partnership ended in 1826 as per this notice in the Circleville Olive Branch, September 23, 1826:

DISSOLUTION
The Co-partnership between
WILDBAHN & CAROLUS
is dissolved by mutual consent. Those persons who have unsettled accounts with said firm, are requested to call one of the subscribers and adjust the same without delay.
GEORGE WILDBAHN & JOHN CAROLUS
Circleville, Sept.23, 1826

---

continued

Samuel Whitemore Estate

Galia County ss.

On the fourteenth day of November in the year of our lord one thousand eight hundred and twenty three William R. Gouler & Thomas Rodgers administrators of the estate of Samuel Whitemore late of Gallipolis Deceased filed in the Clerks Office the Inventory & bill of sale of the personal property of the Estate of the said Deceased and the same is in the word and figures folowing to wit)

		$	
One chery bureau scratch bead		10	00
One " " Cock "		10	00
One Book Case		6	00
One clock & case		18	
One 6 leg Dining Table		6	00
Two chery oval candle stands	@ 1,50	3	00
Three	@ 2 00	6	00
3 dressing tables 2 Draws each	@ 2 50	7	50

Item	$	cts
One	2	00
One kitchen breakfast table	2	00
One Bureau at Mr Howards	16	00
One turnup bedstead	2	00
One Do	2	00
1 bedstead	1	50
One unfinished Bureau	10	00
Carrd over	$102	00

Item	$	cts
Caried Over	$ 102	00
One square Table	5	00
One high top Walnut cradle	2	00
One pine Do		50
Six Red chairs	2	00
2 split botom chairs as Rocking		50
1 London Brown		50
One Evangelical Magazine		25
One sett vilage sermons 2 vols @ 50	1	00
three hymn books 30 one Book of psalms 25		55
One Razor Box 2 old Razors & old Glass	1	25
One large reel 100 one clock Reel 1,00	2	00
one meal & bread tray	1	50
24 Chery & Walnut table legs @ 5 Cents	1	20
five sett hand screws @ 37½	1	88
One clamp 50 one stand table	1	50
One Jointer 100 four fore planes with doublirons 4,00	5	00
One fore plane 75 three Jack planes @ 50 150	2	25
two double Ironed smoothing Planes @ 100	2	00
One tooth plane 75 & 2 Rebbit do @ 75 150	2	25

One large moulding plane	2	00
One sett table planes	2	00
One cut & thrust Do	1	00
One cock bead Do		50
One Philistine	1	50
Two hand @ 150 300 2 do 75 150	4	50
One large Iron tenone saw	1	75
One " Brass " "	2	00
One sash	1	50
One Dovetail do 1.00 One Bows 100 One Key Hole 50	2	50
Two Rasps 12 Two files 13		25
Two mortising chizels 50 12 paring Do 1.00	1	50
Five Gouges 75 two screw drives 1 P compasses	1	62
One hand axe 50 one hold fast 75	1	25
One Oil stone 1.00 one slide rule	1	75
	$ 160	75

Carried Over

Carried Over	$160	75
2 hammers 50 one sett match planes 300	3	50
One steel square 125 one do 50	1	75
One large wooden square		25
One brace with 28 bits	6	00
Three double plane Irons @ 48	1	44
Three new 87 two chizels 38 Two gouges 50	1	75
One half sett bed stead screws		22
Seven Doz half Inch screws @ 6¼		44
Three pair brass bulls 57 two brass drawlocks	1	19
One sett clock case balls eagle top	2	00
Three " " " " @ 137	4	12

One stand springs 12 two gimblets 13		25
two Joiners Benches 200	4	00
One cow	6	00
One grindstone & hangings 200. two sliding boxes 100	3	00
One Fusee 300 1 2 foot Rule 50	3	50
One sign board $200. One calf $100	3	00
1/2 Bbl Spanish brown say 100 lb @ 5	5	00
One Old axe 25		25
	208	41

Whole amount of the personal proper of the late Samuel Whitemore $408.41

Allowed for the support of the widow & 4 children one year from July 21st 1823 } 200.00

$ 208 41

Given under our hands at Gallipolis this 10th day of Nove 1823

N S Cushing
Solomon Hayward
Luther Shepard

George Wildbahn continued on in the business alone, and he was still advertising in the Circleville Herald - Olive Branch, August 21, 1830:

GEORGE WILDBAHN

Informs the public that he prosecutes his business at the new store on West Main street where he offers Cabinetware of any description, also plain and fancy chairs and settees, manufactured of the best materials in the most workmanlike manner, cheap for cash or wheat at market prices, if delivered in Circleville or at Foresman or Boggs Mill. He has lately received a supply of beautiful mahogany and is prepared to execute any orders for furniture on the shortest notice.

This is the last advertisement for George Wildbahn and it is not known whether he remained in Circleville or eventually moved elsewhere.

WILES, EDWIN A.
Lebanon, Warren County

Edwin A. Wiles was the son of William Moon Wiles and he worked as a cabinetmaker in Lebanon probably before 1840 although the author has found no newspaper ad by him. The household inventory may include furniture made by his father or by himself. He had a great deal of furniture.

WILES, WILLIAM MOON......L.1787-1837
Lebanon, Warren County

William Moon Wiles was born June 5,1787, place unknown. He came to Lebanon, Ohio before 1816, for on that date he advertised in the Western Star, April 19, 1816:

Third Sale at Auction
On Saturday the 4th day of May
The subscriber will offer for sale by way of public vendue, a large variety of cabinetwork at his wareroom in Lebanon, at nine months credit. The furniture offered will consist in part of
Secretary and book cases
Desk and book cases
Dining and breakfast tables
Cupboards
Common tables
Chests, stands etc.
The furniture thus offered will be as good a quality as any offered by said Wiles at private sale.
Every attention will be paid by William Wiles to above sale.

At this time Wiles was in partnership with William Halsey and together they were merchants. This partnership was dissolved in March 1816; this was the reason for the big sale. Then, on May 8, 1816, Liberty Hall carried the ad:

Cabinet Work
The subscribed intends keeping on hand and now offers for sale, in the room occupied as the office of the Deputy collector immediately opposite the Bank of Cincinnati, a variety of Walnut, Cherry and Mahogany Furniture of the Most elegant kinds. Persons calling and not being able to suit themselves by leaving their name and the description of such as may be wanted will by supplied in short notice. The furniture will be offered in the room will be low and warranted goods.
Wm. M. Wiles

By June 24, 1816 he was advertising that "two or three journeymen cabinetmakers who are masters of their profession will meet with good and constant employment by application to the subscriber at Lebanon, Warren County, Ohio"(Liberty Hall, June 24, 1816). In the Western Star, on October 18, 1816, he adds:

Come Hither, Woe Haw Dick
The subscriber wants to hire 3 or 4 teams for 9 or 10 days to haul timber to the different saw mills in the vicinity for which he will give any kind of cabinet work at cash prices.

By 1818 he was in business as a major merchant with Trent and Wiles. From the 1820 Federal Manufacturer's Census (Tri-State Trader, September 25, 1971):

Wm. M. Wiles - owner made sideboards, secretaries, desks, book cases, Madison tables, ladies cabinets, wardrobes, Grecian card tables, wash stands with buckets, bedsteads of various quality, bureaus, portable desks, dining and breakfast tables - Used cherry and mahogany, poplar boards and scantling, Glue, nails, beeswax and varnish.

In September of 1821 there appeared an ad in the Western Star indicating that he would take "country produce, flour, wheat, corn meal, corn, whiskey, wool, linsey, sugar, pork, beef, wood, chicken, turkies(sic), geese, eggs - when specie price is asked for he will deduct $.37 from each dollar from present bankable prices for cabinetware".

A month later, in October, 1821, he was bankrupt and the bankruptcy was formally filed in Common Pleas Court in April 1822. Also in 1821, the Henry Clay House, of which William Wiles had been owner and proprietor, was sold to Colonel H. Manger.

By 1824, however, he had returned to the cabinetmaking business as per this advertisement in the Western Star, February 4, 1826:

Boat Ahoy
The subscriber informs his friends that he has come to anchor in the cabinet shop on Main Street in Lebanon one door west of the Clerk's office. Having relinquished all business but that of cabinetmaking will be regarded as the only desideratum for his bread and meat. Country produce will be taken in exchange (as also a little cash)

Through much tribulation, the publics servant
William M. Wiles
At my shop March 29, 1826

In 1828 William Wiles was in partnership with John Hathaway, but this partnership was dissolved on June 28, 1828. During 1827-1830 he was making furniture for the Shires Hotel (The Golden Lamb). Hazel Spencer Phillips in her book *The Golden Lamb - An Authentic History of Ohio's Oldest Inn* notes that:

Other glimpses of tavern life shine through accounts presented to the Administrators. The most revealing of these is the account of cabinetmaker William Wiles, a colorful figure in early Lebanon.

Wiles bill includes a great variety of items purchased prior to 1830. The first, dated January 9, 1827, was:

1 small coffin, lined $5.00
case for do $2.50

other items in 1827 included

1 fancy bedstead(single) $7.00
2 washboards at 50 cents $1.00
stage whip $2.00
salt box $1.50

The variety of services given by these early cabinetmakers is exceedingly interesting:

1 3 tiered Martin box painted $6.00
1 lace frame, for daughter $1.50
new gate frame $1.00
Mending table $2.00
1 fancy bedstead $8.00
1 Ladies cabinet(mahogany) $6.00
1 common bedstead $

The total of this account was $208.68, a sizeable amount for those days.

By 1830, Wiles was auctioning off all of the furniture he had made for The Golden Lamb. An advertisement of April 10, 1830 in the Western Star reads:

Auction
I will sell at auction on Saturday 24th on Broadway (Lebanon) near Mr. Shires Tavern a great variety of second hand furniture consisting in part of bureaus, corner cupboards, tables, bedsteads, one eight day clock, one elegant easy chair, etc., etc.

The furniture offered here is of the first quality and is in good order having been used by a short time.

Terms of sale. Six months credit will be given on all sums over $2. Sale at 10 o'clock.

William M. Wiles
Lebanon, April 9, 1830 Auctioneer

William Moon Wiles died April 16, 1837; no will has been found for him. Wiles has been called erratic and colorful; he certainly had a more unusual and less prosaic career than most.

WILEY, J.D.......1822
Chillicothe, Ross County

From the Scioto Gazette, February 6, 1822:

WANTED IMMEDIATELY...four or five apprentices to learn the house carpenter and joiners trade...boys of about 15 years of age and a good moral character will meet with good encouragement by making application immediately to the subscriber.
J.D. WILEY
He also offers tracts of land on Main, Paint and North streets from Chillicothe.
January 30, 1822

WILHELM, SAMUEL......1840
Lancaster, Fairfield County

Samuel Wilhelm advertised in the Lancaster, Ohio Eagle, December 5, 1840:

SAMUEL WILHELM, CHAIR & BEDSTEAD MANUFACTORY, Lancaster, Fairfield County.

WILSON, -......1811
DUFFIELD, ROBERT E.
Hamilton, Butler County

Hamilton In The Making by Alta Harvey Heiser notes that there was a Wilson & Duffield, who bought a corner lot in 1811 - High and Front. They were cabinetmakers and they built a brick building.

WILSON, AMOS......1816
St. Clairsville, Belmont County

This notice appeared in the Ohio Federalist, November 7, 1816:

---

6 CENTS REWARD
for runaway living in GOSHEN TOWNSHIP, BELMONT COUNTY, OHIO, on the second instant. An indentured apprentice to the cabinetmaking business - JAMES AYRES, about 19 years old, stout made, blue eyes, light hair and complexion.

Nov.4, 1816 AMOS WILSON, CABINETMAKER

WILSON, SAMUEL......1808
Cambridge, Guernsey County

The following information comes from the Guernsey County 175th Celebration Booklet 1973, The Carl Rech Compilation of Cambridge Lots:

In 1808 on lots 14 and 15 there was a one story brick building occupied by Samuel Wilson, chair and cabinetmaker. In the rear of the building was his shop in which was a large lathe, the motive power for the running of the lathe was a large cage wheel in which was used a large dog supplying the power.

WILSON, WILLIAM B.......1808
Washington Township, Preble County

William's *History of Preble County* says that William B. Wilson came from Kentucky to Washington Township in 1808. He was a cabinetmaker and he moved to the country west of town.

WOLCUTT (WALCUTT), JOHN M.......1823
Columbus, Franklin County

From the Columbus Gazette, February 14, 1823:

One dollar Reward and no charges paid Runaway from the subscriber some time in December last, an apprentice boy to the Windsor chair making business by the name of Jesse Grace. He is about 19 years of age, a tolerably good at said business rather addicted to drink, and fond of lewd company. I hereby forewarn any person from harboring or employing in any way whatever said boy for I will prosecute them to the utmost extent of the law.
John M. Walcutt

He was still working in Columbus in 1831 for in the Ohio State Bulletin, January 28 an ad for a tailor stated that they were "one door north of J.M. Wolcutt's chair shop".

WOLTZ, JESSE......1816-1839
Lancaster, Fairfield County

Jesse Woltz was born December 15, 1792 in Hagerstown, Maryland, the fifth son of Dr. Peter Woltz Jr. and his wife Maria Breitengross Woltz. He was also the nephew of George Woltz, the cabinetmaker in Hagerstown (Antiques Magazine, Vol.35, No.3, March, 1939). George Woltz made fine furniture and trained 50 apprentices. Jesse Woltz was undoubtedly one of the craftsmen trained in George Woltz's factory.

Sometime between 1814 and 1816 Jesse Woltz left Hagerstown and came to Lancaster with Samuel Herr. In 1817 he advertised for an apprentice in the Lancaster, Ohio Eagle, July 17, 1817:

WANTED IMMEDIATELY
A boy to learn the cabinetmaking business, of 16 or 17 years old and can come well recommended. Apply to JESSE WOLTZ.

In 1816 he married Elizabeth Canode who was born in Sharpsburg, Maryland in 1799. They were married in Lancaster and lived there for their lifetimes. Jesse had been a private and a sargeant in the Maryland Militia in the War of 1812.

Jesse Woltz continued to advertise as a cabinetmaker in Lancaster. The following is from the Lancaster, Ohio Eagle,April 14, 1818:

JESSE WOLTZ
CABINETMAKER
Respectfully informs his friends and the public in general that he still carries on the Cabinet Making business in all its various branches, on Wheeling street, at his new shop, adjoining Jacob Shaffer's dwelling house, Lancaster, where he has, and intends constantly to keep, a complete assortment of seasoned Cherry and Walnut, suitable for making
ALL KINDS OF
FURNITURE
SUCH AS
Sideboards, Secretary and Common Desks; Clock Cases; Knife Cases; Circular, Strait, Front, & Pannel-end Bureaus; Tables of every Description; Square, Round, & Oval Candle Stands; Wash Stands; High and Low Post Bedsteads, &tc. all of which he will varnish off in style.

He returns his sincere thanks to a generous public for the favors he has heretofore received, and hopes, through unwearied exertions and assiduous attention to business, to give general satisfaction, and thereby to merit a continuance of their favors.

Lancaster, April 14, 1818

N.B. A boy of seventeen or eighteen years of age, will be taken as apprentice to the above business, if immediate application be made.
J.W.

Woltz also made piano cases, household furniture and coffins. Several pieces of his furniture remain in Lancaster; a drop leaf table and a set of chairs are attributed to him. He died March 17, 1839 and his will remains.

After Jesse's death, Elizabeth married Isaac Hollenback in Lancaster. She died in Pulaski County, Indiana. Elizabeth and Jesse had ten children.

Genealogical information from the Woltz Family Manuscript by Mrs. Duncan Woltz, Fort Wayne, Indiana. Courtesy Carolyn B. Lewis, Dayton, Ohio.

WOOD, JOHN......1812
West Union, Adams County

John Wood was the first cabinetmaker to start business in the Village of West Union. His shop stood opposite the brick residence of Mrs. Baldridge. He commenced business as early as 1812. Alexander Woodrow learned the trade with Mr. Wood whom he subsequently bought out. Information from the Adams County Atlas.

WOOD, JOHN G.......1833-1840
Springfield, Clark County

John G. Wood began advertising in the Springfield, Ohio Pioneer and Clark County Advertiser, October 19, 1833:

Give This A Reading

The undersigned begs leave to return his sincere thanks to the citizens of Springfield and vicinity for the liberal encouragement that he has thus received in the

Cabinet Making Business

and further more would inform his friends and those acquainted with his location that he has established himself in the above business on South street, East of Warders Hotel, where he designs manufacturing Cabinet Furniture of every kind and will be thankful to receive such encouragement as he may merit by industry and attention to business.

He also would inform the public that he has been at great expense to add to his establishment the convenience of a first rate

Turning Lathe

worked by horse power for the accomodation of the public as well as himself where he will do all kinds of turning in wood on such terms as cannot fail to please. All those concerned will do well to call, when required he will furnish material to order and the turning shall be done on as short notice as possible.

All kinds of country produce taken in part payment for work in the above business, lumber wanted immediately likewise a good horse for which he will give generously, price will be given in furniture.

The subscriber will take two boys from 14 to 16 years of age as apprentices to the cabinetmaking and turning business immediately Boys from the country would be preferred.

The Undertaking Business

will be attended to as usual and every call taken to render satisfaction to the bereaved survivors. The experience of the subscriber in this business has taught him the necessity and convenience of a suitable hearse and he informs the public that he shall have one completed in short time which will attend without charge upon the burials superintended by him.

John G. Wood

Oct.19, 1833

On Friday, July 17, 1840, John Wood and William J. Baxter went into business together making "Common and fancy chairs of the latest eastern fashion. Old chairs painted and ornamented to order". By May 21, 1841 William Baxter was working alone at the Sign of the Yellow Chair. John G. Wood was either working alone or had moved.

WOOD, ROBERT H.......1825-1826
West Union, Adams County

From the West Union Village Register, June 21, 1825:

CABINET MAKING
ROBERT H. WOOD

Respectfully tenders his thanks to the inhabitants of West Union, and his customers in general, for the liberal encouragement and patronage they have afforded him, informing them that he still continues to carry on the above business in all its various branches, at his old stand on Cherry street, nearly opposite the Steam-Mill; where can be had on a reasonable notice-

Side-Boards, Secretaries,
Bureaus, Desks, Cupboards,
Tables, Stands, Cribs, Cradles, &c. &c.

and any other article in his line of business, from the very first quality down to common, all executed in the neatest, best, and most fashionable manner, and on the reasonable terms.

To those who have not as yet favored him with their custom, he begs leave to suggest to them, that they call and examine the Furniture made in his shop, feeling confident that by his experience in, and attention to business, he will merit their favors.

He receives in exchange for any of the above, Cherry, Walnut, and Poplar Boards, and Country Produce of almost every description.

West Union, June 21, 1825

Robert H. Wood continued advertising on a weekly basis until the paper stopped in June, 1826.

WOODROW, ALEXANDER......1824
West Union, Adams County

Alexander Woodrow apprenticed to John Wood and bought out Mr. Wood. This may have taken place in 1822 for Alexander Woodrow was making enough money in 1823 to buy some property from Andrew Woodrow, a brother or father. On March 8, 1824, the West Union Village Register carried this ad:

REMOVAL - The Subscriber wishes to inform the citizens of West Union that he has removed from his former stand to the west end of Main street opposite John Hayslips Tavern where he intends carrying on the CABINETMAKING business.

N.B. Work in his line will be done in the neatest manner and on the most moderate terms for cash or approved country produce. He will also take plank of different kinds suitable either for cabinetwork or building.

West Union, Mar.8, 1824
ALEXANDER WOODROW

In 1827 Alexander Woodrow married Prudence Stevenson. It is stated in the Adams County Atlas that he moved his shop to Treber premises and finally occupied the property now owned by D.W. Thomas Esq. He worked in West Union for his lifetime. No will has been found for Alexander Woodrow.

WOODS, A.......1819
Charlestown, Clark County

From the Columbus Gazette, July 1, 1819:

One Dollar Reward
Ran away from the subscriber, living in Charlestown, an apprentice to the Cabinet Business, named
JOHN CRAIG.
had on a new fine blue broadcloth coat, brown cashmere pantaloons, yellow vest, etc. Any person who will return said apprentice to the subscriber, shall receive the above reward.
A. WOODS
Charlestown, Feb.

WOOLCOT, JOHNSON......1801
Lancaster, Fairfield County

The following notice appeared in the Scioto Gazette, December 26, 1801:

Ran Away - apprentice in Lancaster, Fairfield County named Johnson Woolcot found by me indentured by trade of cabinetmaking.

Jacob Kirtz - cabinetmaker

YEOMAN, SAMUEL F.......1830
Lebanon, Warren County

From the Western Star, July 23, 1830:

CHEAPER THAN EVER
The partnership between GEOGHEGAN & YEOMAN having been dissolved by mutual consent, the Subscriber takes this method of informing the public that he still carried on the business in the shop formerly by said Geoghagan and intends keeping on hand an assortment of elegant plain and fancy chairs which he will sell at Cincinnati prices. Those wanting any article of his line of business he earnestly invites to call and examine his works. Most kinds of country produce taken in payment and great bargains for cash. He hopes with unremitting attention to business and every exertion to accomodate, to merit and receive a liberal share of patronage.
Samuel F. Yeoman
Lebanon, Jan.20, 1830

YOUNG, -......1812
Chillicothe, Ross County

This advertisement appeared in the Chillicothe Supporter, March 21, 1812:

Chairmaking and Wheelwright Business
The Partnership between Howard and Young has been dissolved and the subscriber intends to carry on at the business in all of its branches in the north end of Mr. Joseph Shepherds house on the corner of Mulberry and 2nd street, on the shortest notice and most reasonable terms.
James Howard

The first name of Mr. Young is unknown.

continued on next page

ZEITZER, GEORGE F.......B.1782
West Alexandria, Preble County

According to the *History of Preble County*, George F. Zeitzer was born in Baden, Germany, August 5, 1782. He married Mrs. Catherine Fry in Lancaster, Pennsylvania. Mr. Zeitzer was a cabinetmaker by trade. He established himself in that trade and continued it for many years with great success. His son, John, and grandson, George, continued in the business.

ZIMMERMAN, JOHN......1830
Kingston, Ross County

John Zimmerman was a cabinetmaker and an undertaker in Kingston, Ross County in 1830. He had the first hearse in Kingston, which was an important crossroad and stage coach stop. John Zimmerman also made wooden planes and several with his stamp still exist.

Information courtesy John Grabb, Chillicothe historian.

Footnotes

[1]*Morris Burbank, Making of a Nation 1783-1860* (New York: American Heritage Publishing Co., Simon and Schuster, 1968),163.

[2]*Diary of Paul Furson,* Courtesy Mrs. Richard Barrett, Carmel, California.

[3]*Melinda Hyde, Ohio Historical Society, Columbus, Ohio.*

[4]*Mrs. Shepherd, interview by Edward Hageman, 1949.*

[5]*1819 Directory, Cincinnati Historical Society, Cincinnati, Ohio.*

[6]*Charles Cist,Sketches and Statistics of Cincinnati, 1859.*

[7]*Melinda Hyde*

[8]*Diary of Benjamin Conrad, privately owned.*

[9]*William Utter, The Frontier State 1803-1825,* Ohio Historical Society, Columbus, Ohio.

[10]*John Lyons, Torrence Papers, Cincinnati Historical Society, Cincinnati, Ohio.*

[11]*R.T. Mayhill, "Federal Manufacturer's Census" Tri-State Trader,* 25 Sept. 1971.

[12]*Yesteryear in Clark County, Ohio,* Vol. II, (1948), 35.

[13]*William Utter, 263.*

[14]*Francis T. Weisenberger, The Passage of the Frontier - The History of Ohio,* Vol. III (Columbus: Ohio Historical Society, 1941), 29.

[15]*Charles R. Hebble and Frank P. Goodevin, eds., The Citizens Book,* Cincinnati Chamber of Commerce (Cincinnati: Steward and Kidd, 1916).

[16]*The History of Clinton County* (Chicago: W.H. Beers & Co., 1882), 264.

[17]*Sarah Worthington King Peter, Private Memoirs of Thomas Worthington (Cincinnati: Robert Clarke & Co., 1882).*

[18]*Smith and Findlay, Cincinnati Historical Society, Cincinnati, Ohio.*

[19]*Backus-Woodbridge Mss, Ohio Historical Society, Columbus, Ohio.*

[20]*Benjamin A. Porter receipt, Cincinnati Public Library, Cincinnati, Ohio.*

[21]*John Henley Ledger Book, Ohio Historical Society, Columbus, Ohio.*

[22]*N.N. Hill, comp., History of Licking County* (Newark: 1881), 232.

[23]*Hebble and Goodevin, 160.*

[24]*Campbell and Williams advertisement, Sentinel of the Northwest Territory,* Cincinnati Historical Society, Cincinnati, Ohio.

[25]*Backus-Woodbridge Mss.*

[26]*Thomas Worthington Papers, Ohio Historical Society, Columbus, Ohio.*

[27]*Arthur St. Clair Papers, Cincinnati Historical Society, Cincinnati, Ohio.*

[28]*Betty Lawson Walters, Furniture Makers of Indiana* (Indianapolis: Indiana Historical Society, 1972), 143.

[29]*Wilkesville Mss., Joseph Thompson Collection, Ohio Historical Society, Columbus, Ohio.*

[30]*Elizah T. Fisher to parents in Wooster, Mass., Ohio Historical Society, Columbus, Ohio.*

[31]*Robert K. Foresman Will, Pickaway County Court House, Circleville, Ohio. Courtesy Carolyn B. Lewis.*

[32]*Charles F. Montgomery, American Furniture - The Federal Period* (New York: The Viking Press, 1966), 18.

[33]*Chillicothe Weekly Recorder 1814-1815, Cincinnati Historical Society, Cincinnati, Ohio, 256.*

[34]*Montgomery, 17*

[35]*Carl W. Dreppard, New Geography of American Antiques* (New York: Doubleday and Company, Inc., 1967).

[36]*Montgomery County Historical Society, Dayton, Ohio, Courtesy Judith Wehn.*

[37]*Courtesy Winterthur Museum Library.*

[38]*1850 Business Schedule, Ohio Historical Society, Columbus, Ohio, Courtesy Sandra Nelson.*

[39]*Sentinel of the Northwest Territory,* 11 Sept. 1795 and 10 Oct. 1795, Cincinnati Historical Society, Cincinnati, Ohio.

[40]*Backus-Woodbridge Mss. and Smith and Findlay Ledger Book.*

[41]*William T. Utter, 233.*

[42]*R.T. Mayhill, "1820 Federal Manufacturer's Census" Tri-State Trader,* 9 Oct. 1971.

[43]*Jesse Woltz advertisement, The Ohio Eagle,* 23 April 1818, 3.

[44]*Sayres and Donohoe advertisement, Eaton Register,* 1 March 1833, 3.

[45]*Robert Pinkerton Ledger Book, Courtesy Robert M. Andrews.*

Newspapers

American Friend and Marietta Gazette. 23 October 1813 - 2 March 1833. Marietta, Ohio.
Athens Mirror and Literary Gazette. 29 October 1825 - 17 December 1825. Athens, Ohio.
Aurora. 25 December 1841. Zanesville, Ohio.
Centinel of the Northwest Territory. 10 May 1794 - 12 February 1796. Cincinnati, Ohio.
Chillicothe Advertiser. 18 May 1833 - 23 July 1858. Chillicothe, Ohio.
Chillicothe Evening Post. 24 April 1830 - 2 October 1830. Chillicothe, Ohio.
Chillicothe Register. 17 March 1810. Chillicothe, Ohio.
Chillicothe Supporter. 6 July 1809. Chillicothe, Ohio.
Chillicothe Times. 28 July 1824. Chillicothe, Ohio.
Cincinnati Advertiser. 15 June 1824. Cincinnati, Ohio.
Clark County Democrat. 18 August 1848. Springfield, Ohio.
Clermont Courrier. 16 January 1838 - 8 April 1839. Batavia, Ohio.
Daily Ohio State Journal. 20 July 1837. Columbus, Ohio.
Dayton Journal and Advertiser. 1 October 1827 - 25 April, 1843. Dayton, Ohio.
Dayton Journal and Herald. 25 December, 1832. Dayton, Ohio.
Dayton Repository (Dayton Journal). 30 September 1808. Dayton, Ohio.
The Democrat and Herald. 7 June 1833. Wilmington, Ohio.
Democratic Standard. 31 October 1839. Georgetown, Ohio.
Eaton Register. 1 March 1833. Eaton, Ohio.
Farmers Chronicle and Clark County Advertiser. 10 January 1833.
The Farmers Friend. 21 July 1821. Williamsburg, Ohio.
Farmers Record and Xenia Gazette. 25 June 1829. Xenia, Ohio.

Flag of 76. 31 March 1843. Somerset, Ohio.
The Fredonian. 6 March 1807 - 28 July 1813. Chillicothe, Ohio.
Gallipolis Journal (Gallia Gazette). 23 July 1819 - 6 October 1820. Gallipolis, Ohio.
Greene County Torchlight. 23 May 1839 - 12 July 1849. Xenia, Ohio.
Guernsey Times. 15 January 1825 - 9 April 1825. Cambridge, Ohio.
Hocking Valley Gazette and Athens Journal. 24 February 1838 - 3 November 1838. Athens, Ohio.
Independent Republican. 2 November 1809. Circleville, Ohio.
Intelligencer. 1 February 1831 - 1 August 1844. Hamilton, Ohio.
Liberty Hall and Cincinnati Gazette. 23 September 1806 - 15 April 1825. Cincinnati, Ohio.
Marietta and the Washington County Pilot. 16 April 1824. Columbus, Ohio.
Miami Herald and Dayton Republican Gazette. 23 December 1828. Dayton, Ohio.
The Morgan Sentinal and McConnelsville Gazette. 1827.
Muskingum Messenger. 2 November 1816. Zanesville, Ohio.
Muskingum Valley. 16 March 1830. Marietta, Ohio.
National Historian. 4 May 1833. St. Clairsville, Ohio.
Ohio Centinel. 14 November 1811 - 5 May 1813. Dayton, Ohio.
Ohio Confederate and Old School Republican. 28 February 1822 - 20 August 1840. Columbus, Ohio.
Ohio Eagle. 13 July 1815 - 5 December 1840. Lancaster, Ohio.
Ohio Federalist. 12 January 1814 - 2 January 1817. St. Clairsville, Ohio.
Ohio Interior Gazette. 13 September 1821 - 8 February 1826. Xenia, Ohio.
Ohio Republican. 27 February 1815 - 9 April 1836. Zanesville, Ohio.
Ohio Vehicle. 10 January 1815 - 24 October 1815. Xenia, Ohio.
Ohio Watchman. 16 October 1817 - 25 January 1825. Dayton, Ohio.
Olive Branch. 10 April 1821 - 25 August 1827. Circleville, Ohio.
Oxford Citizen. 22 March 1856 - 22 November 1856. Oxford, Ohio.
The People's Advocate. 8 June 1833. Wilmington, Ohio.
The People's Press. 29 March 1827 - 24 September 1840. Xenia, Ohio.
Perry Record. 18 August 1826. Somerset, Ohio.
Pioneer and Clark County Advertiser. 27 July 1833 - 18 October 1834. Springfield, Ohio.
The Republic. 13 September 1839 - 21 May 1841. Springfield, Ohio.
St. Clairsville Gazette. 14 November 1835 - 24 December 1835. St. Clairsville, Ohio.
Scioto Gazette. 27 November 1801 - 30 January 1884. Chillicothe, Ohio.
The Spirit of the Times. 11 October 1828. Batavia, Ohio.
The Supporter. 21 March 1812 - 26 April 1820. Chillicothe, Ohio.
The Torchlight. 23 May 1839 - 7 March 1844. Xenia, Ohio.
Tri-State Trader. 18 September 1971, 25 September 1971.
Village Register. 14 October 1823 - 22 December 1828. West Union, Ohio.
Weekly Recorder. 12 July 1814 - 12 April 1815.
Western Argus. 13 January 1825 - 18 November 1825. Wilmington, Ohio.
Western Patriot. 4 December 1824. Batavia, Ohio.
Western Pioneer and Farmers Chronicle. 22 June 1833 - 24 August 1833. Springfield, Ohio.
Western Republican. 17 March 1832. Dayton, Ohio.
Western Spy and Hamilton Gazette. 22 April 1801 - 23 March 1803. Cincinnati, Ohio.
The Western Spy. 29 December 1810 - 6 July 1818. Cincinnati, Ohio.
Western Star. 13 February 1807 - 10 April 1830. Lebanon, Ohio.
Western Telegraph and Hamilton Advertiser. 18 September, 1829 - 22 June 1842. Hamilton, Ohio.
The Western Times. 28 December 1826 - 2 August 1828. Portsmouth, Ohio.
Western Pioneer. 22 January 1830 - 2 March 1833. Springfield, Ohio.
Xenia Patriot. 10 September 1816 - 19 September 1816. Xenia, Ohio.

continued on next page

The Zanesville Aurora. 22 June 1838 - 7 September 1838. Zanesville, Ohio.
Zanesville Express and Republican Standard. 5 January 1813 - 12 September 1820. Zanesville, Ohio.
Zanesville Gazette. 16 March 1831 - 24 February 1847. Zanesville, Ohio.
Zanesville Muskingum Messenger. 17 October 1816. Zanesville, Ohio.

Books

Andrews, Martin R.,ed. *History of Marietta and Washington Counties.* Chicago:Biographical Publishing Co.,1902.
Ayres, Mrs. Edwin. *Hillsboro Story - Sesquicentennial Year 1807-1959.*
Bartlow, Hon. Bert S., W.H. Todhunter, Stephen D. Cone and others, eds. *Centennial History of Butler County, Ohio.* B.F. Bowen & Co.,1905.
Bell, Carol Willsey. *Ohio Genealogical Guide.* Columbus, 1978.
Bjerkoe, Ethel Hall. *The Cabinetmakers of America.* New York:Bonanza Books, 1957.
Broadstone, Hon. M.A. *History of Greene County, Ohio.* Indianapolis:B.F.Bowen & Co., Inc.,1918.
Caldwell, J.A. *History of Belmont and Jefferson Counties.* Wheeling:Historical Publishing Co.,1880.
Colbarn, E.H. and A.A. Graham. *History of Fairfield and Perry County.* Chicago:1883.
Commercial Reference Book for the State of Ohio,1856. Marietta Museum, Marietta, Ohio.
Cummings, Virginia Raymond. *Hamilton County Court House and Other Records.* Cincinnati:General Printing Co.,1966.
Dickinson, Cornelius E. *History of Belpre, Washington County, Ohio.* Parkersburg:Globe Printing,1920.
Dills, R.S. *History of Greene County.* Dayton:Odell and Mayer,1881.
Directory of the City of Springfield. Springfield:John W. Kees and Co.,1852.
Drake, Daniel. *Memoirs of the Miami Country 1779-1794.* Edited by Beverly W. Bond Jr. Cincinnati:The Abingdon Press,1923.
Drinkle, Ruth Wolfey. *Architecture and Arts of Fairfield County.* Lancaster:Pfeifer Printing Co.,1978.
Durant, P.A.,ed. *History of Clinton County, Ohio.* Chicago:W.H.Beers and Co.,1882.
Edgar, John F.*Pioneer Life in Dayton and Vicinity 1796-1840.* Dayton:W.J.Shuey,1896.
Ervin, Edgar. *Pioneer History of Meigs County to 1949.*
Evans, Lyle S. *History of Ross County.* Chicago:Lewis Publishing Co.,1917.
Evans, Nelson W. *A History of Scioto County, Ohio.* Portsmouth, Ohio.
Evans, Nelson W., T. Emmons and E.B. Stivers. *A History of Adams County, Ohio from its Earliest Settlements to the Present Time.* West Union:E.B. Stivers,1900.
Evers, Louis H. *History of Clermont County,1880.*
Fales Jr., Dean A. *American Painted Furniture.* New York:E.P.Dutton and Co.,1972.
Findley, Isaac J. and Rufus Putnam.*Pioneer Record and Reminiscences of Early Settlers and Settlements.* Cincinnati:Robert Clarke and Co.,1871.
Gibbs, James W. *Buckeye Horology.* Columbia:Art Crafters,1971.
Godspeed. *Biographical and Historical Memoirs of Muskingum County,1892.*
Greene County 1803-1908. Xenia:Aldine Publishing Co.,1908.
The Guernsey County 175th Celebration Booklet. The Carl Rech Compilation of Cambridge Lots..
Harden, Ned and W.W. Higgin. *Roundtown Reminiscences - Illustrations and Notes of the History of Circleville, Ohio.* Columbus:Ohio Historical Society.

Heiser, Alta Harvey. *Hamilton in the Making.* Oxford:Mississippi Valley Press,1941.
Hildreth, S.P. *Pioneer History of the Ohio Valley and Early Settlement of the Northwest Territory.* Cincinnati:H.W.Derby and Company,1848.
Historical Cemetery Records of Clinton County 1798-1978. Blanchester:Curless Publishing Co.,1980.
History of Brown County, Ohio. Chicago:W.H.Beers and Co.,1883.
History of Cincinnati and Hamilton County, Their Past and Present. Cincinnati:Nelson,1894.
History of Clark County. Chicago:W.H.Beers and Co.,1881.
History of Lower Scioto Valley, Ohio. Chicago:Interstate Publishing Co.,1884.
History of Pomeroy. Athens:Ohio University Library,1835-1836.
History of Warren County. Chicago:W.H.Beers and Co.,1971.
History of Wayne County. Wooster:Robert Douglas,1878.
Hover,John C. and Joseph D. Barnes, eds. *Memoirs of the Miami Valley. Vol.2.* Chicago:Robert O. Law Company,1919-1920.
Howe Historical Collections of Ohio. Cincinnati:C.J. Krehbiel and Co.,1908.
Hutsler, Donald A. *Gunsmiths of Ohio 18th and 19th Century. Vol.I.* Pennsylvania:George Shumway,1973.
Hutsler, Donald A. *The Log Architecture of Ohio.* Columbus:Ohio Historical Society,1972.
Index of Inscriptions from Gravestones, Pickaway County, Ohio. Circleville:D.A.R.,1936.
Kidney, Walter C. *Historic Buildings of Ohio.* Cincinnati:Art Museum Library,1972.
Knepper, George W. *An Ohio Portrait.* Columbus:Ohio Historical Society,1976.
Knittle, Rhea Mansfield. *Tavern Sign, Barge, Banner, Chair and Settee Painters.* The Ohio Frontier Series, 1787-1847. Cleveland:Calvert-Hatch Company.
Larkin, Stillman Carter. *Pioneer History of Miegs County.* Columbus:Berlin Printing Co.,1908.
*Made In Ohio Furniture 1788-1888.*Columbus:Columbus Museum of Art,1984.
McBride,James. *Pioneer Biographies.* Cincinnati:Robert Clarke,1869.
McGinnis, Ralph.*Oxford Town 1830-1930.* Oxford:Arthur Stewart Press,1930.
Miller, Edgar G. *American Antique Furniture, Vol.I and Vol.II.* New York:Dover Publications,Inc.,1966.
Montgomery, Charles F. *American Furniture - The Federal Period.* New York:The Viking Press,1966.
Ormsbee, Thomas Hamilton. *Early American Furniture Makers - A Social and Biographical Study.* New York:Thomas Y. Crowell,1930.
Phillips, Hazel Spencer. *History of the Golden Lamb.* Oxford:The Oxford Press,1958.
Phillips, Hazel Spencer. *Traditional Architecture of Warren County, Ohio.* Oxford:1969.
Quaker Historical Collections. Springfield Friends Meeting:1959.
Reiter, Edith S. *Marietta and the Northwest Territory 1788.* Marietta:Pettit-Seevers Printing,1968.
Roseboom, Eugene H. and Francis P. Weisenburger. *A History of Ohio.* Columbus: Ohio Historical Society,1976.
Santmyer, Helen Hooven. *Ohio Town.* Columbus:Ohio State University Press,1962.
Sarchet, Cyrus. *History of Guernsey County.Vol.I.* Indianapolis:B.F.Bowen and Co.,1911.
Schneider, Norris F. *Campus Martius.* Marietta:MacDonald Printing Co.,1932.
Schneider, Norris F. *Zanesville Stories 1939-1979.* Reprinted by Bell & Howell.
Sikes, Jane E. *Furniture Makers of Cincinnati 1790-1849.* Cincinnati:The Merten Company,1976.
Smalley, Stephen B. *Historic Homes of Anderson Township, Hamilton County, Ohio.* Cincinnati:1969.
Smith, Ophia D. *Old Oxford Houses and People Who Lived in Them.* Oxford:Oxford Historical Press,1941.
Smith, William E. *History of Southwestern Ohio, The Miami Valleys. Vol.I.* New York:Lewis Historical Publishing Co.,1964.
Steele, Robert W. and Mary Davis Steele. *Early Dayton.* Dayton:W.J.Shuey,1896.

Stout, Frank and Committee. *Once Upon a Hilltop: History of Mt. Healthy, 1817-1967.* sesquicentennial year pamphlet,1967.
Utter, William T. *The Frontier State:1803-1825.* Columbus:Ohio Historical Society,1942.
Walker, Charles Manning. *History of Athens County, Ohio.* Cincinnati: Robert Clarke and Co.,1869.
Walters, Betty Lawson. *Furniture Makers of Indiana 1793-1850.* Indianapolis:Indiana Historical Society,1972.
Webb, David Knowlton. *Reminiscences - A Description of Circleville, Ohio 1825-1840.* Chillicothe: David Knowlton Webb,1944.
Weisenburger, Francis P. *The Passing of the Frontier 1825-1850.* Columbus:Ohio Historical Society,1941.
Whitley, Edna Talbott. *Kentucky Ante-Bellum Portraiture..* The National Society of Colonial Dames in America in the Commonwealth of Kentucky, 1956.
Williams Brothers, comp. *Guernsey County Township Histories.* Cambridge:1882.
Williams Brothers, comp. *History of Franklin and Pickaway Counties.* Cleveland:Williams Brothers,1880.
Williams Brothers, comp. *History of Ross and Highland Counties, Ohio.* Cleveland:1880.
Williams Brothers, comp. *History of Washington County 1788-1881.*
Williams, Stephen Riggs. *Saga of Paddy's Run.* Oxford:Miami University Press,1945.
Wolf, William G. *Stories of Guernsey County, Ohio - History of an Average Ohio County.* Cambridge:William G. Wolf,1943.
Yesteryear in Clark County, Ohio.Vol.I and Vol.II. Springfield:reprinted by Clark County Historical Society,1978.

Periodicals

Bishop, W.W.,ed. *Oxford Chronicle. Vol.I* April 19,1834.
Frary, I.T. The Old Wall Stencils of Ohio. *The Magazine Antiques.* 38(1940):169.
Mackenzie, Donald. Early Ohio Painters - The Pre-War Years. *Ohio Historical Bulletin.* 73(Autumn 1964):254-262.
The Magazine Antiques. 49(January,1946).
Pinckney, Pauline A. George Woltz - Maryland Cabinetmaker. *The Magazine Antiques.* 35(March 1939):124-126.
Remley, Catherine. Marietta Treasures. *Antiques Festival Catalogue - Cincinnati,Ohio.* June, 1980.
Smith, Ophia Delilah. A Survey of Artists in Cincinnati from 1789-1830. *Cincinnati Historical Society Bulletin.* 25(1967):2-21.

Manuscripts

Account Book for Presbyterian Church. Van Cleve-Dover Collection. Dayton Public Library, Dayton.
Appraisement of Personal Property, Franklin County, 1803-1818. Ohio Historical Society, Columbus.
Backus-Woodbridge Collection. Ledger Books, 1804-1807. Ohio Historical Society, Columbus.
Blennerhassett Family Papers. Ohio Historical Society, Columbus.
Blennerhassett, Margaret to Dudley Woodbridge. Letter, 1807. Backus-Woodbridge Collection. Ohio Historical Society, Columbus.

Dallow, Zella Trimble to I.T. Frary. I.T. Frary Collection. Ohio Historical Society, Columbus.
Donaldson, Mary Katherine. Dissertation. *Early Landscapes of the Ohio River Valley, Background and Components.* University of Pittsburg.
Early History of Scioto and Vicinity, Hamilton, Ohio. Butler County, Ohio.
Early Vital Records. Miami University Library, Oxford.
Fisher, Elias T. Manuscript, 1817. Ohio Historical Society, Columbus.
Heiser, Alta Harvey. Manuscript Directory. Hamilton, Ohio.
History of Winchester 1815-1965. Cincinnati Historical Society, Cincinnati.
Kemper Family Papers. Cincinnati Historical Society, Cincinnati.
Lewis Manuscript. Warren County Historical Society, Lebanon.
Mason, Wm. Waste Account Book, 1793-1794. Backus-Woodbridge Collection. Ohio Historical Society, Columbus.
Penitentiary Records. Series 1536. Ohio Historical Society, Columbus.
Rodgers, Sylvester. Pay Book, 1835-1836. Ohio Historical Society, Columbus.
Sander, Samuel and John Henley. Ledger Book, 1823-1824. Ohio Historical Society, Columbus.
Smith, N. Ledger, 1826-1830. Ohio Historical Society, Columbus.
Street, Bertha. History of Gratis, 1902. Ohio Historical Society, Columbus.
Thompson Letters, 1831-1834. Joseph Thompson Manuscript 251. Ohio Historical Society, Columbus.
Torrence Papers. Cincinnati Historical Society, Cincinnati.
Waldsmelt, Christian. Ledger, 1814. Cincinnati Historical Society, Cincinnati.
Woltz, Flora Lee Duncan. Woltz Family. 2nd edition. Fort Wayne Public Library, Fort Wayne.
Worthington, James T. Worthington Family Papers, 1830,1839,1854. Ohio Historical Society, Columbus.

Records and Interviews

Clermont County Court House Records, 1803-1820. Will Book A. Batavia, Ohio.
Devol, Jerry B. Interview with author, 1981.
Ohio Census, 1820,1830,1840,1850. Cincinnati Historical Society, Cincinnati.
Phillips, Hazel Spencer. Interview with author, 1972.
Record of Indentures, Fairfield County, 1830-1840. Ohio Historical Society, Columbus.
Allwine, John. Will,1816. Probate Records, Muskingum County Court House.
Richardson, Peck. Interview with author, 1981.
Schneider, Norris F. Interview with author, 1980.
Xenia Census, 1850. Green County Room, Xenia Public Library, Xenia.

Credits

Editor - Barbara Macke Sikes

Graphic Design - Edward Morton Hageman

Typography - Pagemakers

Printing - The Merten Company

Photography - Frank Lukas, Edward Hageman, Joseph Worley, Todd Weier, Edward Betz, Alan Haines, Nancy Farrar, Judy Morehead, Jeffrey Schenck, Judy Wehn

All photographs by Frank Lukas unless otherwise noted.

Typist - Mary Jane Armstrong

Research Assistants - Carolyn B. Lewis, Suzanne Elder Rogan, Wendy Shepherd, Barbara Macke Sikes, Dawn Vanderzee.